AF339291

Proper BASIC

Proper BASIC

BRIAN C. WALSH

University of Liverpool

JOHN WILEY & SONS

Chichester · New York · Brisbane · Toronto · Singapore

Library of Congress Cataloging in Publication Data:

Walsh, Brian C.
  Proper BASIC.

  Includes index.
  1. Basic (Computer program language) I. Title.
  QA76.73.B3W345 1983   001.64'24   82–17447
  ISBN 0 471 90081 8

British Library Cataloguing in Publication Data:

Walsh, Brian C.
  Proper BASIC.
  1. Basic (Computer program language)
  001.64'24   QA76.73.B3

  ISBN 0 471 90081 8

Phototypeset in Times by Millford Reprographics Int. Ltd, Luton
and printed by Pitman Press, Bath, Avon

Acknowledgements

I wish to thank Prof. J. L. Alty, University of Liverpool, for his encouragement and advice on the preparation of this book, and for permission to use material from the Liverpool Computer Laboratory 'Teach yourself BASIC programming' manual.

Many thanks to Dr P. Craven, University of Essex, for the use of his STORY program in Chapter 5, and also to Dr C. Silk, University of Keele, for the use of his GAUSS program in Chapter 7.

I am indebted to Mr P. Leng, University of Liverpool, for his help and advice with the manuscript, and to Robbie Sutton for patiently preparing it in a readable form.

Acknowledgements and many thanks to the following organizations who supplied the photographs appearing in this book: Cytek (UK) Limited of Old Trafford, Manchester, who are specialist Commodore dealers, Sinclair Research Limited of Cambridge, BBC and Acorn Computers Limited of Cambridge, BASF United Kingdom Limited of London, and Martin Beer of Liverpool University.

'Microsoft' is a registered trademark of the Microsoft Corporation, USA.

Contents

Preface

AIMS

This book is designed to teach the BASIC language to the newcomer to computing and to give the practising programmer an insight into proper computing techniques. At the end of most chapters additional material or complete case studies are presented which may be omitted at a first reading. They are intended to provide a deeper insight into programming and computers. The aim is to provide a knowledge of computing via BASIC, not just a description of the BASIC language, which is available from many books and manuals.

There is a sensible emphasis on design which will provide new and experienced programmers with an excellent basis for developing programs. It is recognized that BASIC is not the best of languages for modern design techniques but a great deal can be achieved through sensible use of both design techniques and the language.

BASIC language elements are presented critically and set in the wider context of modern language developments.

VERSION OF BASIC

Any computer language exposition depends upon a specific implementation of that language in which to present its examples and problems. To make this book useful as widely as possible a reasonable standard has been adopted, together with discussions, tables, and examples for several multi-user mainframe computers and most popular microcomputers available.

USE OF THE BOOK

Here is some guidance if you intend to use this book for self-study. Work through the chapters appropriate to your requirements and keep the book beside you at the computer terminal. Details of the syntax of BASIC statements are highlighted in the text and may be easily found.

CHAPTER 1: introduces the computer and several BASIC programming statements. It explains the functional parts that you will use and develops a simple BASIC program which you should try to run on your computer, perhaps after reading part of Chapter 2.

CHAPTER 2: covers terminal or microcomputer use and program preparation. It describes how to use a terminal or microcomputer, enter a program, and control that program with computer commands. Notice particularly the LIST and RUN commands. Concern yourself only with the section appropriate to your system.

CHAPTER 3: completes the introduction to simple BASIC programming. Having completed this chapter you will be able to construct a wide variety of programs and may wish to stop (at least for a short time). Be sure that you really understand how IF statements work and how loops may be constructed using FOR–NEXT statements. Do not be afraid to spend some time running trivial examples until you are confident you understand them. It is essential to make sure you have a good grasp of the fundamentals before proceeding.

CHAPTER 4: is required reading for those who wish to develop and exploit the full facilities of the BASIC language. It covers arrays and the handling of strings. For later study the end of the chapter gives a complete introduction to searching and sorting techniques.

CHAPTER 5: is essential reading for the correct development of proper programming and design skills. No major programming task should be attempted until you are familiar with the purpose and use of functions and subroutines, as described in this chapter. The main purpose of this chapter is to emphasize the need for correct and sensible design prior to writing any substantial program.

CHAPTER 8: introduces 'files' and gives a thorough description of all the types available via BASIC. Concentrate on using program files and simple sequential files at a first reading. Many different systems are described but select the section appropriate to your computer hardware.

CHAPTER 9: is useful to 'dip into' at any time as it summarizes program development and error correction. Ignore Section 9.2.2 at a first reading, but notice the design summary.

Chapters 6 and 7 deal with extensions to BASIC and matrix handling. More experienced programmers will find these useful. The major division of this book into four sections corresponding to the above layout is clearly indicated by Parts I to IV in the text.

PART I
Introductory

A section particularly for those who are just beginning to use a computer.

1

Introduction

Today the computer is no longer a rather distant and mysterious electronic 'box of tricks' but is rapidly becoming a familiar part of everyday life. This spread of computers is largely due to the microcomputer which is small in size and very cheap to make, yet has all the components and functions of the large computers. If you go round a computer room which contains a large mainframe computer you will see large cabinets which contain the operational parts of the computer. These are also present in the 'chips' which are the packaged microelectronic circuits in the microcomputer. The systems, large and small, are general purpose computers which require a series of instructions to perform a wide variety of tasks. These instructions may be given in many ways. One of the most popular is via the BASIC programming language. It is known as a high level language, as instructions to the computer are given in suitable English type words, and no detailed knowledge of the computer's fundamental electronic features is required. Thus, it should not matter which computer is being used. This means that programs written in BASIC are generally portable; i.e. they can be run on any computer that provides BASIC. Unfortunately, BASIC is not quite the same on all computers, but there is a very large part of it common to all systems and this is treated fully in this book. In addition, many common variants of BASIC are covered, but BASIC keeps expanding, so no attempt has been made to describe all the obscure features of every BASIC you may meet.

BASIC was developed at Dartmouth College (USA) in 1963 by Professors Kemeny and Kurtz who gave us an easy to learn and use computer language. The BASIC vocabulary is very limited compared to English, but unlike English it has to be used correctly. The computer is an inert box of electronic components which performs as it is instructed, no more and no less, so its instructions must be unambiguous. Figure 1.1 illustrates the very broad features of a language like English, the requirements of the computer, and the bridging or intermediary role of a language like BASIC.

Instructions written in BASIC are not in the final form required for the computer machinery to be able to recognize and act on them. They have to be translated into the machine code instructions by a rather complicated program called a *compiler* or *interpreter*. This compiler is usually supplied with the com-

4

puter and is the major part of what appears to you as the 'BASIC system'. The features which the compiler will accept determine the form of BASIC available. Generally, the smaller the compiler, the fewer features which will be available.

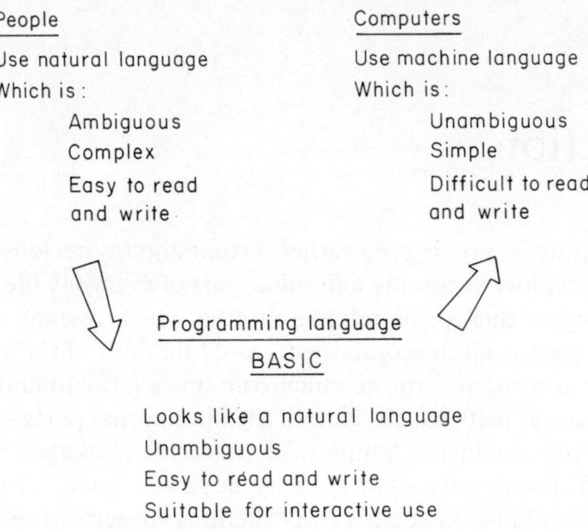

Figure 1.1 A programming language acts as a link between people and computers

1.1 THE COMPUTER

BASIC is a language which was designed for interactive use with a computer. Figure 1.2 illustrates the general set of units which form the basis of a BASIC computer.

The *input unit* is usually a keyboard through which information, instructions and commands can be given to the computer. The *output unit* is usually a video display screen which displays information as text or graphics. As well as displaying the results of a computation, the video screen shows the input from the keyboard as it is typed. Together these two devices are known as the *visual display unit* (VDU).

A large computer system may have many VDUs and other types of input and output devices connected to it which can all be used simultaneously. When many users are each using a VDU to run BASIC, the computer (or more correctly, a specialized program in it called the operating system) keeps the work of each user separate, so that each appears to have the sole use of the computer.

A microcomputer often appears to be a VDU on its own, because the active logic units are so small they can easily be fitted into the keyboard or screen cases.

The active logic units form the most interesting part of the computer; this is called the *central processing unit* in large computers and appears as a separate

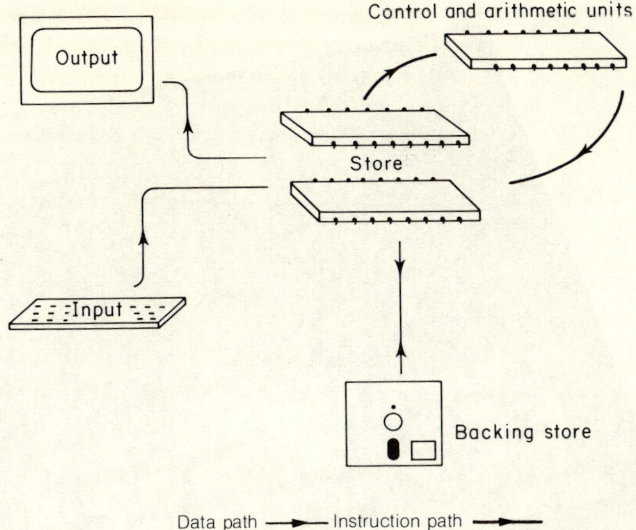

Figure 1.2 The principal computer parts and general data flow

box. However, together with some other features it may appear on a single chip in microcomputers. Within this unit the most important part is the *arithmetic logic unit*, which works rather like a pocket calculator in that it performs additions, subtractions, multiplications, and logical operations on any data which are supplied to it.

The data for the arithmetic logic unit and the instructions on how they are to be processed are stored in the computer *store*. The store is an area which retains the instructions and data supplied to it from the keyboard of a VDU or other input device. During execution the central processing unit will read from the store and write to it. The results of any computation are copied from the store to an output device such as a printer or the screen of the VDU. The store is not a place to keep instructions and data for a long period; it is used as a working area only.

A *program* is the name given to a set of instructions which manipulates the data. Merely putting a program into the store and switching on the arithmetic unit would not achieve very much. There is a need for something which will push the data into the arithmetic unit in synchronization with a program instruction. Such a need is filled by the *control unit*, which interprets the program instructions one at a time, tells the arithmetic unit how to act, and organizes the correct data at the arithmetic unit for each instruction. The actions of the control unit are determined by a kind of 'heart beat' in the computer which is generated by a *clock*. Each clock cycle causes a simple action in the control unit and the overall speed of the system is determined by the clock rate. For microcomputers this is typically 4,000,000 cycles per second. The results after a program has executed for a few seconds may seem quite complex and 'clever' to us using the computer, but in fact consist of a very large number of quite simple operations performed at the very high speed indicated above.

Figure 1.3 The powerful Sinclair ZX81 personal computer. (Reproduced by permission of Sinclair Research Limited)

The computer store does not retain instructions and data permanently. In fact, most computers lose the contents of the store when they are switched off. The store holds the current program which is executing or being prepared for execution. Once this is complete it is deleted so that a new program may be input. Programs and data may be kept permanently on *backing store*, from where they may be copied into the computer store, or copied out of it. Backing store usually operates via some magnetic recording process and takes the form of magnetic tape either in cassettes or on reels, or magnetic discs. The discs may be very expensive rigid discs with a high storage capacity typically tens of millions of characters, or cheap floppy discs with a storage capacity of hundreds of thousands of characters.

1.2 INTO SIMPLE BASIC

The instructions and data must be placed in particular locations within the computer store before the computer can begin work on the problem. All storage locations have detailed machine addresses, in the same way as houses in a street have addresses. Rather than needing to use these inscrutable machine addresses, BASIC provides a convenient way of labelling both instructions and data. Each

Figure 1.4 Details of the chips and electronic layout of the Sinclair ZX81 computer. The chip in the centre of the board is the Z8ØA microprocessor. (Reproduced by permission of Sinclair Research Limited)

instruction, which can be thought of as an English sentence, is labelled by a number assigned by you, the programmer, and each piece of data is addressed by a name (usually a single letter) also chosen by you. Thus an instruction:

    10   LET A=3

is stored in a store location referred to by the number 1Ø and causes the number 3 to be stored in a data location called A. Another instruction:

    2Ø   LET B=A+2

would obtain the data from the location called A, currently 3, add 2 to it, and put the result (5) in the location called B. The equal ($=$) sign in the above instructions is actually an assignment indication to copy the values obtained from the right-hand side to the data location on the left-hand side. Thus:

    3Ø   LET B=A

is

        $B \leftarrow A$

i.e. the value obtained from the data location A is copied to the data location B. The location A is not changed by the instruction and contains whatever value it had before the instruction was obeyed, but the value B contained has been over-written with the new value from A.

The actions of moving values around from one data location (A or B above) to another take place in instructions. Each BASIC instruction is identified by a number. One purpose of these number identifiers on each line is to indicate the order in which the line is processed. A BASIC program consists of a series of instructions which are executed one after the other. BASIC always starts executing the lowest numbered line first and proceeds one line at a time until the end of the programs is reached. A program is rather like a cookery recipe; every action must be done in the right order to produce a successful result.

The data locations A and B discussed above are called *variables* in what follows, as this is a good description of their properties. That is, they contain values which may change during the execution of the program.

Note that BASIC does not execute the lines of instructions when they are typed into the computer, but only when you command it to do so by giving the command RUN. For example, the following lines have been typed into the computer:

```
10   A=1

20   B=-4

30   C=A+B
```

When the command RUN is typed into the computer the variable A will be given the value 1, next the variable B will be given the value −4, and finally the variable C will be given 1−4 which is −3.

1.2.1 A first program

Listed below is a complete program:

```
10   INPUT A

20   LET B=A+2

30   PRINT B

40   END
```

When the program is executed in the computer it proceeds from the lowest numbered instruction present (10) to the highest (40). The first instruction INPUT causes the computer to wait until it receives a number typed in at the VDU keyboard. Next, the location B is given the value of A, which was input, plus 2. The value in B is printed out as a display on the VDU and program execution stops.

Each BASIC statement is typed into the computer on a separate line and preceded by a statement number. Statements are obeyed in order of increasing statement numbers, and not necessarily in the order in which they are written. For example, the above program could equally well have been written:

```
10   INPUT A
40   END
30   PRINT B
20   LET B=A+2
```

Statement numbers do not necessarily have to increase in regular steps of 1Ø, but it is a good practice to do this, so that if any lines have been omitted they can be given an intermediate statement number and will appear in the correct position. If we type:

```
25   LET B=B+1Ø
```

with the above program in store, the result would be:

```
10   INPUT A
20   LET B=A+2
25   LET B=B+1Ø
30   PRINT B
40   END
```

Statement numbers
For microcomputers it is a number from Ø to 65,535 which appears before each statement within a BASIC program.   For many large computers it is a number from 1 to 9999.

The following program would execute in exactly the same way as the one described at the beginning of this section.

```
   1    INPUT A
  29    LET B=A+2
1021    PRINT B
9998    END
```

Section 2.2 gives information on typing in a program and running it. You may wish to try this before proceeding with the following, which describes the statements used above in a little more detail.

1.2.2 INPUT statement

The statement INPUT A causes the program to halt, wait for a number to be typed in, copy the number into the variable (or data location) A, and resume execution.

Only variable names may appear in the INPUT statement. For example:

```
290   INPUT K
```

is valid, but:

```
290   INPUT K+1
```

is invalid.

<table>
<tr><td align="center">INPUT statement</td></tr>
<tr><td>

General form   INPUT item 1, item 2, item 3, . . .

The INPUT statement introduces data into the program from the terminal. Program execution pauses, a question mark (or similar) is displayed on the VDU, and the system waits for values for the items in the input list. The values should be separated by commas and be of the correct type for the corresponding variable.

If insufficient data are provided the system will prompt until all the items in the list have received values.

</td></tr>
</table>

Several numbers might be input in the same statement; e.g.

```
10   INPUT A,B,Z
```

Some kind of prompt is displayed each time additional information is needed by the program; this is usually a question (?) mark. The computer accepts the data only when the *return* key is pressed. In the case of multiple data input, several data values may be input on one line separated by commas. If there are not sufficient data values present, the computer will prompt again. For example, the statement 1Ø above could be provided with data values as (user typed responses are underlined):

> ?1Ø,5Ø   (press return key)
>
> ?-2   (press return key)

or

> ?1Ø   (press return key)
>
> ?5Ø,-2   (press return key)

In both cases the result will be that A contains 1Ø, B contains 5Ø, and Z contains −2.

1.2.3 PRINT statement

The statement PRINT B causes the contents of variable B to be displayed (or printed) on the VDU screen. Unlike the INPUT statement quite complicated expressions can be included in the PRINT statement. These are evaluated and the final result is printed. For example, if B contained 5 then:

    2Ø   PRINT B+1Ø

would display 15.

Several numbers may be output with one PRINT statement. For example:

    3Ø   PRINT B,Z,A

will display the values of the three items on one line.

The PRINT statement is a very versatile statement and with practice you can produce a tremendous range of output layouts, including low resolution graphics. Further aspects of the PRINT statement are discussed in Section 3.5.1.

1.2.4 Assignment, the LET statement

The statement LET B=A*1Ø takes the value from the variable A, multiplies it by 1Ø, and stores it in the variable B. Note that the contents of A are not changed. The basic LET options are given in Table 1.1.

Table 1.1

Action	Operator	Example
Addition	+	LET C=A+B
Subtraction	–	LET C=A–1Ø.5
Multiplication	*	LET Z=A*5
Division	/	LET T=Z/A
Raising to a power (exponentiation)	↑ or ∧ or **	LET B=A↑3
Copy		LET B=A
Copy and negate	–	LET B=–A

The * operator must be present if multiplication is required. The statement LET B=1ØA is not allowed, but must be written LET B=1Ø*A or LET B=A*1Ø. Your computer may accept a statement like LET B=A1Ø but the result is not a multiplication; rather it is a copy from the data location called A1Ø (see variable names, Section 1.2.6).

The numbers presented to the program as data or appearing in program statements, as in the LET examples above, may be positive, zero, or negative and whole numbers (*integers*) such as Ø, –7, 5, 2167 or decimal numbers (*real numbers*) such as 22.1, –Ø.6, 449.3Ø5.

For real numbers, very large or very small values are sometimes more easily expressed in powers of 1Ø (see Table 1.2). Actually, the PRINT statement will automatically output these very large or small numbers in the power of 1Ø format.

Note that the formats 5E5 and 5ØE4 and 0.5E6 are all equivalent, all being equal to 5ØØ,ØØØ.

Table 1.2

Number	Power of ten form	Computer form
5ØØ,ØØØ	$5 \times 1Ø^5$	5.ØE+5 or 5E5
46,927	$4.6927 \times 1Ø^4$	4.6927E+4 or 4.6927E4
Ø.ØØØ42	$4.2 \times 1Ø^{-4}$	4.2E–4
–31.27	$-3.127 \times 1Ø^{-1}$	–3.127E–1

There is a practical limit to the size of the value of the exponent (which is the power of ten and the value to the right of the E) on your computer. Note that the exponent must be a whole number (an integer).

1.2.5 Arithmetic expressions

More than one arithmetic operation can be performed in a single LET statement:

    10   LET A=3.14159*R↑2

    10   LET V=A*B+C/2.1

    10   LET X=(Y+22.7)/180

There is a strict order of performing the arithmetic operations (precedence) in BASIC which follows the rules of algebra reasonably well, but may appear to have some strange results until it is understood. This precedence is not arbitrary, but imposed to guarantee one, and only one, result from any expression occurring in a BASIC statement. Here is a list of the rules in the order in which the operations are performed.

(a)   First, calculate the contents of brackets.
(b)   Next, calculate any exponentiations (raising to a power).
(c)   Next, calculate any multiplications and divisions.
(d)   Lastly, calculate any additions and subtractions.

There is an overriding rule that when two adjacent operations rank equally in the order of precedence, then the calculation is performed from left to right.

Suppose that B is 100, C is 50, and D is 20 in the examples in Table 1.3. The BASIC expression has been constructed to have the same meaning as the algebraic formula, by using the above rules.

Table 1.3

Algebraic formula	BASIC expressions	Result, with the values B=100, C=50, D=20
1. $b+c-d$	B+C−D	(100+50)−20 = 130
2. $b-c-d$	B−C−D	(100−50)−20 = 30
3. $\dfrac{b+c}{d}$	(B+C)/D	(100+50)/20 = 7.5
4. $\dfrac{b}{cd}$	B/(C*D)	100/(50*20) = 0.1
5. $b^{d}/_{10}$	B↑(D/10)	100↑(20/10) = 100↑2 = 10000
6. $bc-\dfrac{d}{c}$	B*C−D/C	(100*50)−(20/50) = 4999.6
7. $b+c^{10}/_{d}$	B+C↑(10/D)	(100+50↑(10/20) = 100+50↑(½) = 107.07107

If the rule of precedence did not exist it would be possible to interpret example 6 as $(100*50-20)/50=4980/50=99.6$ rather than the correct value 4999.6 obtained above. Remember that BASIC will always follow the rule, so that you, the programmer, should always follow it also. The rule would allow us to write example 4 above as B/C/D which becomes $(B/C)/D=(100/50)/20=2/20=0.1$ and is correct, but rather obscure, and thus best avoided.

Take great care with bracketing. Example 3 should not be written $B+C/D=100+(50/20)=102.5$ which represents the algebraic form $b+c/d$ and not the required formula. Likewise, if example 7 had been written $B+C\uparrow10/D$ the result would be $B+(C\uparrow10)/D=100+(50\uparrow10)/20$, a large number which is not the result of the algebraic formula given, but corresponds to $b + c^{10}/_{d}$.

<table>
<tr><td colspan="2" align="center">LET statement</td></tr>
<tr><td>General form</td><td align="right">LET item=expression</td></tr>
</table>

‘Item’ is the name of a (data location) variable which may hold real numbers or integers or strings.
‘Expression’ gives a result of the same type (real or integer or string) as the item.

The LET statement assigns the result to the item after evaluating the expression. All items involved in the expression on the right-hand side must have a working value. That is, they must have previously been given a value by an INPUT, LET, or READ statement (which is considered in Section 4.4).

The word LET is optional for most systems.

Use of LET statements with the same variable on both sides of the assignment sign $(=)$ may cause confusion if you have not fully grasped the fact that the right-hand side is evaluated before the result is copied to the left:

```
LET   N=N+1
```

takes the current value of N, adds 1 to it, then copies the new result back into N. If N originally contained 10, the result of the statement is to leave N with 11. This type of statement is widely used in BASIC as its action is to add 1 to (increment) N each time the statement is executed. In this way N acts as a counter. Similarly, statements of the form:

```
LET   A=A*10
```

are allowed. Here the original value in A is multiplied by 10 and stored back in A again.

The word LET in these statements is usually optional and the rest of this book, apart from Chapter 1, will omit it. Only the Sinclair ZX81 insists on its use.

1.2.6 Variables and names

So far we have considered variables labelled by a single letter name. These variables are the major items which are manipulated by program instructions; they receive data, provide data for manipulation, and receive modified data in the course of program execution.

All BASICs allow variables to be named by a single letter, and a letter followed by a digit from Ø to 9. Thus, the following are valid names for variables:

A, B, N, AØ, Z9, M6, D2

There are $26+26\times10=286$ possible names for the data locations which are known as variables. Invalid names are:

5C   (starts with a digit, not a letter)

A/   (contains an operator)

Some BASICs allow longer names for variables; the main variations are listed below:

Variable names	
Most BASIC systems	One letter (A to Z) or a letter followed by a digit (Ø to 9).
Many micro BASICs	One letter, or letter plus digit, or two letters.
Microsoft BASIC	As above, plus a number of alphanumerics, but only the first two characters are used for recognition. Thus TOTAL and TOTE would be valid, but would be the same variable as TO.
BBC BASIC	One letter or a letter followed by any number of alphanumeric characters. All are significant. Thus TAX and TAXIDERMIST are valid, and names of different variables.

The BBC approach is the only sensible one. Variable names should be able to express the quantity that they represent. This makes a program more readable, and program development less prone to error. However, imagine the serious errors which can result when long variable names are allowed but only the first two characters are used for recognition. The safest approach when using a system of this type is to restrict oneself to using only two letters.

Finally, some BASICs which allow long names do not allow embedded names of BASIC statements (this does not apply to the BBC as long as the name does not start with a keyword).

The choice of names is up to you, the programmer, but careful naming is not enough — the variables must be given a value before they are used. Some BASICs can lull you into a false sense of security by automatically setting all variables to zero before the program is started (see CLR, CLEAR commands in Appendix III). This feature should be treated with care as it can lead to program errors which are very difficult to find.

Note that all the examples in this book use the minimum naming convention for variables, i.e. one letter plus one digit. This ensures that the examples can be run on most systems, which means they are portable, or as close to it as possible. You may wish to follow this practice if you intend to distribute your programs to other computers.

One other matter must be covered before leaving variables, namely the values which they can contain. Most computers have their store organized into groups of eight bits. (Each bit may only contain the value $\emptyset$ or 1, and a combination of eight bits allows a representation of numbers from $\emptyset$ to 255.) These eight bits are called a *byte* and the size of the computer store is usually quoted in terms of thousands of bytes. Actually, the abbreviation K is used, as in 1$\emptyset$K bytes. In the computer context K is taken to be the number 1$\emptyset$24, so a store size of 1$\emptyset$K bytes is actually 1$\emptyset$,24$\emptyset$ bytes.

Variables are given a fixed number of bytes by your BASIC system. The minimum is to provide a variable type to hold numbers to a fixed accuracy (six or seven decimal digits) and another variable type to hold characters. The latter is called a *string* variable, as it may contain a string of characters. For example, A1 could contain the value 1 or 1.237 or 5E+1$\emptyset$, and so on, while A\$ (a string variable, as shown by the \$ sign) could contain the letter B or the string HELLO THERE. Do not worry about string variables too much at the moment; they are discussed fully later in Section 4.2.

Many microcomputer BASICs, for reasons of economy, accuracy, and programming considerations, have introduced additional variable types. They may be shorter than ordinary variables (to save store space) and only contain whole numbers (integers) or may be longer than ordinary variables to give extra accuracy for a sensitive piece of numerical computation. Ignore them until you are competently writing programs which work. For completeness, the main types are given in Table 1.4.

Table 1.4 Types of variables

Numeric (standard; for real values)	A	Numeric, 6 to 7 digits accuracy, exponents allowed between 10^{-38} to 10^{+38}. The usual storage required is 4 bytes per variable. BBC standard is 9 digits accuracy, and 5 bytes per variable.
String (standard; the \$ following the name indicates a string type)	A\$	Character; from $\emptyset$ up to 255 characters. Flexible length, with 1 byte holding each character.

Integer numeric (the % following the name indicates an integer)	A%	Integer values only from −32,767 to +32,767. Storage is usually 2 bytes. BBC values range ± 200 million and occupy 4 bytes per variable.
Double precision numeric (the # following the name indicates double precision)	A#	Numeric; as standard numeric but with 16 to 17 digits accuracy. Few BASIC systems have this feature; one which does is Microsoft.

1.2.7 The END statement

It is desirable that the final program statement is END and that it has the highest statement number in the program so that it is the last instruction to be obeyed. A sensible and tidy approach to programming means that you should follow this rule, for while most BASICs will allow you to omit the END statement, some flag an error if it is absent and refuse to execute the program until one is inserted.

<table>
<tr><td colspan="2" align="center">END statement</td></tr>
<tr><td>General form</td><td align="right">END</td></tr>
<tr><td colspan="2">The statement causes program execution to terminate. Usually the last statement in the program.</td></tr>
<tr><td colspan="2">Some BASICs, mainly micros, do not insist on an END statement.</td></tr>
</table>

1.2.8 Statement layout

Every statement within a program begins the line with a statement number. Some micro BASICs allow multiple statements on a line; each statement following the first is separated by a colon (:) and does not have a statement number. For example:

    10   LET A=1 : LET A=A+1 : PRINT A

The order of execution is from left to right. Multiple statements per line are not recommended in general. They do save space in some computers, and you may need this feature if your computer does not have sufficient store for a program with the normal layout of one statement per line. Later we shall see that multiple statements per line may be used with discrimination when structuring a program.

Within each statement the computer will usually ignore any spaces (does not apply in strings). Thus:

18

        2Ø   LET B=A+C
and
        2 ØLE TB=A+C

are probably equally acceptable. However, reasonable use of spaces obviously
makes the program easy to input. The computer may store the input program in a
compact internal form, removing all the spaces, and expands it to some standard
readable form when you require a listing of it on the VDU. This can be frustrating
when spaces have been deliberately inserted to provide for statement indentation
and they are lost.

1.3 READING A PROGRAM

One of the most important skills that you acquire as a programmer is the ability
to be able to 'read' programs and get some measure of their function. You should
be able to recognize 'chunks' of program statements and realize the purpose
behind them, and not be deflected by the choice of variable names or layout. As
you progress you will find that you will use these chunks of programs, suitably
modified, for your own purposes. As a start on this process consider the following BASIC program, which uses the statements introduced in this chapter. It
calculates the area and circumference of a circle from a value for the radius. (The
area is πr^2 and the circumference $2\pi r$, where r is the radius and π has the value
3.14159 . . ..)

        1Ø   LET P=3.14159

        2Ø   INPUT R

        3Ø   LET A=P*R*R

        4Ø   LET C=2*P*R

        5Ø   PRINT R,A,C

        6Ø   END

Reminder: the first number on each line is a statement number and must be
present, and the statements are obeyed in increasing number order which is from
1Ø to 6Ø in the example above.
  When the computer is instructed to execute this program (see the RUN
command of Section 2.4.1) the value 3.14159 is assigned to the variable P. The
program pauses for input from the keyboard to the variable R, then continues
using these values to calculate A and C. Finally, the values of R (the radius) and
the calculated quantities A (the area) and C (the circumference) are printed out
on the VDU.
  The program remains in the computer store and may be re-run with a different
value of R, and is thus a general purpose program taking the important variable
quantity (the radius) from the keyboard. Note that we do not want to always type

in the value of π, which is a constant, so this is set up in the program. Of course, R could be assigned a value in the program instead of inputing it, but then the program has to be altered to change the value of R each time a different calculation is required. This is quite easy in this case, but not so with more complicated programs, and furthermore we would have lost the generality which is so easily available.

The structure of this program is very simple, yet occurs very often—even in very large programs. It is:

Input

Process

Output

That is, values are input, followed by a processing section, and the results are output. It may seem self-evident that such a layout should be followed. Yet there is such a great gulf between seeing a problem written out and writing the corresponding program to solve it that one of the practices of programming must be to supply the means to bridge this gap. Such design approaches, as above, help to do so. You will find that the input–process–output sequence will apply to a number of programs and may prove a useful starting point when you want to start designing a program.

Let us finish this chapter with another look at the program and a new statement, the REM statement. This statement allows you to introduce any remarks (or comments) that you wish to put into the program. The remarks are ignored by the computer and are there to assist the (human) programmer. For example:

```
10   REM THIS STATEMENT IS A REMARK
20   REM AND SO IS THIS!
30   REMARK AGAIN
```

<table>
<tr><td colspan="2" align="center">REM statement</td></tr>
<tr><td>General form</td><td align="right">REM comments</td></tr>
<tr><td colspan="2">Make comments, using any or all of the symbols you wish. The REM statement is used to add comments to the program listing and is ignored during program execution.</td></tr>
</table>

The hope is that REM statements together with the recognizable structures employed in a program will make the program self-documenting. That is, the programmer will only need a listing of the program, and no other information, to be able to decide exactly what the program does and how to run it.

Unfortunately, this is rarely achieved, but it is a worthwhile goal to strive towards and will certainly produce programs that are easier to modify and develop.

When you run the program above, the output will appear as three numbers on a line. It would be nice to indicate what they represent. This may be done with the PRINT statement on line 46 which displays the names which appear in the quotes above each value.

```
 5    REM FIRST PROGRAM .
10    LET P=3.14159
15    REM
20    INPUT R
25    REM
30       LET A=P*R*R
40       LET C=2*P*R
45    REM
46    PRINT "RADIUS","AREA","CIRCUM"
50    PRINT R,A,C
60    END
```

While it is desirable to include REM statements to illuminate the program layout, they do occupy store and if this is limited you may feel they are best omitted; however, include them where possible.

Note that the BBC BASIC is different from most others in the way it positions strings and numbers on output from a PRINT statement. Thus the headings above, RADIUS, AREA, CIRCUM, will not be correctly aligned with the numeric values below them. One way to overcome this problem is to add some spaces before each heading to shift them to the right. Thus use:

```
46   PRINT "   RADIUS", "   AREA", "   CIRCUM"
```

BBC BASIC users please bear this feature in mind when running other examples in this book.

1.4 EXAMPLE PROGRAMS

The first program below converts gallons to litres. The quantity in gallons is stored in the variable A and converted using the equivalence that 1 gallon is 4.54 litres (user typed responses are underlined):

```
10   REM CONVERSION TO LITRES
```

```
20      LET A=7
30      LET B=A*4.54
40   PRINT B
50   END
RUN      (command execution of the program)
31.78     (the answer)
END AT LINE 50   (the system indicates the termination of the program)
```

The answer given is that 31.78 litres is equivalent to 7 gallons. Note the system termination message END AT LINE 50 ; this varies with different BASIC systems. Some systems just respond OK at the end of a program, but the first form will be used throughout this book.

To achieve a rather nicer program for use let us add some PRINT statements and replace line 20 by an INPUT statement. Only the new lines need be typed into the computer. The full new program becomes:

```
10   REM CONVERSION TO LITRES
18   PRINT "GIVE GALLONS"
20   INPUT A
30    LET B=A*4.54
35   PRINT "GALLONS", "LITRES"
40   PRINT A,B
50   END
RUN
GIVE GALLONS
?   7 (requests input, which is given)
GALLONS    LITRES
7              31.78
END AT LINE 50
```

Finally, here is a quite complicated program where the PRINT statements display text and the answers on the same line, and a new variable type on line 50 is used.

The following payroll program takes as input the number of hours worked in a week (H) and the rate per hour (R), together with the employee name to produce the gross pay (G). (The user responses are underlined.)

```
10    REM PAYROLL PROGRAM
20    PRINT "GIVE HOURS AND RATE"
30    INPUT H,R
40    PRINT "GIVE NAME"
50    INPUT N$
60     LET G=H*R
70    PRINT N$; "HAS GROSS PAY OF";G;"POUNDS"
80    END
RUN
GIVE HOURS AND RATE
?    40 , 4.25
GIVE NAME
?    T. SMITH
T. SMITH HAS A GROSS PAY OF 170 POUNDS
END AT LINE 80
```

Notice the use of the string variable N$ to hold the name of the employee. Such variables hold text in the forms of strings of characters. Semicolons in PRINT statements as shown above have a different effect to commas. This is explained in detail later, but try the different effects for yourself.

Exercises

(The word LET has been omitted from the assignment statement.)

1.1 What final values do the variables contain after the following pieces of program have been run?

```
(a)    10    A=2
       20    B=A
       30    Z=A+2*B
       40    A=B


(b)    10    A=-5
       20    B=-A
       30    Q=1/(A+2)-B
```

(c)   10   B=0
           20   A=(B+1)/(2+B)
           20   Z=-2/(A*(B-A))

(d)   10   A=0
           20   A=A+10
           20   A=A*A
           40   A=A+10

1.2 Write assignment (LET) statements to evaluate the following formulae.

(a) $a = b + c^2$

(b) $a = \dfrac{a+b}{c}$

(c) $y = \dfrac{x + a}{y - b}$

(d) $y = \dfrac{1}{1 - 1/(a+b)}$

1.3 What does the following program seem to do?

```
10   A=22
20   B=-4.1
30   D=7.6
40   C=109.34
50   Z=A+B+C+D
60   Z=Z/4
70   PRINT Z
80   END
```

1.4 Write out the program of 1.3 replacing the statements 10 to 40 by one or several INPUT statements.

1.5 The object is to write a financial program which calculates the simple interest on a given sum of money over a given time. Let the variable M be the money, T the time in years, and R the interest rate (between 0 and 100). The appropriate formula is:

    Interest=M*T*(R/100).

(Hint: consider the standard input-process-output form for programs.)

2
Preparing and running a program

The computer system must be powered up and ready to receive keyboard input for BASIC before you can proceed with program development. This may take several steps to achieve, as it depends on the type of equipment that you are using.

The following section describes the main features of the different systems and why they function as they do.

2.1 READY FOR INPUT

Computer systems can be broadly considered as belonging to two types: the single-user systems with only one terminal and the multi-user systems with many terminals. Within the two types there is a similarity of operation and the following sections describe the features of each type.

Most microcomputers are single-user systems which simplifies their operation considerably. In this group there are two approaches to the provision of BASIC (and other computer languages as well). These are described in the following sections, 2.1.1 and 2.1.2.

2.1.1 Single-user systems (BASIC in ROM)

The simplest way is to build-in the complete BASIC system into ROM memory. This is 'read only memory' (ROM) and is organized in bytes like ordinary memory, but has been manufactured to contain the BASIC system in its memory cells. The contents of the cells are fixed and may be read but not written. No power is required to retain the information in a ROM memory, and you can imagine it as containing 'frozen in' programs.

Any programs may be stored in ROM and the BASIC system is just a rather complicated program or group of programs. Indeed, computer games depend on ROM to retain the games programs. These computers must also contain the usual store which was discussed in Chapter 1. This store is also known as 'random access memory' (RAM) because any part of it may be accessed for a read or write quite at random, without the need to read or write adjacent bytes.

When the power is switched on in these simple systems, part of the BASIC system is automatically copied from ROM (fixed memory) into RAM (the store) and the system is available for immediate use. Here is a typical startup procedure (user typed input is underlined):

(a)   Switch on the power, usually at the rear of the computer box. A slight delay may occur; on some systems the screen may fill with characters as BASIC is loaded from ROM.

(b)   The response will appear something like:

Figure 2.1 The Commodore PET computer with a high quality printer. (This photograph was supplied by Cytek (UK) Limited of Old Trafford, Manchester, who are specialist Commodore dealers)

Figure 2.2 The BBC computer; a powerful self-contained computer system with high resolution colour graphics. (Reproduced by permission of the British Broadcasting Corporation and Acorn Computers Limited)

Figure 2.3 The Sinclair ZX81 personal computer with a Sinclair printer. (Reproduced by permission of Martin Beer, Liverpool University)

HAPPY DAYS INC. BASIC VERSION 2.0

    32767   BYTES FREE

    READY

(c)   At this stage you may type in any BASIC command or instruction. Below is an extract from a session; notes are given in brackets on the right-hand side to help you follow it. The <return> key may be [RETURN] or [CR] or [ACCEPT] or [NEWLINE].

<u>PRINT "HI THERE"</u>	(type in, press <return>)
HI THERE	(response to immediate mode PRINT statement, see Section 2.4)
<u>10 INPUT A</u>	(press <return>)
<u>20 INPUT B</u>	(press <return>)
<u>30 C=A+B</u>	(press <return>)
<u>40 PRINT A;"+";B;"=";C</u>	(press <return>)
<u>50 END</u>	
<u>RUN</u>	
<u>?2</u>	(press <return>)
<u>?27.3</u>	(press <return>)
2+27.3=29.3	(the program result is output)

The number of bytes available in core (RAM) is usually displayed after the startup message. This is the maximum amount that you can use for your programs. As the program, which was typed in executes, it requests input on lines 10 and 20 by means of a ?. Once given the data, the calculation proceeds and the result is output as a simple addition sum. Note that everything within pairs of double quotes ("") in a PRINT statement is output exactly as it appears in the statement.

The advantages of a computer system with BASIC built into ROM are many, including very easy starting, no need to have a disc unit or a tape unit, and the possibility that BASIC may have features designed to suit the particular computer hardware.

2.1.2 Single-user systems (BASIC on disc)

One very versatile way to organize a computer is to provide it with a distinct operating system. This is a program which controls computer hardware by taking care of all hardware addresses and provides a simple series of commands to allow you to control the computer. In particular, the operating system allows

Figure 2.4 The Zenith Data Systems computer based on the Z8Ø microprocessor which runs the CP/M disc operating system. One disc drive is built into the cabinet next to the VDU screen. (Reproduced by permission of Martin Beer, Liverpool University)

you to load the BASIC system or any other program or language system and run it very easily. While running other systems, at least part of the operating system remains in the computer store. Thus there are three distinct states of such a computer:

(a)   The 'naked' state without the operating system or any other program. The computer will usually only accept a single command to load the operating system, generally from disc.

(b)   With the operating system loaded many commands which manipulate programs and data can be given. One of these may be to load a language system such as BASIC.

(c)   In this third state any BASIC statement or command may be given. There is also the option of leaving the BASIC system when required and reverting to interaction with the operating system.

One such operating system which is very widespread is called CP/M produced by Digital Research Inc. It provides a very good environment for the development of programs. Since CP/M itself is adapted to the particular computer hardware, the environment it provides for programs looks the same and is independent of the computer. Here is an initialization session with a computer running CP/M (user typed commands are underlined):

(a)   Switch on the power, usually at the rear of the computer box, on the disc unit if separate, and on the printer if fitted.

(b)   The computer response is minimal, and a single character will appear on the top left of the VDU as:

        H:

(c)   Load the system disc, which contains CP/M and BASIC, into the drive marked A. This is usually the drive next to the screen; discs are inserted with the slot towards the rear and label towards the drive door. Close the drive door. Other disc drives, if present, will be known as B and C.

(d)   Now load the operating system from the disc into the computer store; this is called 'booting' the system. To do this type B and press <return>, and the computer response should be to complete the word BOOT on the screen. The light should flash on drive A, indicating disc activity, and the startup message should then appear:

        H:<u>B</u>OOT   (press <return>)

        64 K   HAPPY DAYS INC. VERSION CPM 2.Ø

        A>

(e)   The CP/M system is now loaded and the prompt (>) indicates that any commands may be given. The A before the prompt shows that drive A is the currently active drive. Any CP/M commands will apply to the files on disc in drive A.

(f)   If the above sequence does not occur, press SHIFT and RESET to return to stage (b) and try again. Check your computer manual; the key in stage (d) may be different on your computer.

(g)   We have only loaded CP/M at this stage, so BASIC is not yet available. To illustrate a CP/M command type DIR which will display a list of files on the current drive (drive A):

        A><u>DIR</u>   (press <return>)

        (a list of file names
         will appear)

        A>

(h)   You will notice one of the files is called MBASIC.COM; this is the Microsoft version of the BASIC system. Type the name MBASIC to load this system:

        A><u>MBASIC</u>   (press <return>)

        BASIC 80 REL 5.21

30

> (CP/M VERSION)
>
> COPYRIGHT BY MICROSOFT
>
> CREATED 12–DEC–83
>
> 30715 BYTES FREE
>
> OK
>
> _

(i) After typing MBASIC, the A drive light should flash, and after a little delay the startup message similar to the one above should appear. The only prompt given in BASIC is the small flashing cursor in the first column of the screen.

(j) You are now ready for a BASIC session. Try the one shown in Section 2.1.1 as part (c) of the startup procedure.

Within BASIC under CP/M you will not notice the operating system and will be able to run, save, and list your BASIC programs as described in Chapter 1. If you wish, you can abandon BASIC by typing SYSTEM and you then return to CP/M alone. This is the state reached at stage (e) of the above procedure and under CP/M you may create, edit, move, delete, list, copy any files that you wish. Any BASIC programs which were not saved during the BASIC session will be lost when you return to CP/M.

A summary of CP/M commands is given in Section 8.5.2 and a discussion of the features of CP/M with BASIC is included in Chapter 8.

2.1.3 Multi-user systems

The computer which is supporting a number of terminals may be near to them or far away; it may be small or very large. Your main concern in this case is the use of a terminal and not the setting up of the system, which is a specialist job.

Like some systems described earlier in this chapter there is an operating system present to support the use of the computer by the many users. One of its tasks is to keep each user's job separate from all the others. Indeed, such operating systems manage to give you the appearance that you are the only user of the system.

The terminal (or VDU) is usually permanently connected to the computer, but may be inactive when you wish to use it. The first task is to activate the terminal, as the computer system does not waste its time checking terminals it considers inactive. Proceed as follows:

(a) Check that the VDU is powered on.

(b) Get the computer to realize that the terminal requires a response. This involves pressing a special key or some combination of keys. Here are some suggestions:

          press RETURN or SEND a few times

or

          press CONTROL and A simultaneously a few times

or

          press CONTROL and C simultaneously a few times

(c)   A response should appear as a new line, or a prompt of some kind, or a startup message.

(d)   To start a session it is necessary to identify yourself to the computer as a valid user of the system. Do this by means of a LOGIN or HELLO command; these vary from system to system but contain a user identification code and perhaps a password. When this has been accepted you are then running a job, one of many, on the system and a heading is usually output giving your user identification, job type, and other details.

(e)   If the system is dedicated to BASIC you may proceed with a session such as the one described in part (c) of Section 2.1.1. Otherwise you will need to load the BASIC system, usually by giving a single command such as BASIC.

After this sequence you will be able to enter and run programs which are described in this book. Before terminating a session you should ensure that any programs or data in store that are to be retained are saved in appropriate files.

In multi-user systems you can do anything you wish to your files, such as erase, copy, and edit, but usually cannot access other users' files unless they allow you to do so. There are commands which allow this sharing of files.

At the end of your BASIC session, remember to terminate your job. If you had to load BASIC explicitly you may have to exit from it before logging out. To do this there will be a BASIC command such as QUIT or BYE. In some systems this will be sufficient to also terminate the job, but if necessary also give the LOGOUT command. A typical system response to this termination procedure is given below:

    username LOGGED OUT AT time, date

    TIME USED = time

2.2 ENTERING A BASIC PROGRAM

Following one of the procedures outlined above, the system should now be ready for you to type in your program.

Type in the first line, not forgetting the statement number and press the <return> key (which may be $\boxed{\text{RETURN}}$ or $\boxed{\text{CR}}$ or $\boxed{\text{ACCEPT}}$ on your keyboard). This transfers control to the computer which will store the line and give a prompt for the next line. Some systems, mainly the multi-user large computers, will check the validity of the line before it is accepted. This is a very useful feature as obvious typing errors and things like missing brackets are detected. In this case the system will not store the incorrect line. Most microcomputer BASIC systems do not have this feature and wait until the program is run before performing this syntax check.

Type in the next line, followed by <return>, and continue until the complete program has been typed in.

Mistakes in statements are inevitable. The process of changing the statements is called editing, and the simplest changes are those made to the current line and are called line editing.

2.2.1 Line editing

There are two ways of correcting a mistake in a single line. Consider the incorrect statement:

    10 INPUS A

(a)   If you have already sent the line to the computer (by pressing <return>), the error is corrected by simply retyping the complete line, including the line number:

       10 INPUT A   press <return>

A line may usually be deleted by inputting a blank line having the same statement number. Thus:

       10   press <return>

will delete line 10. There is often a delete command which will delete lines singly or in groups.

(b)   If the <return> key has not yet been pressed, you may abandon the line or attempt to correct it. If it is simpler to abandon the line there is usually a pair of keys to be pressed; one is the <control> key (marked CTRL or CONTROL) and there is another which depends on your system. Here are a few examples:

    ICL 2903/4 computer <control> and X

    SINCLAIR ZX81 EDIT then NEWLINE

    MICROSOFT BASIC <control> and X

If you notice the mistake soon after it is made you simply press the <delete> key (marked DELETE or ← or RUBOUT or —underline) once for each character that has to be erased. This erases the characters which will be sent to the computer. Some systems leave them still visible on the VDU screen. For example:

    10 INPUS←T   A   press <return>

is equivalent to 10 INPUT A, where the <delete> key shows up as ← and erases the character before it. To change

    10 INPT   A

to the correct form press the <delete> three times (to delete the sequence 'T space A'):

    10 INPT A←←←UT   A press <return>

Remember, the last version of a particular line is the one which is stored and available when the program is run. The lines can be input in any order; omitted lines can be added at any time before running the program.

Most microcomputers provide a way of displaying all or part of the program on the VDU and moving the cursor round the screen changing the program. This is called screen editing and is very system dependent. In the BBC system move the cursor to the line to be changed and use the COPY key to create a new line. Press RETURN when the corrected line is complete.

2.3 SAMPLE PROGRAMS

Three programs are presented here for you to run. After each program is a detailed commentary on its features. The commands, RUN which executes a program and LIST which displays the program on the VDU, will be required, and are described fully in Section 2.4.

The first program performs a simple conversion from imperial units of feet and inches to metric units:

```
10   REM CONVERSION PROGRAM

20   PRINT "GIVE FEET AND INCHES"

30   INPUT F, I

40     I = I+F*12

50     C = I*2.540

60     C = C/100

70   PRINT "THE METRIC EQUIVALENT IS ";C;"METRES"

80   END
```

Line 1Ø is a comment and causes no action.

Line 2Ø displays the output GIVE FEET AND INCHES.

Line 3Ø requires two data items as input; give them on the same line separated by a comma or on separate lines.

Line 4Ø converts the feet to inches and adds it to the inches already input.

Line 5Ø converts all the inches to centimetres (2.54Ø cm to the inch).

Line 6Ø divides the centimetres by 1ØØ to give metres.

Line 7Ø displays the result in the text THE METRIC EQUIVALENT IS XXX.XX METRES.

To display the values as metres and centimetres separately in the output requires a little more knowledge of BASIC than has so far been covered. See the discussion of the INT function in Chapter 3 for further details.

Strings (of any characters) may be used in an analogous way to numbers, but there are some differences between the details of their use between BASIC systems. The following example should run on most machines:

```
10   REM NAME PROGRAM
20   PRINT "PLEASE ENTER YOUR SURNAME"
30   INPUT A$
40   PRINT "PLEASE ENTER YOUR FIRST NAME"
50   INPUT B$
60   C$=B$+" "+A$
70   PRINT "HALLO";C$;"HOW ARE YOU TODAY?"
80   END
```

Line 2Ø displays the output PLEASE ENTER YOUR SURNAME.

Line 3Ø requires some characters as input to variable A$.

Line 4Ø and 5Ø are similar for variable B$.

Line 6Ø puts the text together as first name followed by a space followed by surname. Although the plus sign is used, this operation is called concatenation and is the joining together of strings to form a longer string, which in this case is stored in the variable C$.

Some systems do not use the plus sign for concatenation but the ampersand (&) sign instead.

The final program is similar in structure to the two given above and to all the others we have looked at this far, but has some errors in it. Its purpose is to calculate and display the average value of the three values it accepts as input. If typed in as shown the program should execute but give incorrect values:

```
10    REM  AVERAGE PROGRAM
20    PRINT "PLSE GIVE 3 VALUES"
30    INPUT A,B1,C2
40       A1=A+B+C/3
50    PRINT "AVERAGE OF";A;B;C;"IS";A0
60    END
```

Run this program with test values for the three variables. Examine the result; if it is not correct proceed to 'debug' the program. That is, remove the bugs or errors in the program. Debugging is really an art which develops with practice. However, two things will help you to start debugging a program. Namely, what is the execution path of the program (the trace of those statements which have been executed, or flow of control) and what are the values of internal variables at various points in the program?

Examine the program by typing LIST. An inspection shows that the execution trace can only be from line 10 to line 60 without deviation. Next, examine the variables. The final values of the variables may be examined by means of an immediate PRINT statement (e.g. PRINT A2,A,B,C). Extra PRINT statements can be added to the program by choosing new line numbers such as 25, 35, and so on, to display intermediate values. Run and re-run the program until you have the desired result.

2.4 COMMANDS

Commands are instructions given directly to the BASIC system which is controlling the computer (on some machines there may exist a distinct operating system such as CP/M to which commands are sent) and are distinguished from BASIC language statements by the absence of line numbers.

Remember that statements have line numbers built into programs and are executed only when the program is run. Commands are executed immediately and exist to organize and control the resources of the system. Actually, many BASIC language statements may be given without a line, in which case they are executed immediately, and thus the distinction between statements and commands is a little fuzzy. The instruction:

```
PRINT 10*32        press <return>
```

without a line number is an example of a statement which will be obeyed immediately to give the result 32Ø on the VDU (see Section 9.1.2 for use in debugging).

A selection of the most used commands are given in the following sections. Here is a summary of their meanings.

Command	Meaning	Reference
RUN	Executes the program in store.	Section 2.4.1
Stop execution	Sometimes necessary to abort program execution by means of a 'break in' command from the keyboard.	Section 2.4.1
LIST	Lists all the statements of the program in store.	Section 2.4.2
NEW (or SCRATCH)	Clears the computer store to allow a new program to be entered from the terminal.	Section 2.4.3
OLD (or GET)	Copies a previously stored program from backing store into the computer store.	Section 2.4.4
SAVE	Saves the current program in the computer store by making copy to backing store.	Section 2.4.5
Find names of stored programs	Some systems keep an index of names of the programs which are stored on backing store. This index is called a directory or catalogue. The command is machine dependent.	
HELLO (or LOGIN)	Multi-user systems require a valid authorization code (sometimes called a user name) to use the system. A password may also be required.	
SYSTEM	For CP/M only, this terminates the BASIC session and returns control to the CP/M environment.	
BYE (or QUIT or LOGOUT)	This command terminates a BASIC session which commenced with HELLO or LOGIN.	

2.4.1 The RUN command

A program is loaded into the computer store from backing store, or typed in from the keyboard. It can be executed by merely typing:

RUN   press <return>

On receiving this command the BASIC system will complete its checks on the program and, if there are no errors, execute the statements in order. Consider a run on the full example program described in Section 1.3:

```
 5   REM   FIRST PROGRAM
10       LET P=3.14159
15   REM
20   INPUT R
25   REM
30       LET A=P*R*R
40       LET C=2*P*R
45   REM
46   PRINT "RADIUS","AREA","CIRCUM"
50   PRINT R,A,C
60   END
```

The program has been typed in and now may be executed (user typed information is underlined):

<u>RUN</u>	press <return>	
<u>? 2.4</u>	press <return>	(program requests, and is given, data for R)

```
          RADIUS AREA            CIRCUM

            2.4    18.0956        15.0796
```

END AT LINE 60   (some systems provide this indication of where the program terminates)

The program may be re-run many more times with different values for R, by giving the RUN command and data (as above) as many times as required.

<table>
<tr><td colspan="2" align="center">RUN command</td></tr>
<tr><td>General form</td><td align="right">RUN   line number</td></tr>
<tr><td colspan="2">The command instructs the system to execute the program held in core, starting with the lowest line number. If a line number is given with the command (e.g. RUN 100) then execution begins at this line number, and not the lowest one.</td></tr>
</table>

See the end of Section 2.4.4 for the Microsoft extended RUN command.

Stopping the program when it is running can be more difficult than starting it.

Most systems have some means of allowing a 'break' or 'break in' command to be given which will halt the program. This command also halts other functions such as LISTing a program. But be careful; most microcomputers also have a command to re-start the system from scratch. If this is given instead of the 'break' command you will lose all the program in store at the time. Below are some examples for different systems; consult your computer manual if in doubt.

ICL 2903/4 computer   <control> and ⬚A⬚

Microsoft BASIC

     Stops program   <control> and ⬚C⬚

     Suspends program   <control> and ⬚S⬚

     Re-starts after suspension   <control> and ⬚Q⬚

Sinclair ZX81

     Program waiting for input <shift> and ⬚A⬚ (STOP)

     Program running   ⬚space⬚   (BREAK)

Commodore PET   ⬚STOP⬚

BBC computer   ⬚ESCAPE⬚

2.4.2 The LIST command

This is probably the most frequently used command. LIST displays the program statements, which are in core, on the VDU. The program may be complete or not. You will find it useful during program input to list the previously typed statements so that you obtain a clear view of what has been accepted by the system, in view of editing, mistakes, etc.

By itself:

     LIST   press <return>

will list all the program statements in core on the VDU. The method of output of programs which are longer than the number of lines available on the screen varies. Some systems page the output. That is, they display 16 or 20 lines and wait until an <advance> key is pressed to display the next page of lines, and so on. The advance key may be an up arrow (↑). Others scroll the output continuously by adding lines at the bottom of the screen. In some systems this happens very quickly and there is a key which slows down the speed of the display, e.g. the ⬚REVS⬚ key on the CBM PET. In other systems you must stop the display (e.g. CP/M uses <control> and S), examine the output, and resume the scrolling display (CP/M uses <control> and S to start again).

All BASICs allow selected individual lines or groups of lines to be displayed by allowing start and end line numbers to be included on the LIST command:

LIST 100-110

would display lines 100 to 110 on the screen;

LIST 100-

would display from line 100 up to the end of the program on the screen. Some systems use a comma (,) instead of a hyphen (-) to separate the limits, for example:

LIST 90,110

<table>
<tr><td colspan="2" align="center">LIST command</td></tr>
<tr><td>General form</td><td>LIST lower limit – upper limit
or
LIST lower limit, upper limit</td></tr>
</table>

'Lower limit' and 'upper limit' are optional numbers which set the minimum and maximum of the line numbers to be displayed.

The LIST command displays the current program in store, line by line, starting from zero or the lower limit line number and proceeding to the end of the program or the upper limit line number.

The display mode, page or scroll, applies to the LISTing of programs and may also apply to the output from RUNing a program as well as to inputing a statement or command. The BBC BASIC starts in scroll mode and can be switched to page mode by pressing the CTRL and N keys simultaneously. New 'pages' are displayed by pressing the SHIFT key. CTRL and O keys switch back from page to scroll mode.

2.4.3 The NEW command (or SCRATCH or UNSAVE)

The NEW command clears the working store of any programs or statements it contains. It is used to clear the store so that a new program may be typed in. If the LIST command produces any output then these lines are the current program. NEW will delete these lines and a subsequent LIST will not display anything, indicating the store is clear.

NEW command (also SCRATCH or UNSAVE)

General form   NEW

  Some other names for this command are SCRATCH or UNSAVE.
The command clears the store of BASIC program statements, but does
not delete any part of the BASIC system.

2.4.4 The OLD command (or GET or LOAD)

If this command is available, its action is to obtain the named program from
backing store and load it into core. It always clears the current store contents
before loading the named program. Check its action by issuing a LIST after the
OLD (or GET or LOAD) command.

On the ICL 2904 computer the command:

    GET FRED

will load a copy of the program called FRED into store from the files on disc. On
a microcomputer (the CBM PET) the command:

    LOAD "FRED"

will load the program called FRED into store from the cassette tape; note the
quotes which are needed in this version. Below are summarized the main variants
of this command (for further details see Section 8.1). This command, like SAVE
(see Section 2.4.5), is very computer specific because it depends on the computer
hardware available to your system, and how easily this is operated via your
operating system. This hardware is the backing store media and ranges from
large disc units capable of holding 200 million bytes through floppy discs to
cassette tapes.

OLD command (also GET or LOAD)

For large computers, typically multi-terminal systems:

    OLD filename

        or

    GET filename

For microcomputers with discs:

> LOAD "filename"
>
> or
>
> LOAD "filename", R
>
> For microcomputers with cassette only:
>
> LOAD
>
> or
>
> LOAD "filename"
>
> "Filename" is the name of the file which contains the program. The command clears the store and loads the program, which was previously stored in the file by means of the SAVE command.
>
> The R option, if present, allows data files used by the previous program to be kept open and thus available for use by the new program which it loads and executes.
>
> As cassette tapes are sequential devices a LOAD without a filename can be unambiguously interpreted as 'load the next program on the tape'. A device number may appear after the filename on some systems.

Microsoft BASIC has a MERGE command which is like LOAD, but it does not clear the store. Thus programs, or parts of them, may be put together. It also has an extended RUN command which loads and executes the program, of the form:

RUN "filename", R

The R is optional, as discussed above.

2.4.5 The SAVE command

This command is the reverse of the OLD command in that SAVE copies a program from store onto backing store. As with the OLD command the type of backing store tends to determine the variants of the command (see Section 8.1).

Most systems include the name of the file which is to contain the program on the SAVE command. However, at least one large computer has the command NAME in order to separately name the program which may then be SAVED with various options to allow other users of the system access to it.

SAVE command

For large computers:

    SAVE filename

       or

    SAVE options (of previously NAMED program)

For microcomputers with discs or cassette:

    SAVE "filename"

For microcomputers with cassette:

    SAVE

The command copies the current program from store to backing store and saves it with the given filename.

'Options' if applicable indicate the type of access other users have to your program on a multi-access system.

2.5 STORED PROGRAMS

It is important for a computer system to have a facility to store and retrieve programs and data to or from the area called the backing store. The backing store is some magnetic medium which retains information for many months or even years without power being required. Like the machine addresses for computer core, there are complicated means of locating selected pieces of this media. Tapes simply have track on them, but discs may have tracks and sectors, or even cylinders. Thankfully there are means of leaving the computer to cope with the detail of these items and we can concentrate on using them in any easy manner. Most BASIC systems allow you to imagine the backing store as a large area which retains information. Any part of this area may be given a name chosen by you, subject only to some restrictions, and programs or data may be stored in the named area. Each named part is called a file and the complete area is called the file store.

2.5.1 Obtaining details of your files

The amount of space required for a particular file depends on the size of the program or the amount of data it contains, but there is usually some minimum size set by system characteristics. Since the backing store cannot hold an infinite number of files you will want to know what it contains and how much space has been used. If you have only a cassette tape you must keep a record of the files stored and their positions on the tape on paper, but if you have a disc system, there is a built-in index kept up to date by the BASIC system or the operating system.

Refer to your computer handbook for the commands to display these details. Some widely available systems are documented in Chapter 8.

2.6 AN EXAMPLE SESSION

An example BASIC session is presented below without the startup details for the computer and BASIC, which have been covered in earlier sections of this chapter. The program being developed accepts a number as input and outputs the square, cube, and fourth power of this number.

All the computer input and output is in bold type, with user typed input underlined. Comments are in brackets at the end of each line or between computer lines.

```
Startup BASIC system
```

```
10    REM NUMBER EXAMPLE          (each line typed in)

20    INPUT A

30      B=A*A

40    PRINT "THE SQUARE IS",A

LIST                              (list the program as it exists now)

10    REM NUMBER EXAMPLE

20    INPUT A

30      B=A*A

40    PRINT "THE SQUARE IS",A

RUN                               (execute the program)

? 7                               (request for input)

THE SQUARE IS      7              (the result)

ERROR AT LINE   40
```

(The system may object that no END statement terminated the program. It may not RUN the program unless an END is present. The result is incorrect because variable A has been used on line 40 instead of B.)

```
40    PRINT "THE SQUARE IS",B      (re-type line 40)

50      B=B*A                       (each new line typed in)

60    PRINT "THE CUBE IS",B
```

```
70    B=B*B
80    PRINT "THE FOURTH IS",B
90    PRINT
100   END
RUN                              (execute the program)
? 9                              (request for input)
THE SQUARE IS      81
THE CUBE IS        729
THE FOURTH IS   5.31441E+5       (the results)
END AT LINE 100
```

(The correct results should be 81, 729, and 6561 so investigate the error.)

```
LIST                             (look at program)
  10   REM NUMBER EXAMPLE
  20   INPUT   A
  30     B=A*A
  40   PRINT "THE SQUARE IS",B
  50     B=B*A
  60   PRINT "THE CUBE IS",B
  70     B=B*B
  80   PRINT "THE FOURTH IS",B
  90   PRINT
 100   END
```

(Line 70 is incorrect; it should be B*A. Also tidy up the text on line 80.)

```
70    B=B*A                      (re-type line)
80    PRINT "THE FOURTH POWER IS",B
RUN                              (execute the program)
? 9                              (request for input)
THE SQUARE IS      81
THE CUBE IS        729           (the correct results)
THE FOURTH POWER IS 6561
```

(blank line provided by PRINT on line 9Ø)

END AT LINE 1ØØ

<u>SAVE "EXAMPLE 1"</u> (saves a copy of the current program in store to backing store with the name EXAMPLE 1)

<u>LIST 2Ø</u> (look at one line only of program)

2Ø   INPUT A (the program still exists in store; the SAVE has not removed it, only copied it)

<u>NEW</u> (deletes program from store)

<u>LIST</u>

NO PROGRAM (some systems respond like this)

(There may be no response to LIST when a program is not in store.)

<u>LOAD "EXAMPLE 1"</u> (obtains a copy of the program previously saved)

<u>LIST   8Ø,1ØØ</u> (look at a group of program lines)

 8Ø   PRINT "THE FOURTH POWER IS",B

 9Ø   PRINT

1ØØ   END

The program is now back into store and may be executed again, or modified in any way. Note that some of the details of the SAVE and LOAD commands depend on the medium being used (tape or disc) and the computer system.

Exercises

2.1   The repayment of a loan or mortgage proceeds with a fixed annual payment which pays off both the interest accrued over the year and some of the principal money borrowed.

If m pounds were borrowed for t years at an interest rate i, the annual repayments can be obtained using the following algebraic formula:

$$\text{Repayments} = \frac{mr^{t}(r-1)}{(r^{t}-1)} \quad \text{where } r = 1 + \frac{i}{1ØØ}$$

Write a program to take as input the values of m,t,i and calculate the annual repayments.

2.2   A cardboard box is to be manufactured to given dimensions. Determine the volume, the surface area of cardboard required, and the cost of construction.

    The length L, height H, and width W, all in centimetres, are input to the program. There is a fixed cost of 5 pence for the cutting and folding of the cardboard, irrespective of size, and the cardboard costs Ø.Ø2 pence per square centimetre. Ignore any flaps or tabs required for glueing the edges together. Write the program so that full details are printed, both of input and output.

2.3   The cardboard box of exercise 2.2 above is to be colour printed on the top and adjacent four sides for use as a chocolate box. Printing costs Ø.ØØ5 pence per square centimetre.

    Modify the program solution of 2.2 to incorporate these changes. Choose some dimensions suitable for 1 lb box of chocolates, and vary them to see how the cost changes while the volume remains the same.

2.4   A credit card account is required each month for each card holder. The general form is shown below. It starts with the balance of money owing from the previous month, together with interest charges of 8 per cent per month. Then follows a list of items purchased with the card and their costs. The statement finishes with the total amount of money now owing to the credit card company and the minimum amount payable, which is 10 per cent of this total.

    Write a program to produce such an output for three items purchased. (Use string variables to hold the description of the items.)

TAXHAVEN CREDIT CARD LIMITED

PREVIOUS	BALANCE	XXXX
	INTEREST	XXX
ITEM		*COST*
YYYYY		XXXX
YYYYY		XXXX
YYYYY		XXX
		————
	TOTAL	XXXX
		————
MINIMUM PAYABLE		XXXX

3
More introductory BASIC programming

The first two chapters have introduced the elements of the BASIC language and how to use the computer. In the programs considered so far, execution began with the lowest numbered statement and finished at the highest numbered statement. There has been no facility yet described which can omit a statement under certain conditions or, for example, transfer the execution control to the beginning of the program once the end has been reached. Such changes in the execution of a program can be made by using four BASIC instructions, namely, IF, GOTO, and FOR-NEXT. The common forms of these instructions, available in all BASIC systems, are described in this chapter.

Since the effect of these instructions is to transfer control to another part of the program, it is important to have some way of illustrating these changes. One old, and rather inadequate, method was called flowcharting. A better method, using structograms, is introduced in the next section.

3.1 PROGRAM CONTROL SYMBOLS

The following symbols deserve to be widely accepted as the best way of depicting the flow of (execution) control in structured programs. When suitably combined they give a complete visual picture of the detailed logical operations of groups of program instructions. They are called structograms, or Nassi–Shneiderman diagrams after their creators.

They are not, in themselves, a technique for designing programs but rather an aid to design. They provide a good system for describing and understanding programs and are used to illustrate program control in this chapter.

The simplest symbol is just a rectangular box which contains the description of an action performed by one BASIC statement or a group of statements. Such a box is called a *process* symbol. All assignments, INPUT/OUTPUT statements, calls, or any other collection of sequential operations may be put into this symbol. Control enters at the top of the box and leaves from the bottom, as illustrated in Figure 3.1.

Although it does not show off the value of the symbols, consider the simple program of Section 2.1. Its actions could be represented in process symbols as:

| Input values to A and B |
| Compute the sum |
| Display the results |
| End |

The assignment of the various actions to different boxes is quite arbitrary for this simple program, which only contains a series of sequential statements, so the division into various process symbols is made on the logical steps in the program: input, assignment, output, and end. It could all quite easily have been put into one process symbol. The other point to notice is that the complete program is itself a block—a large process symbol containing others within it. This is a characteristic of this method of describing programs and coincides closely with structured programming.

Control starts at the top of the outer rectangle, proceeds through each box, and finishes at the bottom of the outer rectangle. A complete program, or a logically complete part of one, should fit on one page. There is no provision in this scheme for off-page connectors, as in flowcharting, because of the confusion that they can cause.

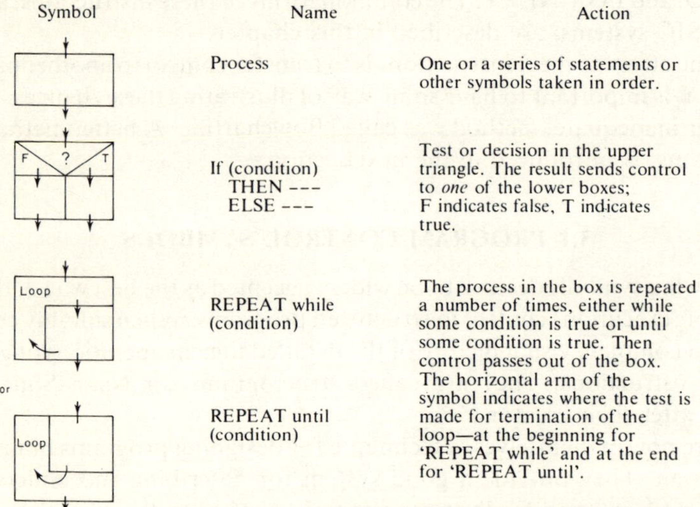

Figure 3.1 Some Structogram symbols. The arrows are *not* part of the symbols; they are included here only to help with the initial appreciation of the symbols

3.2 SIMPLE IF STATEMENTS

The programs discussed thus far have had a very simple structure—the sequence of actions as illustrated in the example above (Section 3.1). This structure, or rather lack of significant structure, does not allow many problems to be solved, but there exists a conditional test, provided by the IF statement, which allows more versatile programs to be developed.

Consider the following program:

```
10   INPUT A,B

20   IF A>B THEN 50

30      PRINT A,B

40   STOP
```

```
50      PRINT B,A

60   END
```

The effect is to accept two numbers as input and print them out in ascending order. Line 2Ø tests if A is greater than B; when this is true control branches to line 5Ø, which prints out the smallest (B) first. If the test is not true, control continues with the next statement on line 3Ø, which prints out the smallest (A). Note the STOP statement which terminates program execution.

STOP statement

General form   **STOP**

    Causes program execution to terminate; it may appear a number of times, or not at all. It is not usually allowed in place of END, which is the last program statement.

When a STOP statement is encountered during program execution, the execution ceases and the system exits from the program and prompts the user for another command. There should be only one END statement in a program (with the highest statement number), but some systems allow multiple END statements and regard it as equivalent to STOP.

Thus the IF statement allows conditional branching of controls; i.e. transfer of control only if some condition is true.

Below is a program which uses two of the allowed forms to construct a conditional in the IF statement. Its purpose is to print out a message indicating the sign of the input number.

```
10      PRINT "INPUT A NUMBER"

20   INPUT N

30   IF N>=Ø THEN 6Ø

40      PRINT "YOUR NUMBER IS NEGATIVE"

50   STOP

60   IF N<>Ø THEN 9Ø

70      PRINT "YOUR NUMBER IS ZERO"

80   STOP

90      PRINT "YOUR NUMBER IS POSITIVE"

100  END
```

50

Simple IF statement

General form   IF e THEN s

e is an expression, which is true or false.
s is a statement number.

If e is true, control is transferred to statement number s, otherwise control continues with the next numbered statement.
Some systems allow the additional form

    IF e GOTO s

which has exactly the same effect as above.
Others, e.g. BBC BASIC, allow any other BASIC statement (except another IF) following the THEN part of the statement. For example:

    IF A=2+B THEN PRINT "TOTAL IS",A

    IF X>Y THEN STOP

If you have a BASIC which allows several statements on a line, then be careful using the IF statement, because the case of the condition not being true causes control to pass to the next line, not the next statement.

The following forms are allowed. Control passes to the statement with number s if the condition is true.

Form		Condition
IF a>b	THEN s	a is greater than b
IF a<b	THEN s	a is less than b
IF a=b	THEN s	a is equal to b
IF a<>b	THEN s	a is not equal to b
IF a>=b	THEN s	a is greater than or
IF a=>b	THEN s	equal to b
IF a<=b	THEN s	a is less than or
IF a=<b	THEN s	equal to b

A frequent use of the IF statement is to set a variable to one of two values. For example, the following program statements set Y to 1 if x is 50, otherwise Y to 0 (on line 70, the GOTO passes control to line 100; see Section 3.2.1 for details).

    50 IF X=50 THEN 80

```
60      Y=Ø

70   GOTO 1ØØ

80      Y=1

1ØØ  ----
```

Referring to Figure 3.1, the above statements may be illustrated as:

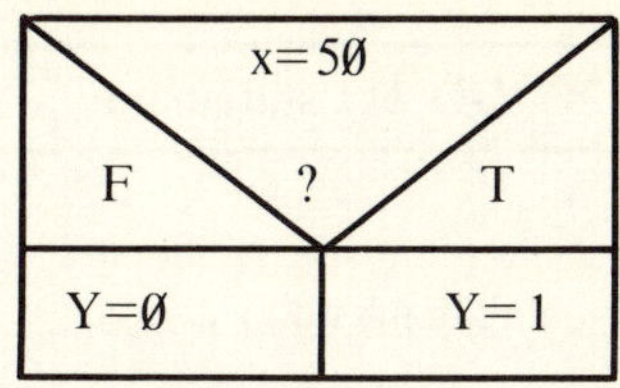

When the condition (x = 5Ø) is true, control passes to the right-hand lower box; otherwise it passes to the left-hand lower box. Whatever follows on line 1ØØ appears below both these boxes.

In the case of only one action being required as a result of an IF statement, one of the lower boxes is left empty. For example:

```
40   IF x=1Ø THEN N=N+1

6Ø   INPUT A
```

could be illustrated as:

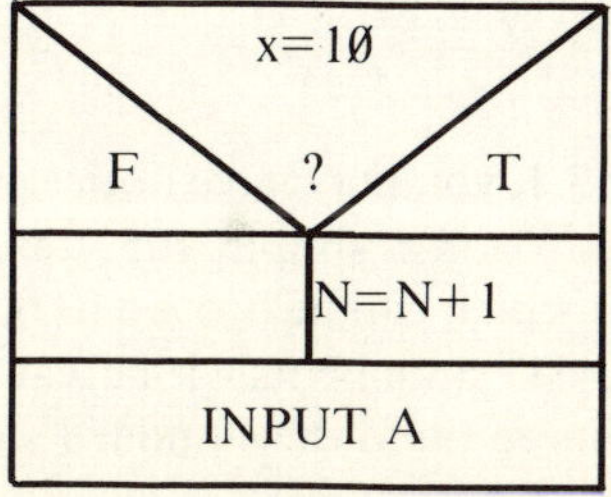

The conditional expression part of the IF statement may be quite complicated. For example:

```
IF A+B>43 THEN 21Ø

IF A/C<=B+1ØØ+D THEN 92

IF 1Ø=A+B THEN A=B/4
```

Conditional expressions may also be combined using the logical operators NOT, AND, OR. These usually have the meaning which seems evident from reading the expression, but see Section 6.1.1 for full details. For example:

    IF X>1 AND Y>1 THEN 9Ø

    IF NOT (X>2) THEN STOP

    IF X>1 OR X<Ø THEN 1ØØ

3.2.1 GO TO statement

The GO TO statement always transfers control to the statement indicated.

<table>
<tr><td colspan="1" align="center">GO TO statement</td></tr>
<tr><td>

General form

GO TO s

or

GOTO s   (one word)

Control is transferred to statement number s.

</td></tr>
</table>

Note that BBC BASIC does not allow the form with a space, GO TO, but requires the form GOTO.

Examples of this statement, which may cause a 'jump' backwards or forwards, are:

    GO TO 5Ø

    GO TO 9999

With reference to Figure 3.1, you may have noticed that no diagram exists for the GO TO statement. The reason is simple; this statement does not fit into the sensible range of structures which can be proved to be sufficient to construct all types of programs. Use GO TO statements with great care, preferably in combination with other statements to build the standard structures referred to in the figure.

3.2.2 Example program

Consider a program to convert a temperature from Centigrade to Fahrenheit, according to:

$$\text{Fahrenheit} = \text{Centigrade} \times \frac{18Ø}{10Ø} + 32$$

The program might be

```
10   INPUT C
20      F=C*180/100+32
30      PRINT C,F
40   END
```

This would produce satisfactory results, but you would have to remember what C and F stand for, and in what order you have printed them out. It would be much better to print out headings. Thus, add the lines:

```
30   PRINT "DEGREES CENTIGRADE = ";C
35   PRINT "DEGREES FAHRENHEIT = ";F
 5   PRINT "PROGRAM TO CONVERT CENTIGRADE TO
     FAHRENHEIT"
 6   PRINT "INPUT TEMPERATURE IN DEGREES CENTIGRADE"
```

This program would now produce the following output, in which user responses are underlined.

```
RUN
PROGRAM TO CONVERT CENTIGRADE TO FAHRENHEIT
INPUT TEMPERATURE IN DEGREES CENTIGRADE
?50
DEGREES CENTIGRADE = 50
DEGREES FAHRENHEIT = 122
END AT LINE 40
```

While useful for conversion of a single temperature value, the program would need to be started each time for a series of values of temperature. To make the program accept a series of values we need to get control back to statement 6, after the print statement on line 35 has been displayed. Adding the line:

```
37   GO TO 6
```

and two REM statements gives the following:

```
LIST
 1   REM CONVERSION OF CENTIGRADE TO FAHRENHEIT
 2   REM C = CENTIGRADE, F = FAHRENHEIT
```

```
  5   PRINT "PROGRAM TO CONVERT CENTIGRADE TO
      FAHRENHEIT"

  6   PRINT "INPUT TEMPERATURE IN DEGREES CENTIGRADE"

 1Ø   INPUT C

 2Ø       F=C*18Ø/1ØØ+32

 3Ø   PRINT "DEGREES CENTIGRADE = ";C

 35       PRINT "DEGREES FAHRENHEIT = ";F

 37   GO TO 6

 4Ø   END

RUN

PROGRAM TO CONVERT CENTIGRADE TO FAHRENHEIT

INPUT TEMPERATURE IN DEGREES CENTIGRADE

?5Ø

DEGREES CENTIGRADE = 5Ø

DEGREES FAHRENHEIT = 122

INPUT TEMPERATURE IN DEGREES CENTIGRADE

?8Ø

DEGREES CENTIGRADE = 8Ø

DEGREES FAHRENHEIT = 176

INPUT etc.
```

The program will loop round between lines 6 to 37 endlessly; inspection of Figure 3.1 indicates that the appropriate diagram is:

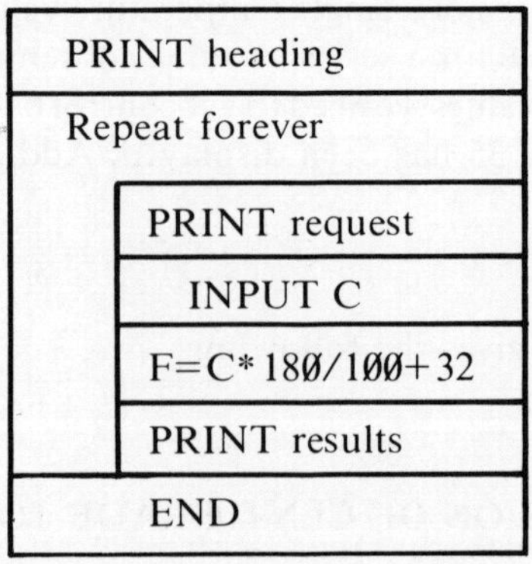

PRINT heading
Repeat forever

	PRINT request
	INPUT C
	F=C*18Ø/1ØØ+32
	PRINT results

END

The only way to stop it is to abandon the program, usually via a 'break in' command. This is not a satisfactory state of affairs for a well-designed program, so we get the program to stop if a certain value of C is given, say 9999. Adding the statement:

    15   IF C = 9999 THEN STOP

we obtain:

<u>LIST</u>

```
 1    REM CONVERSION OF CENTIGRADE TO FAHRENHEIT
 2    REM C = CENTIGRADE, F = FAHRENHEIT
 5    PRINT "PROGRAM TO CONVERT CENTIGRADE TO
      FAHRENHEIT"
 6    PRINT "INPUT TEMPERATURE IN DEGREES CENTIGRADE"
1Ø    INPUT C
15      IF C = 9999 THEN STOP
2Ø      F=C*18Ø/1ØØ+32
3Ø      PRINT "DEGREES CENTIGRADE =";C
35      PRINT "DEGREES FAHRENHEIT =";F
37    GO TO 6
4Ø    END
```

<u>RUN</u>

```
PROGRAM TO CONVERT CENTIGRADE TO FAHRENHEIT
INPUT TEMPERATURE IN DEGREES CENTIGRADE
?5Ø
DEGREES CENTIGRADE = 5Ø
DEGREES FAHRENHEIT = 122
INPUT TEMPERATURE IN DEGREES CENTIGRADE
?8Ø
DEGREES CENTIGRADE = 8Ø
DEGREES FAHRENHEIT = 176
INPUT TEMPERATURE IN DEGREES CENTIGRADE
```

56

?9999

END AT LINE 40

The appropriate diagram for this program is:

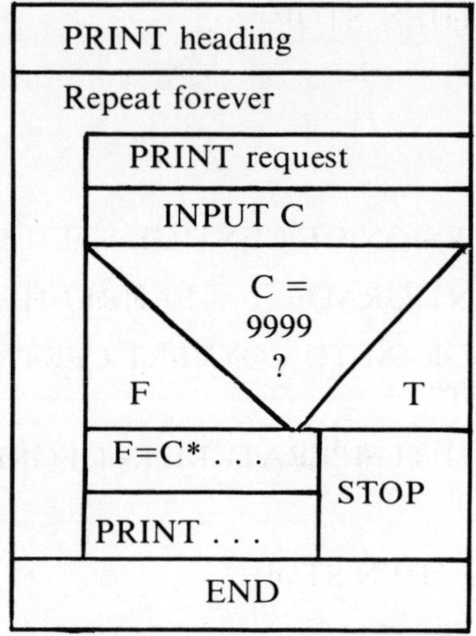

which is much more satisfactory, as it has a proper termination point.

3.3 LOOPS

The previous section showed how it was possible to set up a means of repeating a series of statements and controlling the termination of what is in fact a loop.

If we know how many temperatures we are going to convert, we could count the temperatures as we convert them and jump to the end when we have performed the required number of calculations. The loop could be programmed using an IF statement, a counter variable I which records the number of iterations, and a variable N containing the desired number of iterations:

```
10    INPUT N
20    I=1
30    IF I>N THEN 90
40       INPUT C
50       F=C*180/100+32
60       PRINT F
70       I=I+1
```

80   GO TO 30

90   END

Apart from the input value N, the statements controlling the loop are: line 20 to set up the counter I to one, line 30 tests if N iterations have been made, line 70 adds one to counter I each time it is used, and line 80 branches back to the start of the loop at line 30. Again the GO TO is not represented by the structograms except as loop feature, so this program appears as:

<table>
<tr><td colspan="2">INPUT N</td></tr>
<tr><td colspan="2">Initialize I to 1</td></tr>
<tr><td colspan="2">REPEAT WHILE I ≤ N</td></tr>
<tr><td></td><td>INPUT C</td></tr>
<tr><td></td><td>F = C* . . .</td></tr>
<tr><td></td><td>PRINT</td></tr>
<tr><td></td><td>Increase I by 1</td></tr>
<tr><td colspan="2">END</td></tr>
</table>

There is a confusing loss of the IF statement in the above. This is because it is included in the 'REPEAT WHILE' symbol and as indicated by the horizontal part this test appears before the 'INPUT C'.

There are several ways of creating the loop, apart from the method above. For example, delete lines 30 and 80 and add:

80   IF I<=N THEN 30

which tests at the end of each computation of a value for Fahrenheit. The revised structogram is:

<table>
<tr><td colspan="2">INPUT N</td></tr>
<tr><td colspan="2">Initialize I to 1</td></tr>
<tr><td></td><td>INPUT C</td></tr>
<tr><td></td><td>F = C*</td></tr>
<tr><td></td><td>PRINT</td></tr>
<tr><td></td><td>Increase I by 1</td></tr>
<tr><td colspan="2">REPEAT UNTIL I>N</td></tr>
<tr><td colspan="2">END</td></tr>
</table>

Again the final IF statement is incorporated into the structogram symbol, in this case the 'REPEAT UNTIL'. Many programming languages, and some extended BASICs, provide statements to perform these loops easily, thus avoiding the slightly clumsy use of IF and GO TO statements.

The first form corresponds closely with the action of the FOR–NEXT statements described in the next section.

3.3.1 FOR–NEXT statements

The BASIC language provides a pair of statements to give the looping effect in the example above (Section 3.3). These are the FOR statement and the NEXT statement which surround, or bracket, the group of statements which are inside the loop.

For example, the above program could be written:

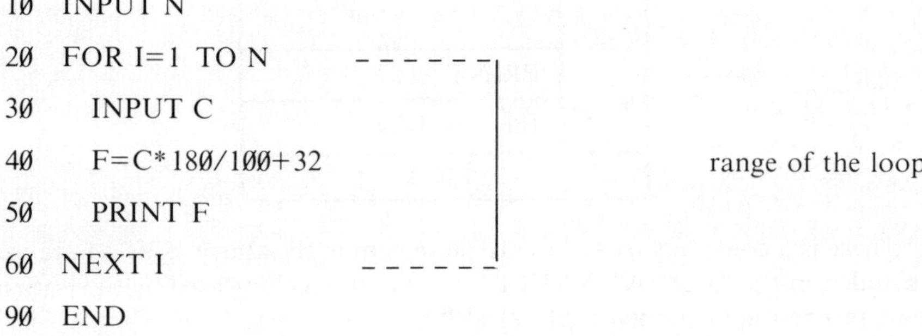

```
10   INPUT N
20   FOR I=1 TO N
30      INPUT C
40      F=C*180/100+32          range of the loop
50      PRINT F
60   NEXT I
90   END
```

Line 20 automatically takes care of the business of starting I at 1, and incrementing it by 1 each time the loop is executed. Line 60 indicates the extent of the loop.

All statements between the FOR statement and the NEXT statement are obeyed for I=1, I=2, I=3, and so on to I=N. Control is then passed to the statement following the NEXT statement. Hence, in our example, N temperatures are input, converted and printed, and then the program ends.

This program may be illustrated with the following diagram:

| INPUT N |
| FOR I=1 TO N |
| INPUT C |
| F=C* . . . |
| PRINT F |
| END |

<table>
<tr><td align="center">FOR statement</td></tr>
</table>

General form

$$\text{FOR } i = j \text{ TO } k$$
$$\text{or}$$
$$\text{FOR } i = j \text{ TO } k \text{ STEP } m$$

where i is the control numeric variable and j, k, m may be numeric expressions (i.e. constants, variables, or combinations of these).

The loop started by the FOR statement is limited by the NEXT i statement. All the statements between FOR and NEXT are executed for

$$i = j, i = j + m, i = j + 2m, i = j + 3m, i = \ldots$$

until the limit k is reached.

That is, if m is positive the loop continues as long as $i \leqslant k$. If m is negative the loop continues as long as $i \geqslant k$. If the STEP option is not present, then the step size m is assumed to be $+1$.

Here are some examples:

```
10   FOR I=1 TO 10
20      PRINT I
30   NEXT I
```

Will print out all the numbers between 1 and 10.

```
10   FOR K=1 TO 10 STEP 2
20      PRINT K
30   NEXT K
```

Will print out all the odd numbers between 1 and 10.

```
10   X=2
20   Y=3
30   FOR P=X+Y TO X*Y
40      PRINT P
50   NEXT P
```

Will print the values 5 and 6.

```
10   FOR A=10 TO 1 STEP -1
```

```
20      PRINT A

30   NEXT A
```

Will print the numbers, in descending order, 1Ø to 1.

Many BASICs, for example Sinclair ZX81, follow the standard and test the loop limits at the beginning of the loop, so that:

```
1Ø   FOR I=3 TO 2

2Ø      PRINT I

3Ø   NEXT I

4Ø   ----
```

will not print anything, but will continue with statement 4Ø. This corresponds with the example program of Section 3.3 with the 'REPEAT WHILE' structogram.

Other BASICs, such as the BBC, do not follow the standard; always execute the loop at least once and effectively test at the end of the loop. The suggested modifications to the example in Section 3.3 with the 'REPEAT UNTIL' structogram follow this rule. In this case the program would print 3.

In all the examples which follow, the first form of structogram 'REPEAT WHILE' will be used to represent the FOR–NEXT loop as this is the way the Minimal BASIC standard defines its operation. That is, the test is at the beginning of the loop. If your system tests at the end you could use the other symbol 'REPEAT UNTIL' marked with FOR at the bottom. Do not worry about this difference; it will only cause differences of operation in about one program in a thousand between the two types of system. Just be aware of how your system operates.

Some warnings follow. Do not alter the value of the control variable inside the loop. The system will automatically increment this variable and make the test at each cycle of the loop. This means that the control variable should not appear on the left of a LET statement, in an INPUT or READ statement, or be used in an interior nested loop. The following examples are *wrong*:

```
1Ø   FOR  I=1 TO 1Ø

2Ø      I=I+1                        (control variable I is changed)

3Ø   NEXT I


1Ø   FOR A=2 TO 8 STEP 2

2Ø   INPUT I,A             (control variable A appears in an INPUT)

3Ø      I=1Ø+I+A

4Ø   NEXT A
```

You should *not* depend on the control variable having a set value when the loop has finished. In the example:

```
10   FOR L=1 TO 10
20      PRINT L
30   NEXT L
40   PRINT L
```

the value printed out at line 40 may be 10 or 11 or just rubbish. The results vary for different systems, although the Minimal BASIC standard indicates that the control variable may contain the next unused value in the FOR sequence of increments.

Be wary of changing the FOR numeric limits inside the FOR loop although it *should not* affect the operation of the loop; for example:

```
10   A=2
20   FOR I=A TO 4
30      A=A+1
40      PRINT I
50   NEXT I
```

should produce the results 2, 3, and 4 correctly.

<table>
<tr><td colspan="2" align="center">NEXT statement</td></tr>
<tr><td>General form</td><td align="right">NEXT i
or
NEXT</td></tr>
<tr><td colspan="2" align="center">where i is a numeric variable</td></tr>
<tr><td colspan="2">Terminates a FOR loop. Most BASICs require a separate NEXT, with the control variable name, for each FOR statement. Some will accept NEXT without the control variable name, or even with several variable names, to terminate nested loops.</td></tr>
</table>

It is quite possible to use an IF or GO TO statement to jump out of a FOR–NEXT loop before it has completed all its iterations, but is not recommended as this is not a clear and unambiguous exit from the loop, and as such is virtually impossible to represent as a structogram. However, you should *never* jump into a loop from outside the FOR–NEXT statements as the results would be unpredictable.

3.3.2 Nested FOR loops

The following example shows how one FOR loop can be used inside another. Note that the inner loop must be completely contained within the outer loop. This is known as nesting of FOR loops.

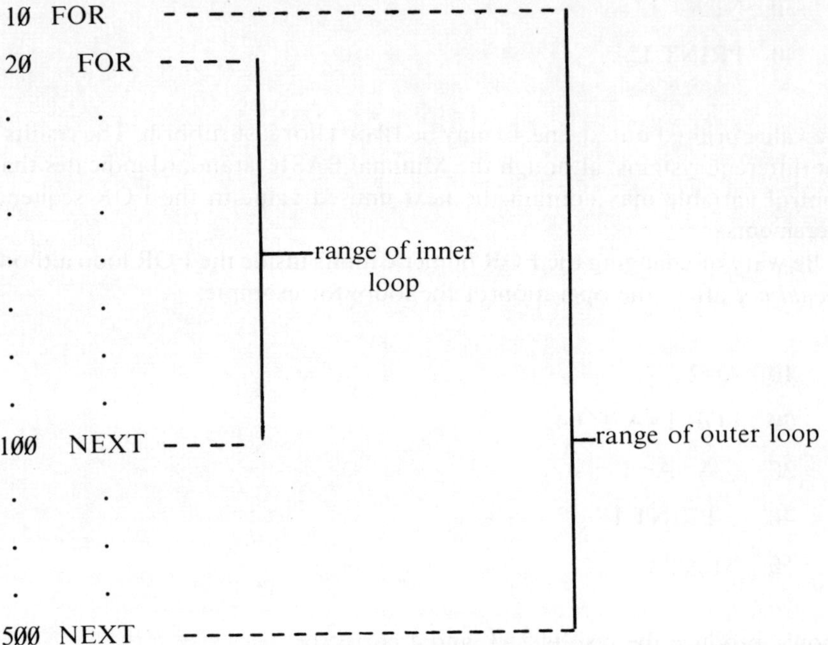

The diagram for such a nesting is given below.

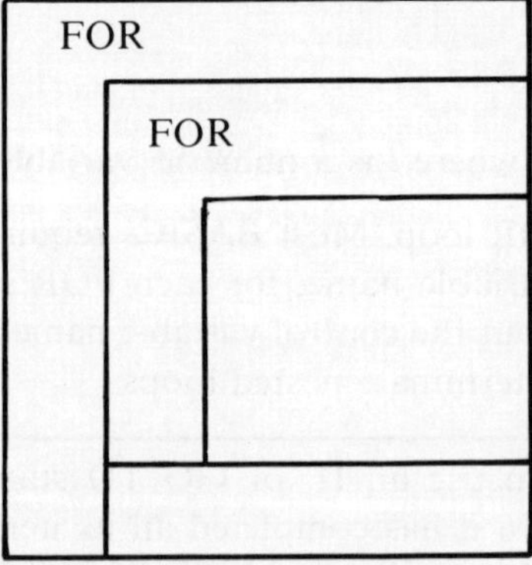

The loops must be completely nested. The inner one must terminate inside the outer one. The following program prints out a multiplication table:

```
10    FOR I=1 TO 5
20      FOR J=1 TØ 5
30        Z=I*J
40          PRINT Z;
50      NEXT J
60    PRINT
70    NEXT I
```

The semicolon in the PRINT statement on line 4Ø causes all the Z values for a complete inner loop to be printed on one line. Each time this finishes the PRINT statement on line 6Ø starts a new line for the I loop. Thus:

<u>RUN</u>

1	2	3	4	5
2	4	6	8	1Ø
3	6	9	12	15
4	8	12	16	2Ø
5	1Ø	15	2Ø	25

Note that the BBC BASIC print layout causes the columns of results to 'run together', so either limit the multiplication to a maximum of 4 or use the following PRINT statement in place of line 4Ø:

```
40    PRINT " ";Z;
```

Another example demonstrates the many options available with FOR–NEXT statements while nesting three loops:

```
10    A=2
20    B=4
30      FOR I=100 to 200 STEP 60
40        PRINT "I IS NOW";I
50        FOR J=.3 TO .2 STEP -.1
60          PRINT "           J IS NOW";J
70          FOR K=A TO B
80            PRINT "                K IS NOW";K
```

```
90        NEXT K
100       NEXT J
110     NEXT I
120   END
RUN
  I   IS NOW 100
```

                                 J IS NOW .3

                                     K IS NOW 2
                                     K IS NOW 3
                                     K IS NOW 4

                                 J IS NOW .2

                                     K IS NOW 2
                                     K IS NOW 3
                                     K IS NOW 4

```
  I   IS NOW 160
```

                                 J IS NOW .3

                                     K IS NOW 2
                                     K IS NOW 3
                                     K IS NOW 4

                                 J IS NOW .2

                                     K IS NOW 2
                                     K IS NOW 3
                                     K IS NOW 4

```
     END AT LINE 120
```

Where extended NEXT options are available, a NEXT without a variable refers to the most recent FOR. Thus lines 90, 100, 110 could be written:

```
90   NEXT
100   NEXT
110   NEXT
```

or, when available, with all the variables (first variables for inner loops):

    9Ø   NEXT I, J, K

showing all the loops terminate at the same point.

A final point—unless integer numeric variables are used in the FOR statement, the arithmetic is only approximate and the loop will execute to the best of the machine arithmetic. This is very limied, so there may occasionally be some surprising results when, for example, a decimal step length is used with a large number of iterations in the loop.

3.3.3 Example program

Here is an illustration of the use of three nested loops. The program calculates the probability of a particular total occurring when three dice are rolled. It does this by looking at all the possible values occurring ($6 \times 6 \times 6 = 216$ values) and only selecting those values which equal the given total N. These are counted on line 8Ø and the combination printed out on line 9Ø. Totals not equal to N cause a jump from line 7Ø to 1ØØ and are thus ignored (user responses are underlined):

```
 1Ø   INPUT N
 2Ø   PRINT
 3Ø    C=Ø
 4Ø     FOR D1=1 TO 6
 5Ø      FOR D2=1 TO 6
 6Ø       FOR D3=1 TO 6
 7Ø        IF (D1+D2+D3)<>N THEN 1ØØ
 8Ø         C=C+1
 9Ø          PRINT D1;D2;D3
1ØØ         NEXT D3
11Ø       NEXT D2
12Ø     NEXT D1
13Ø   PRINT N;" OCCURS IN";C;" WAYS"
14Ø   PRINT "THUS THE PROBABILITY OF A";N;" IS";C/216
15Ø   END
RUN
?6

 1   1   4
```

1	2	3
1	3	2
1	4	1
2	1	3
2	2	2
2	3	1
3	1	2
3	2	1
4	1	1

6 OCCURS IN 1Ø WAYS

THUS THE PROBABILITY OF A 6 IS 4.62963E–2

END AT LINE 15Ø

The diagram below illustrates the structure of this program:

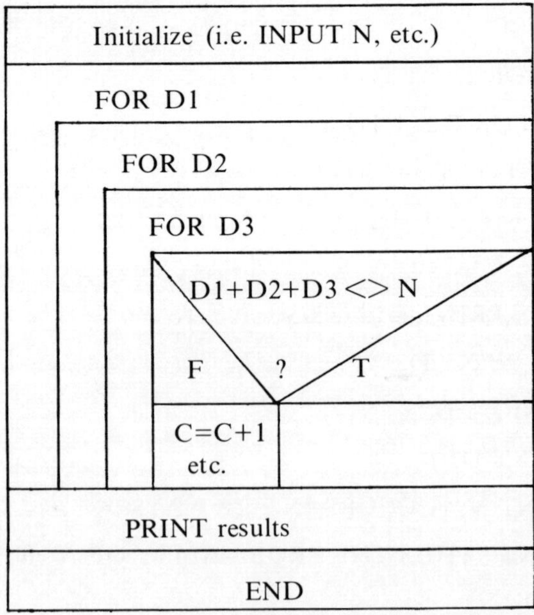

For correct BBC print layout modify line 9Ø to become:

9Ø   PRINT D1;" ";D2;" ";D3

3.4 INTRINSIC NUMERIC FUNCTIONS

Many calculations involve expressions which cannot be easily stated in terms of the simple arithmetic functions $+, -, *, /, \uparrow$. A particular example would be the square root of a number. The BASIC language provides special functions to perform some of these calculations for the user. For example:

        2Ø   A=SQR(X)

calculates the square root of the value in X and stores the result in A. Functions such as SQR can appear in expressions; the value computed by the function is substituted for the function reference. The input to the function, X in the example, can be replaced by an expression provided that for SQR its value is not negative. Thus:

        2Ø   A=SQR(A+B*3.1)

        2Ø   A=B–SQR(14.7)

        2Ø   A=SQR(3+SQR (X))

are allowed.

The list of intrinsic functions in Table 3.1 are those recommended as standard, and should be found in all versions of BASIC. In all cases X stands for a numeric expression.

Table 3.1 Standard numeric functions in BASIC

Function	Action
ABS (X)	Gives the absolute value of X, i.e. the value after changing its sign to positive: $$\text{ABS } (-3.7)=3.7$$
ATN (X)	Gives the arctangent of X, i.e. the angle whose tangent is X. The result is an angle in radians in the range $-\pi/2$ to $\pi/2$. To convert to degrees from radians use $(18Ø/\pi=57.29577951)$: $$\text{Degrees} = \frac{18Ø}{\pi} * \text{radians}$$
COS (X)	Gives the cosine of X, where X is in radians. To convert from degrees to radians use $(\pi/18Ø=1.745329252E{-}2)$: $$\text{Radians} = \frac{\pi}{18Ø} * \text{degrees}$$
EXP (X)	Gives e ($= 2.718281828$) raised to the power X, that is e^X. Note that e is the base for natural logarithms, and EXP, LOG are inverse functions; thus: $$\text{LOG(EXP (X))} = X = \text{EXP(LOG(X))}$$

INT (X)   Gives the largest integer not greater than X, i.e. the whole number N such that:

$$N \leqslant X \leqslant N+1$$

Thus:

$$INT \quad (3.7) = 3$$

$$INT \ (-3.7) = -4$$

LOG (X)   Gives the natural logarithm of X; X must be greater than zero. To convert to the common logarithm (of base 10) use:

Common log (X)=0.434294481 * natural log (X)

RND
or
RND (X)   The RND form has no input value. It returns the next value in a pseudo-random number sequence. That is, numbers uniformly distributed in the range 0 to 1. See also RANDOMIZE below. The RND (X) form may have X as a dummy parameter, or may use it to set or alter a random number sequence. See tables following for details of particular systems.

SGN (X)   Gives the sign of X as:

$$-1 \text{ if } X < 0$$

$$0 \text{ if } X = 0$$

$$+1 \text{ if } X > 0$$

SIN (X)   Gives the sine of X, where X is in radians (see also ATN, COS).

SQR (X)   Gives the non-negative square root of X; X must be positive or zero.

TAN (X)   Gives the tangent of X, where X is in radians (see also SIN, ATN, COS).

Note: RANDOMIZE N, where N is a constant or variable, is a statement, not a function, which is used to produce a different random number sequence for the RND function.

The following trignometric identities may be useful when using the above functions:

$$\tan (x) = \frac{\sin (x)}{\cos (x)} \qquad\qquad \cot (x) = \frac{\cos (x)}{\sin (x)}$$

$$\sec (x) = \frac{1}{\cos (x)} \qquad\qquad \csc (x) = \frac{1}{\sin (x)}$$

$$\sinh (x) = \frac{e^{x} - e^{-x}}{2} \qquad\qquad \cosh (x) = \frac{e^{x} + e^{-x}}{2}$$

$$\tanh(x) = \frac{\sinh(x)}{\cosh(x)}$$

Since only ATN (X), the arctan (x), is provided the other functions can be derived from:

$$\arcsin(x) = 2 \arctan\left[\frac{1 - \sqrt{(1-x^2)}}{x}\right]$$

$$\arccos(x) = \frac{\pi}{2} - \arcsin(x)$$

The following program illustrates the use of some of the intrinsic functions:

```
10   REM USING FUNCTIONS
20   PRINT "X", "ABS(X)", "INT(X)", "SGN(X)"
30   FOR X=-1.5 TO 1.5 STEP .5
40      PRINT X, ABS(X), INT(X), SGN(X)
50   NEXT X
60   END
RUN
```

X	ABS(X)	INT(X)	SGN(X)
-1.5	1.5	-2	-1
-1	1	-1	-1
-.5	.5	-1	-1
0	0	0	0
.5	.5	0	1
1	1	1	1
1.5	1.5	1	1

```
END AT LINE 60
```

For correct BBC print layout modify line 20 to print one string with appropriate spaces for the headings:

```
20   PRINT " X      ABS(X)     INT(X)     SGN(X)"
```

Many BASICs provide additional functions; Tables 3.2 to 3.4 give the functions available in some popular versions.

70

Table 3.2 Sinclair ZX81 BASIC numeric functions, additional to the standard functions of Table 3.1

Function	Action
ACS(X)	Gives arc cosine of X, i.e. the angle in radians whose cosine is X. See ATN in Table 3.1.
ASN(X)	Gives arc sine of X, i.e. the angle in radians whose sine is X. See ATN in Table 3.1.
LOG	Does not exist. This function is called LN.
LN(X)	Gives the natural logarithm of X. See LOG in Table 3.1.
PI	Has no input value. Gives the value of $\pi = 3.141592654$.
RND	Gives next random number in a sequence. Has no input value. The statement RAND N initializes a new random number sequence.

Table 3.3 Microsoft BASIC numeric functions, additional to the standard functions of Table 3.1

Function	Action
CDBL(X)	Converts a standard real value X to a double precision value. Thus: A #=CDBL (454.67) Then A# has the value 454.67 padded out to double precision length.
CINT(X)	Converts a standard real value X to an integer (same effect as INT). Note X must be in the range −32,768 to 32,767.
CSNG(X#)	Converts a double precision value X# to a standard real value.
FIX(X)	Gives the truncated integer part of X. It is equivalent to SGN(X)*INT (ABS(X)) and is like INT(X) when X is positive.
RND(X) or RND	Gives the next random number between Ø and 1. For X<Ø restarts a new sequence; X=Ø gives the last random number generated again. If X>Ø or X is omitted it gives the next random number. There is also a RANDOMIZE N statement to initiate a new sequence.

Table 3.4 BBC BASIC numeric functions, additional to the functions of Table 3.1

Function	Action
ACS(X)	Gives arc cosine of X, i.e. the angle in radians whose cosine is X. See ATN in Table 3.1.
ASN(X)	Gives the arc sine of X, i.e. the angle in radians whose sine is X. See ATN in Table 3.1.

DEG(X)   Gives the degrees equivalent to X in radians.

LN(X)   Gives the natural logarithm of X. Equivalent to LOG in Table 3.1.

LOG(X)   Gives the common (base 1Ø) logarithm of X. Notice the difference from the
            standard in Table 3.1.

RAD(X)   Gives the radians equivalent to X in degrees.

RND(1)   Gives the next real random number in the range of Ø.Ø to Ø.999999.

RND(Ø)   Gives the previous random number from RND(1).

RND(–K)   Uses the negative value to reset the random number sequence (like
            RANDOMIZE) and returns this value.

RND(N)   For N a positive integer, gives an integer in the range 1 to N.

RND   No argument, gives an integer in the range ±2,147,483,647 (the size of the
            machine's 32 bit integer).

The following program uses the INT function to test if a number is exactly
divisible by another number. If this is the case then N1/N2=integer (N1/N2):

```
10   INPUT A,B
20     D=A/B
30     IF  INT (D)<>D  THEN 60
40        PRINT A;"IS EXACTLY DIVISIBLE BY";B
50     GO TO 70
60        PRINT A;"IS NOT EXACTLY DIVISIBLE BY";B
70   END
RUN
? 96,12
96 IS EXACTLY DIVISIBLE BY 12
END AT LINE 70

RUN
? 21,4
21 IS NOT EXACTLY DIVISIBLE BY 4
END AT LINE 70
```

The structogram for this program is:

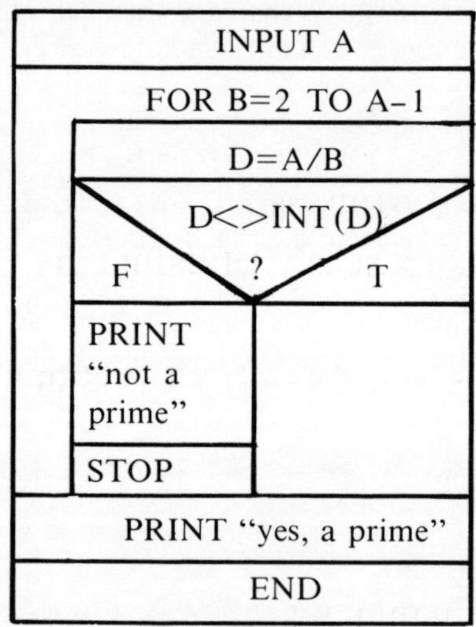

Prime numbers have been the subject of study for many years and the program discussed above shows some potential for solving the problem of whether a number is prime or not. A prime number is an integer which has no divisors other than 1 and itself. The following structogram illustrates a program to determine if an input integer A is prime or not:

The program is:

```
10    REM PROGRAM TO DETERMINE IF A IS PRIME
20      INPUT A
30        FOR B=2 TO A-1
40          D=A/B
50            IF INT (D)<>D  THEN 80
60              PRINT A;"IS NOT A PRIME"
```

```
70        STOP
80        NEXT B
90        PRINT A;"IS A PRIME"
100  END
```

Although there are changes to the first divisor testing part, both the structo-gram and the program statements clearly show how the previous program is used as a block within the larger program.

3.4.1 Random numbers

The generation of random numbers certainly needs some explanation, not least because almost every system chooses a slightly different way of presenting the RND function. It is a well-used function because many games and computer simulations involve choosing items at random rather than in a preset order. Computers do not have a true random number generator (which would be a hardware feature), but generate the numbers by software using a recursion formula. Although these numbers are only pseudo-random, they usually form quite acceptable sequences. They are usually presented within the range 0 to 1, but there are exceptions, e.g. the BBC BASIC provides several options (see Table 3.4).

The main point about the function RND is that each time it is used it produces a different value. Here is a simple example program (your system will produce a different sequence).

```
10   REM SIMPLE RANDOM NUMBERS
20   FOR I=1 TO 8
30     X=RND
40     PRINT I,X
50   NEXT I
60   END
RUN
1              0.586078
2              0.966241
3              0.579484
4              0.437442
5              0.191831
```

6	Ø.799346
7	Ø.617701
8	Ø.109323

END AT LINE 60

For correct BBC print layout modify line 40 to become:

```
40   PRINT ;I,X
```

Because the numbers are generated by a formula which always starts in the same initial state, you will get the same sequence each time you RUN the program, except in the BBC case which continues the sequence until initialized again. While this is a useful feature for testing and debugging a program, it is not acceptable when the program is put into service. The random number generator algorithm usually contains an initial 'seed' value, which may be altered by the RANDOMIZE statement, or RND(X) where X is negative, or in some other way (see Tables 3.1 to 3.4). A new sequence of pseudo-random numbers is then generated. The following are examples of initializing a new sequence for different systems:

```
100   RANDOMIZE 92
100   RAND 4
100   X=RND (–42)
```

Amending the simple example given above to input a value, and using this to reset the random number generator gives:

```
10   REM SIMPLE RANDOM NUMBERS
15   INPUT B
17   RANDOMIZE B
20   FOR I=1 TO 8
30      X=RND
40      PRINT I,X
50   NEXT I
60   END
RUN
?12
```

1	Ø.25
2	Ø.77Ø436
3	Ø.663104
4	Ø.612Ø85
5	Ø.4Ø2334
6	Ø.576949
7	Ø.964517
8	Ø.72Ø529

3.5 OUTPUT LAYOUT

This section is concerned with producing satisfactory control over output for programs intended for general inter-active use. When important tables and reports are produced for printing, very careful control is sometimes necessary over the field widths and formats of numbers. This is provided by the PRINT USING statement described in Section 6.3. Some similar control is provided in BBC BASIC (see the next section).

3.5.1 PRINT again

An introduction to the PRINT statement was given in Section 1.2.3. The PRINT statement can display both text and numbers to the output device which is usually the VDU. The text may appear as a string constant in the PRINT statement as:

```
1Ø   PRINT "THE RESULT IS",A
```

or in a string variable as:

```
1Ø   A$="FINAL TOTAL"
2Ø   PRINT A$;B
```

Any items in the PRINT list may be separated by either a semicolon or a comma.

If the separator is a semicolon the values are printed close together. Numeric values may be preceded by a space or minus sign and have a trailing space. Thus, if A=1, B=2, C=−3:

```
1Ø   PRINT "START";A;B;C;"END"
```

will produce:

    START 1 2 –3 END

Note that there are no spaces printed around numeric values in BBC BASIC which will produce:

    START12–3END

String values separated by a semicolon have no leading or trailing spaces. Thus:

    10   PRINT "START";"END"

will produce:

    STARTEND

Data are spaced across the VDU screen into preset columns when a comma is used as separator. Typically, the display width on the screen may be divided into 14 or 15 character-wide zones, and the comma causes the value, string or numeric, to be printed out at the beginning of the next zone, which may be a new line if the current line is exceeded. Thus:

    10   PRINT A,B,C

will produce:

    1   2   –3

Note that BBC BASIC differs from all the others in that it left justifies strings but it right justifies numeric values in zones, so the BBC result would be:

                       1   2   –3

It has the slight advantage of producing nicely lined up columns of numeric values, but does tend to run adjacent values together.

Any combination of separators can be used; all of the following are acceptable:

    100   PRINT A;B;C

    100   PRINT A,B;C

    100   PRINT A;B,C

By itself a PRINT statement without any list of variables will cause a new line to be generated.

Conversely, if the PRINT list of variables ends with a comma or semicolon then the next PRINT continues on the same line. For example:

    10   PRINT A;"AND";

    20   PRINT B;"GIVES";

    30   PRINT A+B

produces

    1 AND 2 GIVES 3

The following program uses the features above to produce a semi-graphics effect by giving a bar chart corresponding to points related by the formula $y = x^2 + 3$:

```
 5   REM HISTOGRAM DISPLAY PROGRAM
10   PRINT"--------------------Y AXIS--------------------"
20   FOR X=0 TO 7 STEP .5
30      Y=X↑2+3
38      PRINT "!";
40      FOR H=1 TO INT (Y)
44         PRINT "*";
46      NEXT H
48      PRINT
50   NEXT X
60   END
RUN
--------------------Y AXIS--------------------
!***
!***
!****
!*****
!*******
```

```
!********
!**********
!**************
!******************
!**********************
!******************************
!**********************************
!**********************************************
!**************************************************
```

END AT LINE 6Ø

Each line of output is started by the PRINT statement on line 38 with a vertical bar. As many *s as necessary are added (up to the integer value of Y) by the loop on lines 4Ø to 46—all printed on the same line.

The PRINT statement on line 48 is required to provide a new line for the next X value. The example assumes that the screen display scrolls upwards as new lines are added at the bottom. This is not the case with some systems unless a keyboard switch is set (to control the PAGE mode) or via a BASIC instruction. See Table 3.5 for the SCROLL instructions in Sinclair BASIC, which should be inserted at line 35 in the above program.

<table>
<tr><td colspan="2" align="center">Print separators</td></tr>
<tr><td>General form</td><td align="right">, or ;</td></tr>
<tr><td colspan="2">(,) A comma skips to the start of the next print zone to print the item (i.e. output is left justified, but BBC is different).</td></tr>
<tr><td colspan="2">(;) A semicolon prints the item immediately after the preceding one. If the list of items to be printed has a comma or semicolon at the end of it then no new line is generated. Thus, the next PRINT statement continues on the same line.
A PRINT statement with no item list (i.e. blank) will generate a new line.
Zones are generally 15 characters wide and are usually fixed.</td></tr>
<tr><td colspan="2">Notes</td></tr>
<tr><td colspan="2">(a) Sinclair BASIC divides the screen into 32 character-wide lines (numbered from Ø to 31), with zones starting in columns Ø and 16.</td></tr>
</table>

> (b) Microsoft and BBC BASICs allow the overall line width to be re-set by means of a statement, WIDTH N, where N is a constant or expression giving the width in characters.
>
> (c) BBC BASIC *RIGHT* justifies strings, but *LEFT* justifies numeric values in zones.
>
> BBC additional features:
>
> (') An apostrophe separator generates a new line.
> A degree of control over print layout is provided via a four-byte integer variable ■%. The value (Ø to 255) of the least significant byte determines zone widths. The other three bytes from right to left control the number of digits printed (Ø to 9), the numeric format printed (Ø,1 or 2), and the result of the function STR$.
> Two hexadecimal characters are provided for each byte, so the value runs from ØØ through to FF. Leaving the other three bytes at zero for these examples and looking at the zone byte only:
>
> @%=&ØØ ØØ ØØ Ø9 sets zone width to 9.
>
> @%=&ØØ ØØ ØØ ØC sets zone width to 12.
>
> @%=&ØØ ØØ ØØ 14   sets zone width to 2Ø.
>
> (& indicates hexadecimal value)

Control over the display on any part of the screen as in cursor control and semi-graphic display are available via the PRINT statement on a number of systems (see Section 6.6).

3.5.2 INPUT output

Quite often, when input is requested by a program, some message describing the form of the input, or its range of values, is displayed. Thus:

```
1Ø   PRINT "GIVE NUMBER OF YEARS"

2Ø   INPUT Y
```

produces:

```
GIVE NUMBER OF YEARS

?_
```

and the value is typed following the question mark. It is often nicer and tidier to be able to input immediately after the text, and a PRINT statement with a semi-colon after the text will produce this effect. Thus:

```
10   PRINT "GIVE NUMBER OF YEARS";
20   INPUT Y
```

produces:

```
GIVE NUMBER OF YEARS? __
```

and the input is typed after the question mark, on the same line as the text.

A number of microcomputer systems allow an enhancement of the INPUT statement which has exactly the same effect as the last example above. The form is generally:

```
INPUT "text"; item list
```

Thus:

```
10   INPUT "GIVE NUMBER OF YEARS";Y
```

produces GIVE NUMBER OF YEARS?__, exactly as above. BBC BASIC is more flexible than most systems and allows text and input items to be mixed in the INPUT list, either separated by commas or immediately following the string. For example:

```
10   INPUT "GIVE NUMBER OF YEARS",Y,"AND INTEREST"I
```

See Section 4.1.6 for the further use of a comma or semicolon with INPUT to input a list of values on one line.

3.5.3 PRINT control functions

So far, the layout of text and results has been controlled by the use of commas or semicolons. However, it is possible to exercise greater control by the use of functions such as TAB and SPC.

The TAB function does not simply generate a certain number of spaces; it tries to move to the column position specified by its input value. It is generally available, takes as input a value N, and tries to move the print position forwards (from left to right) to column position N. If this is not possible because the print position already exceeds N, the function generates a new line and positions the print output at column N in the new line. Thus:

```
PRINT A;TAB(12);B;TAB(24);C
```

would print the value of A starting in the first column, the value of B starting in column 12, and the value of C starting in column 24.

Since the TAB function does not output any spaces, but moves to columns, it is ideal for setting out correctly adjusted tables of values where the lengths of the items vary. For example, the following PRINT statements could appear in an estate agent's program giving the costs of houses:

```
PRINT "TOWN HOUSE";TAB(25);P1

PRINT "SEMI DETACHED HOUSE";TAB(25);P2

PRINT "EXCLUSIVE BUNGALOW";TAB(25);P3

PRINT "SHED NEEDS ATTENTION";TAB(25);P4
```

The effect would be to line up the prices (P1 to P4) irrespective of the lengths of the descriptions:

```
TOWN HOUSE               1ØØØ

SEMI DETACHED HOUSE      2ØØØ

EXCLUSIVE BUNGALOW       3ØØØ

SHED NEEDS ATTENTION     2ØØ
```

Implementations of the TAB function vary, and one or two systems do not give the new line mentioned above. In these cases if the print position exceeds N, the TAB function is merely ignored.

The TAB may be used for printing rough graphs using TAB (X) where X is calculated within the program. X may be any expression and the value of this expression is truncated to an integer since printing can only take place in integer steps.

The histogram example in Section 3.5.1 can be easily modified to give:

```
 5   REM ROUGH GRAPH PROGRAM

10   PRINT "------------Y AXIS--------------------------"

20   FOR X=Ø TO 7 STEP .5

30     Y=X↑2+3

40     PRINT "!";TAB(Y);"*"

50   NEXT X

60   END
```

and produces the following output. (Note the comment made about scrolling in Section 3.5.1.)

RUN

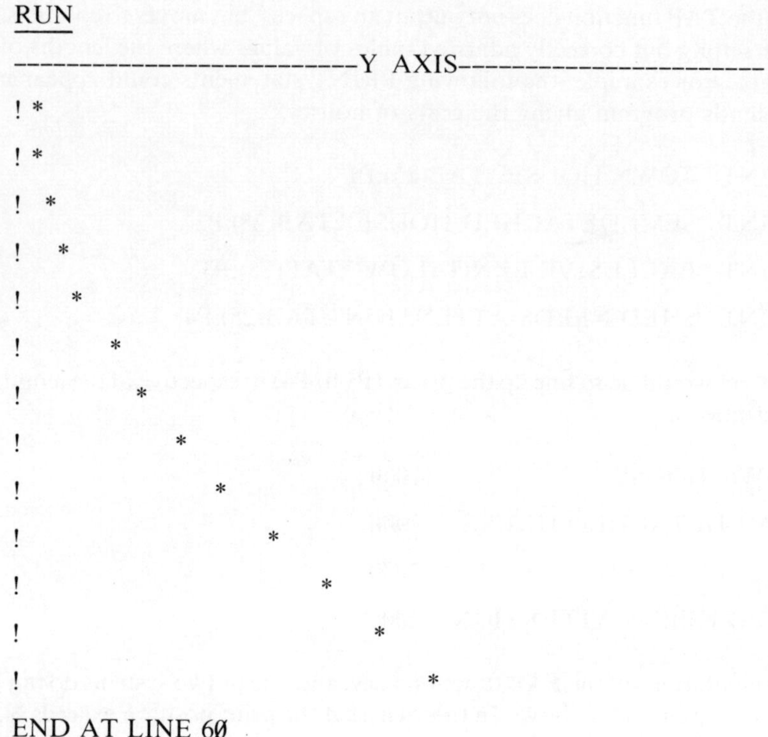

END AT LINE 6∅

Several other useful output functions may be available which are not in standard BASIC. Tables 3.5 to 3.8 list the output functions for different systems. Notice the SPC(N) function which outputs N spaces, with N limited to the range ∅ to 255.

Rather different functions allow you to move the cursor (print position) backwards, forwards, or to other lines on the screen, and overwrite existing material.

There may also be a function CLS which clears the screen and leaves the cursor at the top left corner. Together these functions give a BASIC program complete control over the positioning of output at any point on the VDU. They may be used to give a semi-graphic output which is animated in some way, such as in games programs or in applications showing flow through pipes, etc. See Section 6.6 for semi-graphics.

Table 3.5 Sinclair ZX81 BASIC output functions

Function/statement	Meaning
AT X,Y	Not a real function, but appears in the PRINT statement followed by the line, column at which the next item is to be printed. (Top is line ∅, left is column ∅, bottom is line 21, right is column 31.)

CLS	A statement which clears the screen.
SCROLL	A statement which scrolls the display up one line.
TAB Y	Not a real function, but moves the print position to column Y.

Table 3.6 Microsoft BASIC output functions

Function/statement	Meaning
HOME	A statement which clears the screen and leaves the cursor at upper left.
HTAB X	A statement which positions the cursor at the column given by the integer part of X (left is 1, right is 40) (see VTAB).
POS (X)	A function with dummy argument X which returns the cursor position (column) in a line (see VPOS(X)).
SPC (X)	A function which outputs the integer value of X spaces.
TAB (X)	A function which moves the print position to the column given by the integer part of X.
VPOS (X)	A function with dummy argument X which returns the cursor line position (vertically).
VTAB X	A statement which positions the cursor vertically at the line given by the integer part of X (top is 1, bottom is 24).

Table 3.7 BBC BASIC output control functions

Function/statement	Meaning
CLS	A statement which clears the screen leaving the cursor at top left (0,0).
COUNT	A function with no arguments (input values) which returns the number of characters printed on the current line.
POS	A function with no arguments which returns the horizontal position of the cursor (left is column 0).
SPC (X)	A function which takes the integer part of X and outputs X spaces.
TAB (X)	A function which moves the print position to the column given by the integer part of X.
TAB (X,Y)	A function which positions the cursor at X,Y (see POS, VPOS).
VPOS	A function with no arguments which returns the vertical position of the cursor (top is line 0).

Table 3.8 Commodore PET BASIC output functions

Function/statement	Meaning
1Ø PRINT "text",A;B	The usual PRINT statement, and text plus numeric values to be output. However, within the text string if any of the cursor control keys are pressed a special symbol is generated, and when the statement is executed in a program the appropriate movement takes place. For example: PRINT " ♥ S TOP LEFT" will clear the screen and display the message at the top left. Remember, the string must be closed by the second pair of quotes before the cursor control keys work as normal.
SPC (X)	A function which outputs the integer part of X (spaces).
TAB (X)	A function which moves to the column given by the integer part of X. If the current position exceeds this, then no action is taken.

3.6 STARTING DESIGN

You may think that when you have become familiar with the statements which make up a programming language you are almost at the stage of being a fully qualified programmer, lacking perhaps only some experience. In a way this is true, because you have implicitly acquired a knowledge of design from following the examples and exercises during the study of the language. In fact, a thorough knowledge of the techniques of design forms the major part of the skills of a qualified programmer. Once acquired they can be applied to solving problems in a wide variety of programming languages. Thus, correct design techniques are too important to be left to develop only by example. A number of parts of this book discuss the modern techniques available.

Firstly, what is programming all about? Surely its main aim is to solve problems and produce systems which work. And not only work, but do so correctly, all the time! The worst case which can occur is that a program seems to work correctly and in fact is thoroughly tested, but (say) in one run in a thousand produces invalid results. Users and the authors of such a program tend to believe in it, and may make expensive or serious mistakes using the occasionally erroneous results. Thus correctness is the first criterion for a program.

Problems change and develop, data changes, and computing hardware changes, so even a straightforward program may need modifications during its working life. Change is the norm for programming systems, not the exception, so the next feature that we should aim at when designing a program is ease of modification.

Since the advent of the microelectronics revolution the cost of the computer hardware has become much less than the cost of developing the software. The reverse was true in the 1950s and 1960s, and various 'clever' programming practices developed to save computer store space, save execution time, or minimize disc accesses. Unfortunately the other aspect of these practices meant that programs became unreadable, prone to error, and almost impossible to modify. So the lesson is clear—by all means design programs to be efficient, but do not strive to achieve this at all costs. The aims of correctness and modification are more important than efficiency. What of achieving these laudable aims? The mechanism for producing programs is, today, still mostly via human beings who are irrational and individual. Therefore, any assessment of the output of programmers and their efficiency in meeting the aims above is very difficult. However, a large body of opinion now supports the design techniques which come under the heading of *structured design*. Where studies have been carried out comparing structured techniques with other methods, substantial gains have been shown in favour of the former.

There are several distinct techniques available today which come under the category of structure design. One technique applies to problems which have a large volume of structured data and fits the structure of the program to these data. Another, which we shall follow here, starts with a very general view of the problem and develops step by step to include more detail until there is sufficient to be able to write out the program. This is often called 'stepwise refinement', and since it proceeds from the general view through to the specific program it is said to be 'top-down' in its development. All structured design techniques proceed 'top-down'. Section 1.3 described a simple program structure as:

   Input

    Process

   Output

which corresponds to the top level of a design. The simple BASIC programs described in Chapter 1 correspond to the bottom level of a design. This chapter has provided several new elements which may be used in design. These are:

   FOR loop

    Action

   NEXT end of loop

   IF condition THEN Action

   IF condition THEN $Action_1$ ELSE $Action_2$

where 'action' represents one or many statements which do not cause jumps to other parts of the program. The original three descriptions, input, process, output, are all examples of an action. The corresponding structograms are:

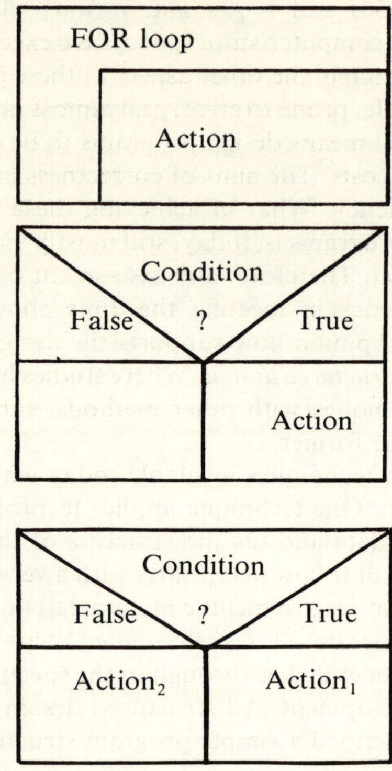

Of course, action can be a FOR–NEXT or IF structure itself. The example already discussed in detail was of nested loops in Section 3.3.2, while the example program in Section 3.3.3 used FOR–NEXT and IF structures nested together.

In terms of the structograms, action is a rectangular box, and as you have seen demonstrated in this chapter all the programming options described so far form rectangular boxes externally. Thus they can all be nested or combined together very easily.

One way of considering a rectangular box of actions given in a structogram is as a module; i.e. a group of actions which form a logical whole. The division program and the prime number programs in Section 3.4 illustrate the module principle, for the division program with slight changes forms a module which fits inside the prime number program. The inner module, which is the slightly altered division program, is shown outlined in heavy black lines in the full structogram for the prime number program below:

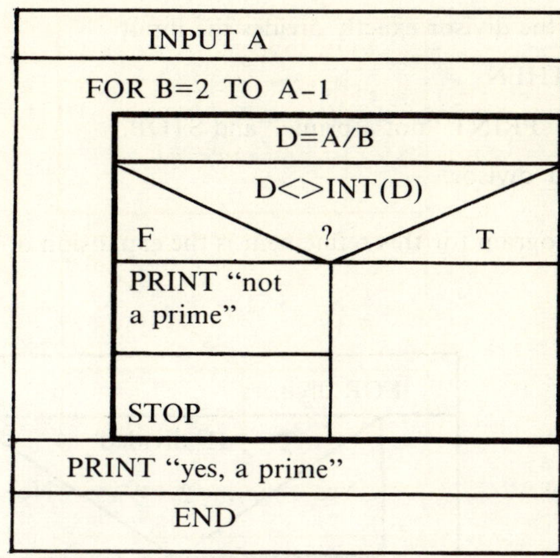

Not every action is a module, only those actions which form a more or less complete logical group, as illustrated above.

Let us follow through the method of stepwise refinement for the prime number problem. The first task is to write down the general method, which is to see if the input value has any divisors apart from 1 and itself. This description is called level 1.

Level 1

Input a number.

Test if it is divisible.

Output result.

Various parts of Level 1 are considered for expansion; these are called refinements. They are produced for everything which is not immediately expressible in BASIC statements. The structogram for this level is:

Input
Test
Output

Refinement 1.1. Test if it is divisible.

FOR all the possible divisors, of the input number.

88

IF the divisor exactly divides the input.

THEN

PRINT "not a prime" and STOP.

NEXT divisor.

The structogram for this refinement is the expansion of the centre 'test' box of level 1.

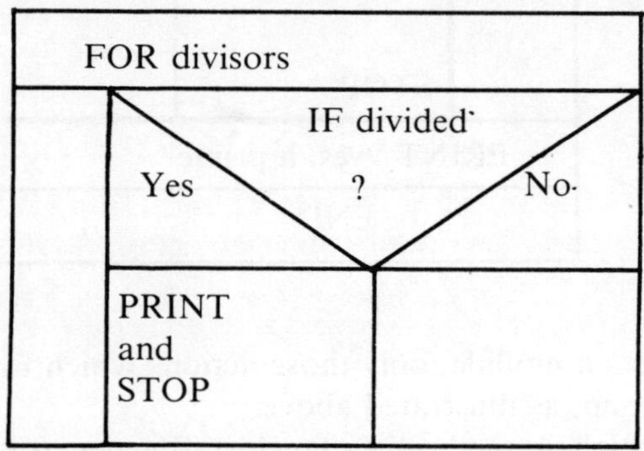

There are no other major parts to refine, but the 'output result' in level 1 can be written in full now that we have decided in 1.1 that on exit from the FOR–NEXT loop all possible divisors have been tested and have not divided the number exactly. Putting all the parts together and using the names of BASIC statements in capital letters, the next level may be written out in full.

Level 2

INPUT a number.

FOR all the possible divisors, of the input number.

IF the divisor exactly divides the input.

THEN

PRINT "not a prime" and STOP.

NEXT divisor.

PRINT "yes, is a prime".

END

This is almost at the level of BASIC statements. The only phrase which needs to be clarified follows the IF.

Refinement 2.1. IF the divisor exactly divides the input.

    IF (A/B)=INT (A/B) THEN . . .

or this may be written more efficiently, avoiding a division, as:

    D=A/B

    IF D=INT(D) THEN . . .

This introduces a process box above the slightly altered IF box in the above structogram.

Thus the program can be written out in full in BASIC statements (see Section 3.4). There are not many levels in this example, but it does illustrate the method quite well.

This design technique is developed in succeeding chapters, but it is worth noting a few comments here.

The approach taken above works with structures in both words and diagrams. Some programmers work with only one form, e.g. using words only. You may find it more convenient to work in one or other of the forms, rather than both.

Sometimes the structures contain a GO TO statement. Notice, however, that there are no symbols which correspond to the GO TO statement used on its own. Thus the rule is: by all means use GO TO statements to form correct structures, but never use GO TO statements in an arbitrary way.

You will probably have noticed that some of the structures look a bit cumbersome when expressed in BASIC statements, e.g. the IF–THEN–ELSE structure. You may have felt a little uneasy about it. If so, you were right to do so, because BASIC is not suited to structured design and must be carefully used. Extended features in some BASIC systems, help to overcome some problems in this area.

No design is ever purely top-down. There must always be a certain amount of look-ahead, i.e. downwards, to arrange for what can be actually provided at lower levels, and ultimately what is available at the lowest level of the programming language. For example, there is no sense in designing a data retrieval program from the top-down which requires a random access method of accessing data items in a file at the lowest level, if this feature is not available on your system. (Files and data access methods are discussed in Chapter 8.)

Exercises

3.1   Taxi fares are calculated as the sum of a standing charge of 25p, plus 8p for every half-mile over two miles. Design a program, in words or structograms, which accepts as input the length of the journey in complete miles and outputs the cost.

One answer is given in the solutions in Appendix I. Code this solution or your own into BASIC and run it. What happens if the input is not complete miles but includes parts of a mile? Examples would be 2.4 miles and 2.7 miles. The problem would be clearer for these cases if it set the rate as 8p for every half-mile or part thereof. One of the numeric functions may be helpful in this case.

3.2 The following structogram illustrates a very simple program which prints a number, its square, and its cube:

<table>
<tr><td>INPUT N</td></tr>
<tr><td>PRINT N,N*N,N*N*N</td></tr>
<tr><td>END</td></tr>
</table>

Draw the structogram, using the above as a basis, which represents a program to print a table of the squares and cubes of all the numbers from 1 to 10. Add suitable headings to show which column is which.

3.3 Develop the program from exercise 3.2 above to print out in each line the powers of the number up to the fifth by using an additional FOR–NEXT loop and the print control options. That is, in each line print out N^I where I goes from 1 to 5. When N=4 the output should appear as:

$$4 \qquad 16 \qquad 64 \qquad 256 \qquad 1024$$

Add suitable headings to the columns. The columns will not appear neatly lined up because of the different magnitudes of the numbers. You may wish to try the output functions available on your computer to remedy this defect.

3.4 Design and write a program to calculate the factorial of N, where N is a whole number. This factorial is sometimes written as N! and defined as

$$N! = 1*2*3*4*\ldots*N$$

Thus:

$$2! = 1*2 = 2$$

$$5! = 1*2*3*4*5 = 120$$

The program should input a value N and print it and its factorial with suitable explanations. The factorial has a direct application in many problems. For example, if we wish to arrange N unlike objects R at a time, the number of arrangements (sometimes called permutations and written $_NP_R$) is $N!/(N-R)!$. Note $0!$ is defined to be 1.

As an illustration, if a shopkeeper has eight different new books to display in his shop window for the Christmas season, but can only fit five of them in his display at a time, then the number of arrangements of 5 from 8 is 8!/(8–5)! = 6720 ways.

3.5 Design and write a program to calculate the average of a set of examination marks of a class of students. The mark is a percentage one, so ranges from 0 to 100. The program is to be flexible enough to accept any number of input values. One way of achieving this is to use a special input value to indicate the end of the set of values. This special value is not used in the calculations and to be recognized must be outside the range of the normal values. In the present problem you could choose a negative number, or a number greater than 100, as the special value.

3.6 Design and write a program which accepts a whole number as input and tests to see if it is odd or even, displaying the number and result.

3.7 Design and write a program which counts the number of even numbers which must be added together before the sum is greater than 100.

Some thought is required to make the program do exactly as you want, and this is as much an exercise in exactness as it is of programming.

3.8 Design and write a program to produce a table to enable traders to calculate VAT (Value Added Tax) on their goods. The tax is 15 per cent of the cost of the goods. All the values are expressed in pence (100p = £1) and the table should range from 0p to £2 in steps of 2p, with appropriate headings:

VAT for Øp to 2ØØp

	Ø	2	4	6	8
Ø	Ø	Ø	Ø	Ø	1
1Ø	1	1	2	2	2
2Ø	3				
3Ø					
4Ø					
.					
.					
.					
1ØØ					
.					
.					
.					
.					
2ØØ					

etc.

Note that fractions of a pence are discarded (i.e. truncated) and layout is an important consideration. This problem has a lot in common with the structures used in problem 3.3.

If you are mathematically inclined you could use a similar program structure to produce a table such as is published in a book of trignometric functions. That is, a table of sines for the angles Ø degrees to 9Ø degrees in steps of two degrees.

3.9   Design and write a program to solve the following simulation problem.

A train you take to work may be between 1Ø minutes early and 5 minutes late. If you reach the station always exactly on time for a month (equals 2Ø working days), on how many of these days will you catch the train?

Use the random number generator to simulate the real situation. Assume that all the times in whole minutes are equally probable. Thus there are 15 one-minute intervals from 1Ø minutes early, through exact time, to 5 minutes late, and you catch the train only if it is at the exact time or late.

3.10   In one type of darts game the object is to score exactly 3Ø1. A novice is throwing the darts so that they hit the board at random and score between Ø (off the board) and 2Ø with equal probability. Design and write a program to simulate this game and count the number of throws of the darts.

Assume that there are no doubles or trebles. To reach the score 3Ø1 exactly, the values obtained at the end of the game are not counted if they would put the total above 3Ø1, and the throws continue until it is reached.

PART II
Intermediate

A section for those with some previous practical experience of using BASIC and writing programs.

4
More programming concepts

Like most programming languages BASIC has a number of important features which are best considered when the elementary parts are completely understood and familiar. This chapter introduces several of these important features, which although different are in a sense very simply related. The theme of this chapter is the consideration of computing objects, meaning the 'things' which a programming language manipulates.

The 'things' so far manipulated have mainly been numbers, in numeric variables and as constants. If we can happily manipulate these simple things, then why not invent more complicated things, and when appropriate, use these in the same kind of fashion. BASIC allows a sequence (or array, or list) of numeric values to be easily used. It also provides another type of single variable which holds characters, not numbers, and the means to manipulate these string variables in a powerful way.

While the detail of their use is quite complicated in some instances, do not let this hide from you the essential simplicity that what follows is the description of some objects and how to use them.

Some advanced programming languages offer the feature of defining your own 'things' (objects or structures) and their relations, but it takes a skilled programmer to use this feature efficiently. Practice with BASIC should lead you to realize its restrictions in this area, and this will be the time to look at other languages.

4.1 ARRAYS

The power of a computer, via its program, is the ability to repeat a sequence of operations very quickly, for as many times as we require it. This feature was examined and developed in the looping instructions of the last chapter. For example, the following program fragment will produce the average value of the six items input:

```
50   S=0
60   FOR I=1 TO 6
70      INPUT A
80      S=S+A
90   NEXT I
100   S=S/6
```

Each new value is input to the same variable (A) on line 7Ø and added to the total in line 8Ø. All the early values input to A are lost as each new one replaces the old one. Only the very last value is available in A at the end of the loop. The only alternative method open to us, up to this point, would be to write:

```
5Ø   INPUT A,B,C,D,E,F

6Ø   S=A+B+C+D+E+F

8Ø   S=S/6
```

which gives the same result, and leaves all six values available in the six variables for subsequent use. It might even seem shorter to program, but try writing the same program to average 1ØØØ values!

Computer store

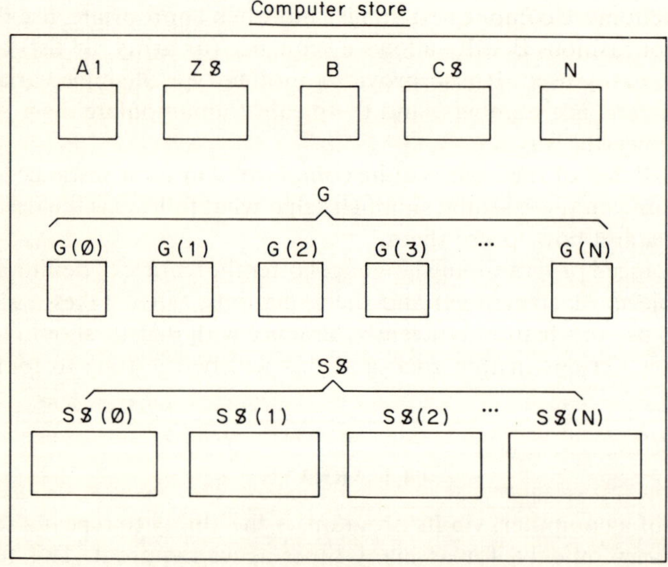

Figure 4.1 Arrays in the computer store

In the above case, and in many other different circumstances, we must be able to use a whole set of numbers, without destroying their values, as easily as we used the simple variable A in the first example above. The object we require is an **ARRAY**, which gives one name to a series of neighbouring locations in the computer store and allows access to each individual location by means of a subscript value. Figure 4.1 shows some individual variables, such as A1 and N, together with an array called G. This is a group name given to the collection of locations, each of which is the same as a single variable. Thus the first variable in the array is called G(Ø), the second is G(1), the third G(2), and so on. These individual variables which make up the array are called **ARRAY ELEMENTS**, and the number within the brackets is the **ARRAY SUBSCRIPT**. The individual array elements may be used exactly as variables were used previously. In the fragment:

```
10   INPUT  G(1)

20   G(2)=G(1)

30   PRINT  G(1),G(2)
```

a value input on line 10 is copied on line 20, and both values are displayed from line 30; G(1) and G(2) are separate variables. Another program with simple variables such as A or Z, so that:

```
10   INPUT  Z

20   A=Z

30   PRINT  Z,A
```

has exactly the same effect.

Arrays are often used to hold related values. For example, in an array M we could record the number of pints of milk we received on each day of the week. Thus M(1)=1 for the Sunday delivery, M(2)=3, M(3)=0, M(4)=2, M(5)=1, M(6)=2, and M(7)=1. From these values stored in array M the statement PRINT M(4) would produce 2, but we could also have:

```
100   D=4

114   PRINT M(D)
```

with the same result. The power of the array lies in this ability to use a variable as the subscript. Consider the program fragment:

```
50   FOR D=1 to 7

60      PRINT M(D);

70   NEXT D
```

If the array M had the values given above the first cycle of the loop would set D = 1 and thus PRINT M(1), the next would set D=2 and PRINT M(2), and so on. With the semicolon print control putting all the values on one line, the result would be:

```
1   3   0   2   1   2   1
```

4.1.1 The DIM statement

Before an array is used a DIM statement giving the maximum allowed subscript should be included in the program so that the BASIC system can reserve the store spaces. For example:

        10   DIM M(7)

would reserve space for the array mentioned above. A list of arrays may be declared in one statement if desired. Thus:

        30   DIM A(14),M(7),Z(100)

The word DIM is used as it specifies the DIMension or size of the array. DIM statements may appear anywhere within a BASIC program though they are best grouped together at the beginning of the program where they are easily seen by the programmer. They must appear before the array referred to in the DIM statement used.

<table>
<tr><td colspan="2" align="center">DIM statement</td></tr>
<tr><td>General form</td><td>DIM array name (maximum subscript)</td></tr>
</table>

The 'array name' is usually chosen according to the same rules as for simple variables. Both numeric and string arrays are allowed. There may be a list of array items separated by commas.

The 'maximum subscript' gives the maximum subscript that may be used, which must be positive, and is sometimes restricted to be a constant integer value. The array subscripts usually run from 0 to the maximum subscript, but some systems have them run from 1 to the maximum subscript (see Section 4.1.2).

Arrays with more than one dimension can be used, by indicating several maximum subscripts in the brackets after the name. There is a limit on the number of dimensions allowed.

Where an array is not declared in a DIM statement a default size of 10 is assumed for a one-dimensional array and 10,10 for a two-dimensional array.

Both string and numeric arrays are allowed and may have one or two dimensions (most implementations allow more dimensions). If an array element is used before a DIM statement for that particular array is encountered, then most systems assume a default value of (10) for a one-dimensional array and (10,10) for a two-dimensional array. It is very poor programming practice to rely on these default values, rather than to declare all arrays to be used at the beginning of each program. Here are some examples:

        10   DIM A(50),Z(6)   (numeric, one-dimensional)

        20   DIM P$(5)   (string, one-dimensional)

        30   DIM C(10,5),D(10,20),E$(5,5)   (two-dimensional matrices)

Before passing on to use arrays, let us look at array names. These are usually of the same type and length as simple variable names.

If A9 is allowed for a variable, so is DIM Z2(1Ø), i.e. a maximum one letter plus a digit as usual, but at least one system only allows single letter names for arrays.

If PINTOFMILK is allowed for a variable, so is DIM DAILYPINTA(7).

Where integer or double precision variables are allowed, so are arrays of these types. Do not worry about using the same name for a single variable, array, and string variable, as your system *should* treat them as separate items. Thus:

```
 5   DIM A(4)
1Ø   A=1Ø
2Ø   A(Ø)=-9
3Ø   A$="OK"
4Ø   PRINT A,A(Ø),A$
```

should produce:

```
1Ø                              -9                              OK
```

If it does not, then take great care.

Next, the use of variable dimensions. It is very convenient to use the exact array size to fit the problem, so that situations like:

```
1ØØ   INPUT K
12Ø   DIM A(K)
13Ø   .......
```

can be used to set the size of A during program execution to fit the data. Most systems allow variable dimensions. For those which do not, some suitable large size has to be fixed, even though most runs of the program will only use part of the array.

Here is an example of array use. In a stock control system 2Ø different items are held in stock, with item numbers running from 1 to 2Ø. The array S is to hold, in each array element, the current stock level for that item. A program accepts as input the stock levels, calculates the total stock, and prints the item number, its stock level and its stock level as a percentage of the total stock.

```
1Ø   REM STOCK REPORT
2Ø   DIM S(2Ø)
3Ø   REM INPUT 2Ø STOCK LEVELS
4Ø   REM FIND TOTAL AT SAME TIME
```

```
50   T=Ø
60   PRINT "PLEASE GIVE NUMBER IN STOCK"
70   FOR I=1 TO 20
80      PRINT "FOR ITEM";I;
90      INPUT S(I)
100     T=T+S(I)
110  NEXT I
120  PRINT
130  PRINT "TOTAL STOCK IS";T
140  REM
150  REM PRINT THE THREE OUTPUT VALUES FOR EACH ITEM
160  PRINT "ITEM","NO.IN STOCK","% OF TOTAL"
170  FOR I=1 TO 20
180     PRINT I,S(I),S(I)*1ØØ/T;"%"
190  NEXT I
200  END
```

Note that this program has a very simple structure of two separate loops.

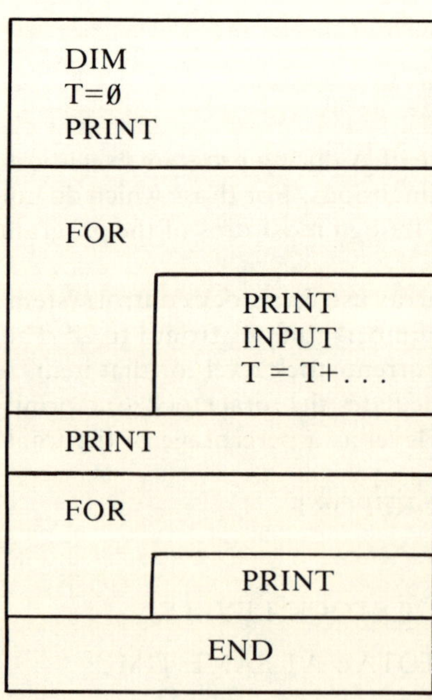

If you are fortunate to have an extended BASIC you can write the program as:

```
10   REM STOCK REPORT
20   DIM STOCKITEM(20)
30   TOTAL=0
40   PRINT "PLEASE GIVE NUMBER IN STOCK"
50   FOR ITEM=1 TO 20 :REM INPUT STOCK LEVELS
60      PRINT "FOR ITEM";ITEM;
70      INPUT STOCKITEM(ITEM)
80      TOTAL=TOTAL+STOCKITEM(ITEM) :REM ADD TO
        TOTAL
90   NEXT ITEM
100  ......
```

and so on, using meaningful names for variables and the multiple statement facility (via the colon separator) to put comments where they belong.

4.1.2 Array store space

Standard (minimal) BASIC expects all array subscripts to start at 0, which is the convention adopted by most systems. For the 0 system:

DIM P(4)   reserves 5 locations P(0),P(1),P(3),P(4)

DIM A(2, 3) reserves 12 locations
      A(0, 0) A(0, 1) A(0, 2) A(0, 3)
      A(1, 0) A(1, 1) A(1, 2) A(1, 3)
      A(2, 0) A(2, 1) A(2, 2) A(2, 3)

Thus the default size for a one-dimensional array which has 10 as the upper limit, reserves 11 locations, the subscripts going from 0 to 10. Likewise, the default size for a two-dimensional array of 10,10 reserves 121 locations.

The other system starts arrays with the subscript 1. For this 1 system:

DIM P(4)   reserves four locations P(1),P(2),P(3),P(4)

DIM A(2, 3) reserves six locations
      A(1, 1) A(1, 2) A(1, 3)
      A(2, 1) A(2, 2) A(2, 3)

The OPTION BASE statement is available in most systems (but not BBC) to allow alteration of the default lower subscript limit. Thus

    1Ø OPTION BASE 1

in an initially minimum subscript Ø system will reduce the space taken up by a two-dimensional (2,3) array from 12 down to 6 locations.

<table>
<tr><td colspan="2" align="center">OPTION statement</td></tr>
<tr><td>General form</td><td align="right">OPTION BASE N</td></tr>
<tr><td colspan="2">N is either Ø or 1.

Sets the lower limit of all arrays used in the program to be Ø or 1. A program may contain at most one option statement.</td></tr>
</table>

The choice of the Ø or 1 system, if available, should be made to fit in with the problem. For example, in the milk example above we can naturally identify days of the week with the numbers 1 to 7, but not as easily with the seven numbers Ø to 6. Thus 1 would be a sensible minimum array subscript in that program.

If you are not aware of the Ø base for an array and use only subscripts from 1 upwards you can waste a lot of computer store. For example, a real numeric array such as DIM A(1ØØ,1ØØ) would require at least 4 bytes per array element (5 bytes in BBC BASIC), so the total store space required is $4 \times 1Ø1 \times 1Ø1 = 4Ø,8Ø4$ bytes in the BASE Ø system (51,ØØ5 for BBC). The space used when working with subscripts 1 upwards is $4 \times 1ØØ \times 1ØØ = 4Ø,ØØØ$ bytes (5Ø,ØØØ for BBC). Thus 8Ø4 (1ØØ5 for BBC) bytes are never used, and are not available for other uses such as more program instructions or strings. In this case, using the OPTION BASE 1 statement at the beginning of the program would have saved a lot of space.

Some systems provide matrix handling functions, which begin with the letters MAT, e.g. MAT INPUT. All these functions operate on array elements from 1 upwards, regardless of whether any elements with Ø subscripts exist (see Chapter 7).

4.1.3 Array subscripts

In addition to allowing a variable as a subscript, such as M(D), most BASICs allow any arithmetic expression. Thus, if D has the value 3, then:

    M(D+2) is M(5)

    M(6*D–12) is M(6)

    M(2*(D–4)+5) is M(7)

Be careful that proper whole values result from the expressions, because systems differ in their action with decimal parts. Some truncate, so 7.2, 7.5, and 7.9 would all be treated as 7, whereas others round the value to the nearest integer, by taking Ø.5 and upwards to the higher value. In this case 7.2, 7.5, and 7.9 would be treated as 7, 8, and 8 respectively.

Either use an integer variable if available as a subscript or use the INT function and your own rounding system. You might expect 2*(D–4)+5 to give 7 when D is 5, but the actual result could be 6.999999 and truncation leaves this as 6. This is the wrong array element and gives a very difficult error to locate. Thus, in the case of D=5:

$$INT(2*(D–4)+5+\emptyset.5) = INT(6.999999+.5)$$
$$= INT(7.499999)$$
$$= 7$$

The above array elements are thus best used as M(INT(D+2.5)), M(INT(6*D–12 +$\emptyset$.5)), and M(INT(2*(D–4)+5.5)).

4.1.4 Use arrays economically

In some problems there is no need to use an array, yet nine out of ten beginner programmers will use one. This presents no difficulty, because all the example programs likely to be written by such programmers are small and should easily fit in the store available. However, if the practice is continued valuable space may be wasted later in larger programs. In this context, the essential question you should ask is 'are the array element values required more than once'. If the answer is no, then you probably do not need an array. Look at the program in Section 4.1.1. If we do not have a requirement for the display of each stock level as a percentage of the total, then the program changes. In the original form we had to input all the values, find the total, then output the values including a column where each value is divided by the total. Thus two loops were required. Change the problem by removing the percentage requirement, and all that is needed is:

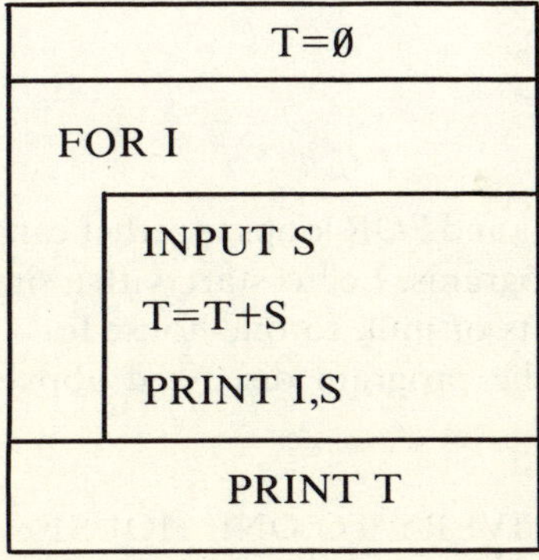

which is:

```
10   REM STOCK REPORT, PRINT IMMEDIATELY
20   T=Ø
```

```
30    FOR I=1 TO 20
40       INPUT S
50       T=T+S
60       PRINT "ITEM";I;"STOCK IS";S
70    NEXT I
80    PRINT "TOTAL STOCK IS";T
90    END
```

It is clear that the above form is not easy to use as the input values and output displays are mixed up. Thus:

```
RUN
? 6
ITEM 1 STOCK IS 6
? 4
ITEM 2 STOCK IS 4
.
.
.
etc.
```

However, a saving of 19 array elements has been made by using the one variable S again and again.

4.1.5 A program example

An example of how arrays and FOR loops together can simplify programming is given in the following programs. Let us start with a simple program to total a milkman's deliveries of pints of milk to one house for one week. Actually, the structure is the same as the program discussed above in Section 4.1.4; the program is:

```
10    REM MILK DELIVERY TO ONE HOUSE
20    T=0
30    FOR D=1 TO 7
40       INPUT M ,
```

```
5Ø      T=T+M
6Ø    NEXT D
7Ø    PRINT "TOTAL DELIVERIES =";T
8Ø    END
RUN
? 1,3,Ø,2,1,2,1
TOTAL DELIVERIES=1Ø
END AT LINE 8Ø
```

Notice the comma separator on line 4Ø in the INPUT statement. It means that no line feed is generated each time the INPUT is used, so that the values required can be input on one line separated by commas. Some systems allow a semicolon to appear on INPUT instead of the comma. BBC BASIC does not provide either form, so each value is given on a new line. Now generalize the program. In a street of eight houses the milkman wishes to produce a total for each house at the end of the week. So the simple variable T in the above program becomes an array of dimension 8, with each array element recording the total for each house. The structogram is:

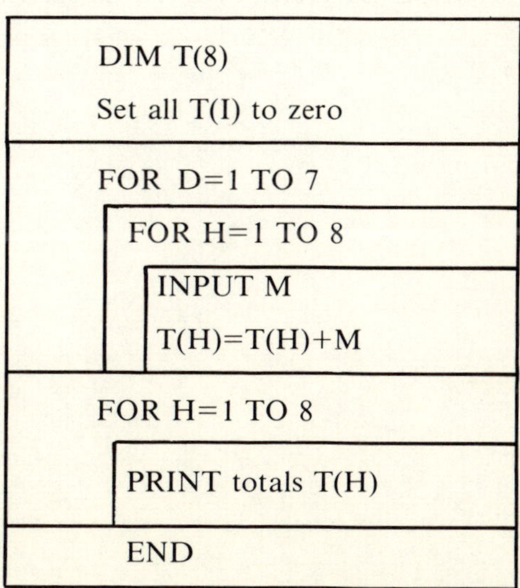

The first box is really a loop to set all the parts of the array T to zero, but since it is a self-contained action which does not illuminate the working of the problem it has been written as a block. The program expanded from the structogram is:

```
5   REM MILK DELIVERY TO 8 HOUSES
1Ø   OPTION BASE 1
```

```
 20   DIM T(8)
 30   FOR I=1 TO 8
 40     T(I)=0
 50   NEXT I
 60   REM
 70   FOR D=1 TO 7
 80     PRINT "DAY";D
 90     FOR H=1 TO 8
100       INPUT S,
110       T(H)=T(H)+S
120     NEXT H
130   NEXT D
140   REM
150   FOR H=1 TO 8
160     PRINT "HOUSE";H;T(H);"PRINTS OF MILK DELIVERED"
170   NEXT H
180   END
RUN
DAY 1
? 1,4,1,3,2,0,5,2
DAY 2
? 3,0,1,1,1,2,0,1
DAY 3
? 0,2,0,1,4,0,0,1
DAY 4
? 2,1,1,0,1,1,2,1
DAY 5
? 1,1,2,1,0,0,1,0
DAY 6
? 2,1,0,0,0,3,4,1
DAY 7
? 1,5,2,0,1,1,3,1
```

HOUSE 1 1Ø PINTS OF MILK DELIVERED

HOUSE 2 14 PINTS OF MILK DELIVERED

HOUSE 3   7 PINTS OF MILK DELIVERED

HOUSE 4   6 PINTS OF MILK DELIVERED

HOUSE 5   9 PINTS OF MILK DELIVERED

HOUSE 6   7 PINTS OF MILK DELIVERED

HOUSE 7 15 PINTS OF MILK DELIVERED

HOUSE 8   7 PINTS OF MILK DELIVERED

END AT LINE 18Ø

The milkman types in the pints delivered on each day for the eight houses. The first house, number 1, is the house whose data were calculated with the simple program. The action of the program is simply to add up all the values in each column and display the individual totals.

4.1.6 MAT input and output

The MAT statements are designed to operate on all the elements of an array, from subscript 1 upwards, in one statement. Many systems do not supply the full range of these instructions, as described in Chapter 7, but some systems do at least provide the MAT input and output statements.

Quite simply, the statements:

```
1Ø   DIM A(5)

2Ø   MAT INPUT A
```

will input to the five array elements A(1), A(2), A(3), A(4), and A(5). The values can be typed on one line or over several lines. If your computer does not have this feature, the equivalent statements are:

```
1Ø   DIM A(5)

2Ø   FOR I=1 TO 5

3Ø      INPUT A(I),

4Ø   NEXT I
```

The comma after A(I) just allows you to input several values on one line separated by commas. If your system does not accept it, you will have to input the values one on each line.

Output works in the same way:

```
10   DIM P(8)
20   MAT PRINT P
```

will output the eight values of P(1) to P(8), each on a new line. Adding a comma or semicolon after the P causes the output to be on one line and the values to be widely or closed spaced. If your computer does not have this feature the equivalent statements are:

```
10   DIM P(8)
20   FOR I=1 TO 8
30      PRINT P(I)
40   NEXT I
```

Both MAT INPUT and MAT PRINT also operate on two-dimensional arrays. Take care on INPUT to note how the values are assigned to individual array elements; the usual method is with the second subscript varying fastest. Thus:

```
10   DIM A(2,3)
20   MAT INPUT A
```

is equivalent to:

```
10   DIM A(2,3)
20   FOR I=1 TO 2
30      FOR J=1 TO 3
40         INPUT A(I,J),
50      NEXT J
60   NEXT I
```

Output is in a similar fashion with the second subscript varying fastest. For example:

```
10   REM FRAGMENT TO SHOW MAT FEATURES
20   DIM A(2,3)
30   MAT INPUT A
40   REM
50   MAT PRINT A,
60   END
```

```
RUN
? 1,2,3,4,5,6
1              2              3
4              5              6
END AT LINE 60
```

The 2 by 3 matrix A is displayed in the usual algebraic form of rows and columns, and the comma on the MAT INPUT statement causes the output to be produced row by row as shown.

BBC BASIC does not have these statements, but unlike most other systems it does provide a 'procedure' feature (see Section 6.5), and it may be useful to define the procedures MATINPUT(A) and MATPRINT(A) to operate as above.

4.2 STRINGS OF CHARACTERS

Text, or strings of characters, may be manipulated in a BASIC program quite easily. Although this manipulation is not elegant, as it is achieved through a library of built-in functions, it is very powerful.

Thus, strings may be regarded as another type of object that BASIC can use and operate on. Some computer languages try as far as possible to keep the same sort of operations on all the objects available, but not many succeed in doing this properly. BASIC does not even try! Each type of object and its associated operations are usually separate from the others, so BASIC appears like a series of separate bits loosely fastened together. One advantage is that BASIC can, and does, grow and change fairly easily.

4.2.1 String variables

A string is regarded as a group of characters. Within a program, strings are groups of characters bounded by double quotes, and have been used extensively in PRINT statements. For example:

```
10   PRINT "HOUSE";H;T(H);"PINTS OF MILK DELIVERED"
```

A string may contain any letter of the alphabet, any digit, and any of the special characters such as " / £ ? ; &=$ @ + – # . , space. It may also contain non-printable characters which may cause some action, such as moving the cursor, when the string is printed. Unlike most BASIC statements a space in a string is significant.

Up to this point the variables we have concentrated on have stored numeric values only, but a second type of variable is available which stores strings only. This is a string variable and has the usual form of a variable name, but ending with a $ sign. There should be no connection between a numeric and string variable which share the same name. Thus the string variable A$ should be

112

completely different from the numeric variable A. Here is a mini-program illustrating the use of a string variable:

```
10   REM STRING EXAMPLE
20   PRINT "PLEASE TELL ME YOUR NAME";
30   INPUT A$
40   PRINT "HELLO";A$;"HOW ARE YOU TODAY?"
50   END
RUN
PLEASE TELL ME YOUR NAME? LARA
HELLO LARA HOW ARE YOU TODAY?
END AT LINE 50
```

Try it again:

```
RUN
PLEASE TELL ME YOUR NAME? 27.6!
HELLO 27.6! HOW ARE YOU TODAY?
END AT LINE 50
```

Whatever is given as input is placed into the string variable and later printed out. The only limitation is that BASIC takes a comma as a separator for items given in response to an INPUT request. Thus, re-run the above program:

```
RUN
PLEASE TELL ME YOUR NAME? WALSH,LARA
WARNING – EXTRA INPUT IGNORED
HELLO WALSH HOW ARE YOU TODAY?
END AT LINE 50
```

If line 30 had been INPUT A$,B$ then the first item above (WALSH) would be put into A$ and the second item (LARA) into B$. There is a means of getting the whole line into one variable regardless of the number of commas in it; this is discussed in Section 4.2.4.

Another way of getting a complicated string into one variable is to make it appear as one string by putting double quotes round it. Re-run the above program:

<u>RUN</u>

PLEASE TELL ME YOUR NAME? <u>"WALSH,LARA"</u>

HELLO WALSH,LARA HOW ARE YOU TODAY?

END AT LINE 5Ø

Just as numeric variables can be assigned values within a program, so can string variables. The following are valid statements:

    1Ø   A$="LARA"

    1Ø   C$="£25.6"

    1Ø   B$=C$

    1Ø   IF Y$="YES" THEN 2ØØ

    1Ø   IF X$<>A$ THEN PRINT "OK"

The above IF statements will check if the strings are identically equal or not. Spaces are significant. If Y$ contained "   YES" (note initial space), then Y$ is not equal to "YES".

   Strings can contain from zero to very many characters. The string containing zero characters is "", and is known as the null string. The maximum allowed length for a string differs between systems and some values are given in Table 4.1.

Table 4.1 Maximum string lengths

System	Maximum string length (characters)
BBC	255
Microsoft	255
CBM PET	255
Sinclair	No limit
ICL 2903/4	511

   There may be a restriction on the number of characters which you can put into the string in one operation, either in response to an input or within a program statement. This usually has something to do with the implementation of the system in terms of the line length of the VDU. Typically the maximum allowed is this length (perhaps 4Ø or 6Ø characters), and longer strings must be built up by adding strings together.

114

The following program works in a rather elementary way as a word counting program. The word to be recognized is first input, followed by a sentence ending with a full stop, each part of which is on a new line.

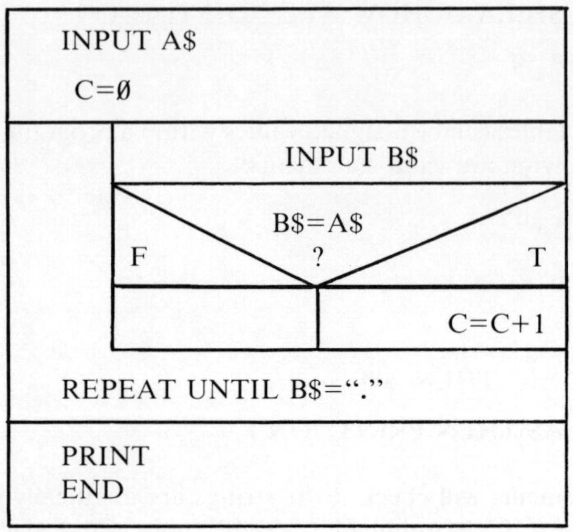

Notice the 'repeat until' diagram which is used above. It indicates that the test is at the end of the loop and may be implemented using an IF statement in most systems, but some BASIC systems do provide a REPEAT–UNTIL statement (see Chapter 6). The program is:

```
10   REM ELEMENTARY WORD COUNTING
20   INPUT A$
30   C=Ø
40     INPUT B$
50     IF B$=A$ THEN C=C+1
60   IF B$<>"." THEN 40
70   REM
80   PRINT "THE WORD   ";A$;"   OCCURS";C;"TIMES"
90   END
RUN
? TWO                                    ←——————————————— this is input to A$
```

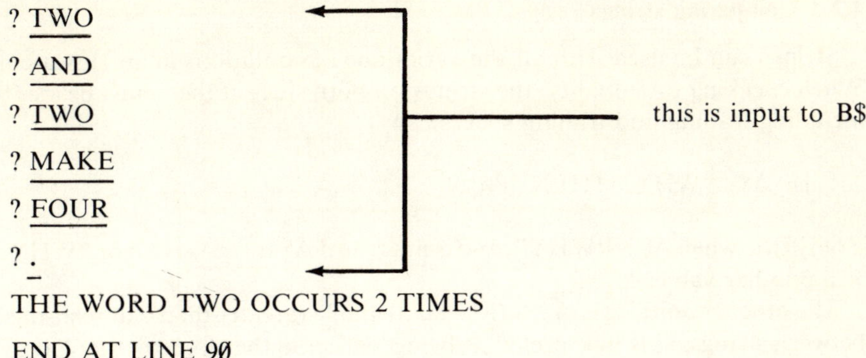

THE WORD TWO OCCURS 2 TIMES

END AT LINE 90

4.2.2 Concatenation of strings

Strings may be put together, rather like adding carriages to a train, to form longer strings. This action is called concatenation. It is done using the & operator on some systems or the+operator on others between two strings. For example:

```
10   A$="WALT"
20   B$=A$+" DISNEY"
30   PRINT B$
40   END
RUN
WALT DISNEY
END AT LINE 40
```

Quite complicated expressions may be constructed as in:

```
10 A$=C$+" "+D$+" AND "+Z8$+"."
```

Spaces are significant and may have to be added into the appropriate places to stop words running together in the final string.

Because the+operator is so easily thought of as numeric addition some systems use another operator such as &, but as you see the action of concatenation is one of joining together rather than addition. Thus the other numeric operators *,/,– are not applicable to strings. If you wish to break up a string into parts, which is the reverse of concatenation, you must use the string functions provided (see Section 4.2.6).

4.2.3 Comparing strings

Strings can be used with all the variations of conditions in an IF statement. When checking for equality, the strings on both sides of the=must be identical, including leading and trailing spaces. So:

    IF A$="WHY" THEN 100

is only true when A$ is "WHY", and is not true if A$ is "   WHY" or "WHY   ", or any other value.

The other conditionals are $<$ (less than) and $>$ (greater than). In relationships between strings, $<$ is interpreted as being 'earlier in the alphabet than' and $>$ as 'later in the alphabet than'.

That being said, it needs some qualification, for where do special symbols or number digits fit in? The answer is simple. The computer compares string values by looking at the internal numeric code of the characters, and the correctness of the comparisons $<$ and $>$ is based on this numeric code. Thus, look up the numeric code for 'character 1' and if it is less than the code for 'character 2', then 'character 1'$<$ 'character 2'. Most, but not all, computers use the ASCII code to represent their internal characters (see Appendix II). In any case, your system should provide a function to enable you to find the numeric code corresponding to each character. Some examples of ASCII codes are given in Table 4.2.

Table 4.2 Some examples of ASCII codes

Character	Code (decimal)
*	42
+	43
–	45
Ø	48
9	57
A	65
H	72
Z	90
a	97
h	104
z	122

Notice that some special characters appear before the digits Ø to 9, which in turn appear before the capital alphabetic letters. The lower case alphabetic letters appear near the end of the list.

Strings can be easily sorted into alphabetical order since a string beginning with A is $<$ one beginning with B, and so on. The following is thus correct:

"CAR" $<$ "CARD" $<$ "CARTER" $<$ "CAT"

and so is:

"Ø" $<$ "1" $<$ "2"

The following is a simple program which demonstrates some of these relations. Try it on your computer.

```
10   REM STRING TEST DEMO
20   IF "A"<"B" THEN PRINT "A<B"
30   IF "Ø"<"8" THEN PRINT "Ø<8"
40   IF "Ø"<"D" THEN PRINT "Ø<D"
50   IF "X"="XX" THEN PRINT "X=XX"
60   IF "X"<"XX" THEN PRINT "X<XX"
70   IF "CART HORSE"<"CARTER" THEN PRINT "CART HORSE
     <CARTER"
80   END
RUN
A<B
Ø<8
Ø<D
X<XX
CART HORSE<CARTER
END AT LINE 80
```

The next program illustrates an elementary method of sorting three strings into alphabetical order. If numeric variables were used in place of string variables the program would sort three numbers into ascending order. The technique used in this program would not be used to sort a number of strings. A much more comprehensive sorting program is given in Section 4.5.

```
10    REM ELEMENTARY SORT
20    INPUT A$,B$,C$
30    REM TEST FIRST PAIR, SWAP IF OUT OF ORDER
40    IF A$<B$ THEN 90
50      X$=A$
60      A$=B$
70      B$=X$
80    REM TEST SECOND PAIR, SWAP IF OUT OF ORDER
90    IF B$<C$ THEN 150
100     X$=B$
110     B$=C$
120     C$=X$
130   REM HAVING SWAPPED THESE, NEED TO CHECK NEW
      FIRST PAIR
140   GO TO 40
150   PRINT "WORDS IN ALPHABETICAL ORDER ARE"
160   PRINT A$,B$,C$
170   END
RUN
? LARA, ANN, BETTY
WORDS IN ALPHABETICAL ORDER ARE
ANN              BETTY              LARA
END AT LINE 170
```

4.2.4 Line INPUT

As discussed in Section 4.2.1 there are difficulties in putting a string to an INPUT request when that string contains commas. The comma acts as a separator which makes the INPUT regard it as several strings. It can be forced to appear as one string if it is enclosed in double quotes, but this is tedious, and even may be impossible if the INPUT is coming from a file not the terminal. To overcome this problem many BASIC systems supply a line INPUT statement which takes the next complete line of text regardless of its contents and puts it into a single string variable. Table 4.3 gives the differing names used. The action of each type is the same as the ordinary INPUT for that system, and may contain a prompt string where appropriate.

Table 4.3 Line INPUT statements for various systems

System	Line INPUT statement
BBC	INPUT LINE A$,B$,....
Microsoft	LINE INPUT A$,BS,....
ICL 2903/4	LINPUT A$,B$,....

The effects of the statements may be judged from the action of the following program, using the Microsoft form:

```
10   REM LINE INPUT
20   LINE INPUT A$,B$
30   PRINT
40   PRINT "FIRST LINE IS:";A$
50   PRINT "SECOND LINE IS:";B$
60   END
RUN
THIS IS AN EXAMPLE, SEVERAL CHRS., " AND !&
NEXT LINE, MORE CHRS., $"";
FIRST LINE IS: THIS IS AN EXAMPLE, SEVERAL CHRS., " AND !&
SECOND LINE IS: NEXT LINE, MORE CHRS., $"";
END AT LINE 60
```

4.2.5 Numeric string functions

All the string functions in BASIC are computer dependent. In what follows the commonly available functions are described.

This section deals with those functions which act on strings but return a numeric value, e.g. the length of the string. Being functions they require one or more input values and return a single numeric value via the function name. Thus:

```
10   A=LEN ("DON'T GIVE UP")
```

places the value 13 into the variable A by using the function LEN which returns the length of a string. Tables of the various alternative names, and sometimes slightly different actions, for the common functions are given in Tables 4.4 to 4.8. For consistency, the Microsoft functions will be used to illustrate the function actions. The strings A$ and B$ in the tables may be a variable, an expression, or a constant.

Table 4.4 Sinclair ZX81 functions

Action	Function	Use
Code value	CODE A$	Gives the internal computer code of the first character of A$. If the string is null Ø is given.
Length	LEN A$	Gives the number of characters in A$.
Value	VAL A$	Gives the numeric result obtained by evaluating the numbers in A$, which may be a complicated arithmetic expression.

Table 4.5 Microsoft functions; several others are used with random file handling (see Section 8.6.2)

Action	Function	Use
Code value	ASC(A$)	Gives the (internal computer) ASCII code for the first character of A$.
Length	LEN(A$)	Gives number of characters in A$.
Position	INSTR(A$,B$) INSTR(I,A$,B$)	Gives the position of the start of the occurrence of B$ in A$, else Ø. If I is present, the search starts from character position I.
Value	VAL(A$)	Gives a number corresponding to A$, which can contain only +,−,&, or a digit. Blanks and linefeeds are removed from the string.

Table 4.6 BBC functions

Action	Function	Use
Code value	ASC(A$)	Gives the (internal computer) ASCII code for the first character of A$ (i.e. positive or zero). If the string is null −1 is given.
Length	LEN(A$)	Gives the number of characters in A$.
Position	INSTR(A$,B$) INSTR(A$,B$,I)	Gives the position of the start of the occurrence of B$ in A$, else Ø. If I is present, the search starts from character position I.
Value	VAL(A$)	Gives a number corresponding to A$, which can contain only numeric characters, else Ø.

Table 4.7 CBM PET functions

Action	Function	Use
Code value	ASC(A$)	Gives the (internal computer) ASCII code for the first character of A$.
Length	LEN(A$)	Gives the number of characters in A$.
Value	VAL(A$)	Gives a number corresponding to A$, which can contain only numeric characters, else Ø.

Table 4.8 ICL 29Ø3/4 functions

Action	Function	Use
Code value	CHR(A$)	Gives the internal computer code of the first character of A$.
Length	LEN(A$)	Gives the number of characters in A$.
Occurrences	OCC(A$,B$)	Gives the number of non-overlapping occurrences of B$ in A$.
Position	POS(A$,B$) POS(A$,B$,N)	Gives the position of the start of the occurrence of B$ in A$, else Ø. If N is present, then the Nth occurrence.
Value	VAL(A$)	Gives a number corresponding to A$, which can contain only numeric characters.

If A$ contains "PHOTOGRAPH" then:

    B=LEN(A$)

    C=ASC(A$)

    D=INSTR (A$,"P")

    E=INSTR (6,A$,"PH")

leaves B with 1Ø, C with 8Ø which is the decimal ASCII code for P, D with 1 which is the character position in A$ of the beginning of the match, with E and 9 which is the character position in A$ of the beginning of the match where the search started from character position 6 onwards. The use VAL(A$) is invalid, and for this system will give the value zero.

If A$ contained "−12356" then VAL(A$) gives the number −12,356, which may be processed numerically if required. There is a function which is the reverse of VAL and converts a numeric value to a string containing the number. It may help to think of the string containing a number as the picture of the number. If A\$ contains "1234" and B\$ contains "5678", and:

C\$=A\$+B\$

E=VAL(A\$)+VAL(B\$)

then C\$ contains "12345678" and E contains 6912. This VAL seems a strange function, but proves to be very useful in two areas. Firstly, it can be used to format output. The numbers to be output are formed into strings, manipulated to add or delete spaces and drop unwanted digits, then PRINT ed, or put together as a single string and PRINT ed.

Secondly, some file processing to disc requires that only strings be passed as input and output from the disc. Thus numeric values are converted into strings for a write to the disc and converted back from strings after a read from the disc.

The OCC function (see Table 4.8) is quite useful but if you require it and it is not available on your system the following program fragment does the same job. It assumes A\$ as input and B\$ which contains the search string, and the result is returned in the variable O as zero or the number of non-overlapping occurrences found. Note that the INSTR function as described in Table 4.5 is used. In the solution to this problem which is illustrated in the structogram below, we would like to continue testing string B\$ against string A\$ until one of two things occurs. Either there are no more matches of the strings or we have run off the end of string A\$. There is no structure symbol which allows this termination of the loop from different places inside the loop sequence unless we write the conditions at the end of the loop, which in practice is done by introducing another variable M. This starts as zero and is set to 1 if either of the conditions occur. The loop is then controlled as 'repeat until the end of string A\$ would be exceeded or no more position matches found' which becomes 'repeat until M equals 1'.

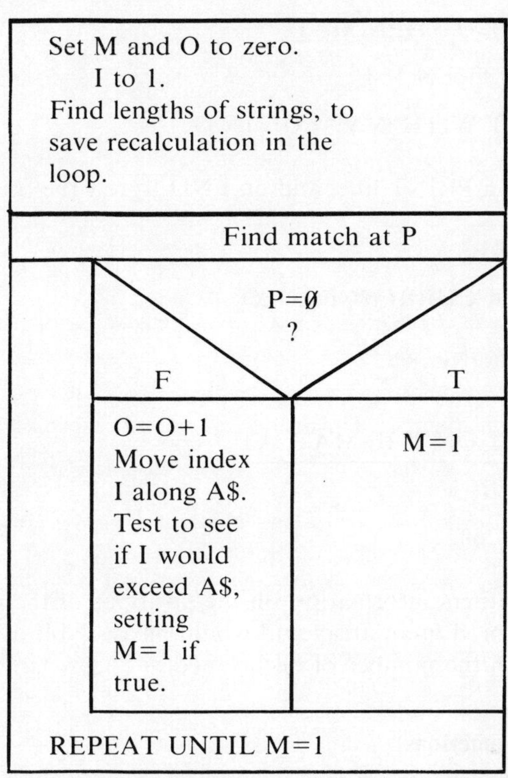

The program code corresponding to this structogram is given below. It is not a complete program as it is likely to be used as a part of a larger program—perhaps as a subroutine or function discussed in Chapter 5:

```
100    REM OCCURRENCES FRAGMENT
110    O=Ø
120    I=1
130    J=LEN(A$)
140    K=LEN(B$)
150    M=Ø
160    P=INSTR(I,A$,B$)
170      IF P<>Ø THEN 200
180        M=1
190        GO TO 230
200      O=O+1
210      I=P+K
```

124

```
220    IF (I+K)>J THEN M=1

230   IF M<>1 THEN 160

240   REM EXIT WITH A VALUE IN O
```

Add an INPUT line, a PRINT line, and an END to test the fragment.

```
 10   INPUT A$,B$

250   PRINT "OCCURRENCES=";O

260   END

RUN

? THE CAT SAT ON THE MAT, AT

OCCURRENCES=3

END AT LINE 260
```

The program also gathers information on the positions of the matches; these positions could be stored in an array and would be available at the end of the process, together with the number of occurrences.

4.2.6 Substrings and functions

This section deals with those functions which return strings, either substrings of existing strings or new ones, as, for example, the result of a conversion process from a numeric value. Only the generally available functions are described, and the Microsoft functions will be used in the examples unless otherwise stated. Tables of the various functions classified by general action are given in Tables 4.9 to 4.13.

The principal interest is focused on those functions which produce parts of strings or, more correctly, substrings. A substring is a sequence of consecutive characters taken from another string. So "HAPPY" and "Y BIRTH" are substrings of "HAPPY BIRTHDAY", but "HAP DAY" and "PP BIRTH" are not, although they are new strings which can be built up out of several substrings of the original.

Table 4.9 Sinclair ZX81 string functions

Action	Function	Use
Conversion to character	CHR$ N	Gives the character whose code is N, range from Ø to 255.
Parts of strings	Uses a technique of slicing a string; not a function	
	String (N TO M)	The expression in brackets gives a substring from the Nth to the Mth characters. If N is absent, 1 is assumed. If M is absent, end of string is assumed.
	String (N)	The form (N) gives one character, the Nth.
Number string	STR$ N	Gives a string corresponding to the number in A. The opposite function is VAL (which is more general in that it can deal with expressions).
Special character input	INKEY$	No arguments, gives a single character from the keyboard.

Table 4.1Ø Microsoft string functions

Action	Function	Use
Conversion to character	CHR$(N)	Gives the character whose ASCII code is N.
Parts of strings	LEFT$(A$,N) RIGHT$(A$,N)	Gives the N left or right characters of string A$.
	MID$(A$,N,M)	Gives the M characters of A$ starting from position N.
Number string	STR$(A)	Gives a string corresponding to the number in A. The opposite of VAL.
Special character input	INKEY$	No arguments, gives a single character from the keyboard.
	INPUT$(N)	Gives a string of N characters from the keyboard. (May also be used for files.)
Format aids	SPACE$(N)	Gives a string of N spaces.
	STRING$(N,M) STRING$(N,A$)	Gives a string containing N characters of ASCII code M, or of the first character of A$.
Others	HEX$(A) OCT$(A)	Gives a string containing the hexadecimal or octal value of A, rounded to an integer.

Table 4.11 BBC string functions

Action	Function	Use
Conversion to character	CHR$(N)	Gives the character with internal code N, effectively modulo 256.
Parts of strings	LEFT$(A$,N) RIGHT$(A$,N)	Gives the N left or right characters of string A$.
	MID$(A$,N,M)	Gives the M character of A$ starting from position N.
Number string	STR$(M)	Gives a string corresponding to the number in A. The opposite of VAL.
Special character input	GET$	No arguments, waits for next character in the input, which it then supplies.
	INKEY$(N)	As GET$ but waits for a maximum of N clock cycles. If there is no character it returns the null string (there are numeric versions of both functions).
Formatting aids	STRING$(N,A$)	Gives a string comprising N copies of A$.

Table 4.12 CBM PET string functions

Action	Function	Use
Conversion to character	CHR$(N)	Gives the character whose ASCII code is N.
Parts of strings	LEFT$(A$,N) RIGHT$(A$,N)	Gives the N left or right characters of string A$.
	MID$(A$,N,M)	Gives the M characters of A$ starting from position N.
Number string	STR$(A)	Gives the string corresponding to the number in A. The opposite of VAL.
Special character input	Not a function but a normal statement, e.g. 1Ø GET A$	Can be used with a string variable to obtain the next character from the keyboard.

Table 4.13 ICL 2903/4 string functions

Action	Function	Use
Conversion to character	CHR$(N)	Gives the character with internal code N, evaluated to modulo 64.
Parts of strings	SEG$(A$,N,M) SUB$(A$,N,M)	Gives a substring of A$ from position N to position M. In the case of SUB$, from position N for M characters.
Number string	STR$(A)	Gives a string corresponding to the number in A. This is the opposite of VAL.
Formatting aids	GAP$(N)	Gives a string of N spaces.
	SGN$(X)	Gives the character +,– or space, as X is positive, negative, or zero.
	LIN$(N)	Gives N new line characters.
Others	DEL$(A$,B$,N) SDL$(A$,B$,N)	Delete single or multiple occurrences of B$ in A$.
	REP$(A$,B$,C$,N) SRP$(A$,B$,C$,N)	Replaces single or multiple occurrences of B$ by C$ in A$.

If A$ contained "HAVE A GOOD DAY" and:

```
A1$=LEFT$(A$,11)
A2$=LEFT$(A$,2)

B1$=RIGHT$(A$,3)
B2$=RIGHT$(A$,1Ø)
```

then A1$ contains "HAVE A GOOD", A2$ contains "HA", B1$ contains "DAY", and B2$ contains "A GOOD DAY". If we have the assignments:

```
C1$=MID$(A$,8,4)
C2$=MID$(A$,8,8)

C3$=MID$(A$,8)
```

then C1$ contains "GOOD", C2$ contains "GOOD DAY", and C3$ takes all the rightmost characters from the eighth to contain "GOOD DAY" again.

A combination of selection of substrings and concatenation usually solves most string handling problems. For example:

```
1Ø   REM STRING FUNCTION FRAGMENT
```

128

```
20   A$="SUN MON FRI"
30   B$="DAY"
40   FOR I=1 TO 9 STEP 4
50      C$=MID$(A$,I,3)
60      C$=C$+B$
70      PRINT C$
80   NEXT I
90   END
RUN
SUNDAY
MONDAY
FRIDAY
END AT LINE 90
```

The loop picks up the starting positions of the first part of the weekday names, and they are extracted as substrings on line 50, put together with "DAY" on line 60, and printed on line 70. These three lines could be put together as one statement PRINT MID$(A$,I,3)+B$ if required.

If you contemplate a task such as designing a program for word processing or editing a text file then the supplied string functions are not convenient, acting as they do on numeric character positions. The exact form of the program components will depend on the detailed requirements such as the type of material to be changed and where it is stored (store or disc); thus the following are suggestions. It is assumed that the material is worked on line by line and the current line is stored in A$. Instructions given to the system change the current line or instruct it to be replaced by the next one.

(a) In a sensible system the user does not want to count character positions to perform some action on part of the line. Thus the first feature required is *FIND* B$ *IN* A$, where A$ is the current line and B$ is some substring. The INSTR, or similar function, will do this quite adequately.

(b) The next feature is *INSERT* C$ *AT POSITION* I *IN* A$, which usually means add the new string immediately before position I, as:

$$LEFT\$(A\$,I-1)+C\$+RIGHT\$(A\$,LEN(A\$)-I+1)$$

will produce a new string with the insertion.

(c) The next feature is *DELETE* B$ *FROM* A$. The position of the start of B$ in A$ can be found as in (a); if this is I the amended string is:

$$LEFT\$(A\$,I-1)+RIGHT\$(A\$, LEN(A\$)-LEN(B\$)-I+1)$$

(d) The actions (a), (b), and (c) occur together often enough to be useful as a single replacement feature, ***REPLACE*** B\$ ***BY*** C\$ ***IN*** A\$. First find I, the start of B\$ in A\$, then delete B\$, and finally add C\$.

Some systems such as the ICL 2903/4 (see Table 4.13) provide functions similar to the above, and on others such as the BBC they may be created as special procedures not unlike functions; however, in all systems they can be created as subroutines.

The Sinclair ZX81 system for obtaining substrings is both simple and elegant. Brackets after the string variable indicate the range of character positions selected, as:

A\$="OKAY"

B\$=A\$(1 TO 2)

leaves B\$ containing "OK". The substrings may also be used on the left-hand side of an assignment (=) to receive characters into a set length substring. It is a shame that so many BASIC systems have opted for the clumsy function system, rather than adopting the above approach which is called slicing.

Returning to look at some of the remaining string functions, the action of CHR\$ is illustrated in the following program:

```
10   REM CHR$ DEMO
20   FOR I=45 TO 69
30     PRINT CHR$(I);
40   NEXT I
50   END
RUN
-./0123456789:;=?@ABCDE
END AT LINE 50
```

In fact all types of characters, even non-printable ones, can be generated by CHR\$. For example, 13 is the decimal ASCII code for carriage return so PRINT CHR\$(13) causes a carriage return to be generated. All types of line printer control features such as form feed and overprinting can be produced using CHR\$, which cannot be done in any other way. If you try running the program above for I=0 TO 255, which is the complete set of ASCII codes, you will see some very strange results as the display responds to the control characters which are generated. You may even lose BASIC and have to start the machine again!

STR$ and VAL are complementary functions. VAL is very useful in extracting numbers, for subsequent numeric computation, from strings. Thus:

B=VAL(RIGHT$("THE COST IS £105.12",6))

leaves B containing 105.12 as a number. And STR$ can always be used to pack a number back into a string. If B contains 105.12 and a tax of 15 per cent is added, we obtain 120.888, but since we want this to represent pounds and whole pence we discard the final 8 digit before putting it all into a string. Thus:

```
100   B=105.12
110   B=B*1.15
120   B$=STR$(B)
130   B$=LEFT$(B,6)
140   A$="THE COST IS £"+B$+"INCLUDING TAX"
```

Note that lines 110 to 140 can be written as one line:

A$="THE COST IS £"+LEFT$(STR$(B*1.15),6)+"INCLUDING TAX"

Finally, the special character input facility is useful in a number of situations. In normal input, the program halts and one or many characters are typed; these are only sent to the program when the return key is pressed. However, this character input does not wait for a **SEND** command. The program halts for a few milliseconds for input and when any key is pressed this is immediately accepted, or the first character previously typed and waiting in the input buffer is taken.

As the tables show, there are many different forms for character input; the following have the same effect:

```
10     A$=GET$
10     B$=INKEY$
10   LET C$=INKEY$
10   GET D$
```

for the BBC, Microsoft, Sinclair, and PET systems respectively. The PET feature is a statement not a function and may be used with a numeric variable. The BBC system has an additional function which has a limited wait period specified. If this is exceeded the program resumes with a null string.

The function is almost always used in a loop to wait for input. For the Microsoft function:

```
50    B$=INKEY$
60    IF LEN(B$)=0 THEN 50
70    . . . . . .
```

the loop will continue indefinitely until a key is pressed. You may organize your own input by building up characters into a string until a special character or carriage return (which is CHR$(13)) is received:

```
100   I$=""
110   B$=INKEY$
120   IF LEN(B$)=0 THEN 110
130   IF CHR$(13)=B$ THEN 200
140   I$=I$+B$
150   GO TO 110
200   REM A SET OF CHARACTERS IS IN I$
210   . . . . . .
```

The loop to B$ on line 110 may be replaced by a limited number of cycles in a FOR–NEXT loop, which is thus a limited waiting time. So the program will accept a line of input terminated by a carriage return, or if this is not given after a suitable time it will continue.

Since INKEY$ (or GET$) allows full control over input you can construct your own input features such as free format, etc.

4.3 STRING ARRAYS

In Section 4.1 we saw that several numbers can be stored in an array, say A, with the numbers held in the elements of A which are A(1),A(2),A(3), and so on. Similarly, we can store several strings in a string array A$ and refer to the individual strings as A$(1),A$(2), and so on. The names which are allowed for string arrays are usually the same as those allowed for ordinary arrays, plus the final $ sign.

The most restrictive is ICL 2903/4 BASIC which restricts all array names to one letter; this applies to string arrays as well. Normally, properly significant names may be used such as RESPONSE$, TOTAL$, and ADDRESSES$. As with numeric arrays, a DIM statement giving the maximum subscript must be included in the program. There should not be any connection between a string array and a numeric array which share the same name.

Let us be clear about string arrays. Each element of a string array acts as a string variable and can hold between zero and many characters. The number is given in Table 4.1. The string array element may be used with all the string functions discussed in the previous sections.

A one-dimensional string array may be thought of as a list of items; e.g. a list of names as in a telephone directory or a shopping list. The trivial example below reads and then prints items in such a list:

```
10    REM STRING ARRAY DEMO
20    DIM A$(1Ø)
30    FOR I=Ø TO 3
40       INPUT A$(I)
50    NEXT I
60    REM
70    PRINT
80    PRINT "OUTPUT FROM ARRAY IN REVERSE ORDER"
90    FOR I=3 TO Ø STEP -1
100      PRINT A$(I)
110   NEXT I
120   END
RUN
? 1lb POTATOES
? 2oz MUSHROOMS
? 1 CABBAGE
? 6 APPLES

OUTPUT FROM ARRAY IN REVERSE ORDER
6 APPLES
1 CABBAGE
2oz MUSHROOMS
1lb POTATOES
END AT LINE 12Ø
```

Two-dimensional string arrays and higher dimensions may be used as the problem dictates. Do not forget that higher dimensional arrays take up a lot of space, even more so in the case of strings where each element may contain a large number of characters and each character requires one byte of store. An array A$(9,9,9) with an average of 20 characters per element would consume at least 2Ø×1Ø×1Ø×1Ø=2Ø,ØØØ bytes of store!

4.3.1 String program example

The program converts from a decimal integer to a Roman number. String usage is chosen because of the characters which make up Roman numbers. The solution is not a straightforward one of replacing the decimal digits by the Roman numerals because of the quite different assumptions in the two systems. For example:

1Ø25   becomes   MXXV

1982   becomes   MCMLXXXII

2ØØØ   becomes   MM

The decimal system is based on a value determined by the position of the digit in the number, but the Roman system is based on adding (and subtracting) the values of the numerals. There is a repetitive rule which allows a repeat up to three times, so III is 3 and XX is 2Ø. There is a subtractive rule which, when reading from left to right, says that the smaller values are subtracted from the larger ones on the right; so XL is 4Ø. There is an additive rule which accumulates the values of the numbers obeying the above rules; so CXLIII is 1ØØ+4Ø+3=143. The decimal values of the Roman numerals are:

I=   1

V=   5

X=   1Ø

L=   5Ø

C=   1ØØ

D=   5ØØ

M=1ØØØ

It is the combination of the three rules which causes the complexity in the program, which must follow the changes in layout. The Roman sequence from 1 to 1Ø illustrates this:

I II III IV V VI VII VIII IX X

which shows a symmetry up to each new symbol, so that 1,2,3 and 6,7,8 are repetitions (plus addition), 4 and 9 are subtractions, and 5 and 1Ø are new symbols.

A string array is chosen to act as a 'look-up' table containing the Roman numerals, and is set out as follows:

I   X   C   M

V   L   D   null

X   C   M   null

134

The first column will be used for decimal values Ø to 9, the second for 1Ø to 9Ø, the third for 1ØØ to 9ØØ, and the fourth for numbers 1ØØØ and upwards. Because the higher symbols are not easily printable this program will fail with numbers higher than 3999, but if you wish you may include the following for the higher values of the fourth column.

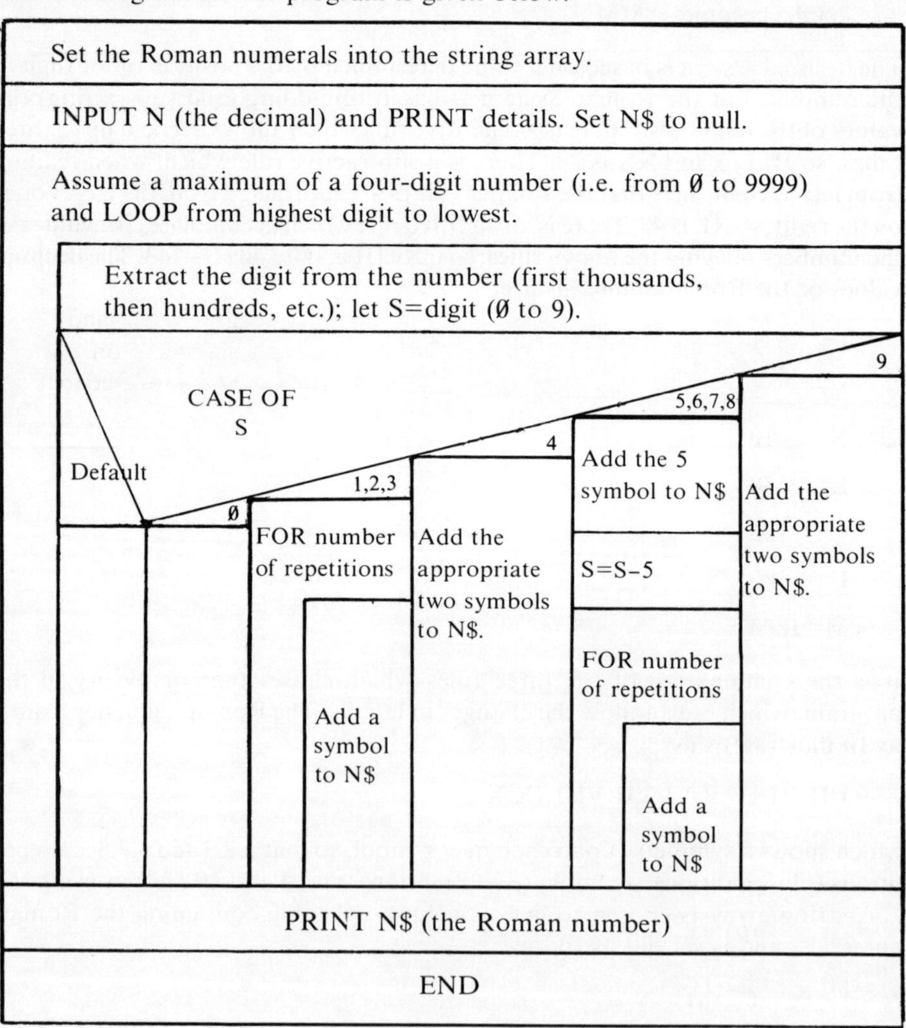

The structogram for the program is given below.

The main loop extracts the digits from the input decimal, first for the thousands, then for the hundreds, then for the tens, and finally the units. Inside the loop the new box is an example of the case statement. In BASIC it is called ON–GOTO and is rather like an expanded IF statement; hence the similar appearance. The expression after the ON is evaluated and should be rounded to an integer whose value is used to select one of the line numbers after the GOTO. If the expression has value 1 the first line number is selected, if 2 then the second number is selected, if 3 the third, and so on. Execution then jumps to the line number specified.

ON–GOTO statement

General form $\qquad\qquad\qquad$ ON e GOTO $s_1, s_2, s_3, \ldots\ldots\ldots s_n$

where e is an arithmetic expression

$\quad$ s_1 to s_n are statement numbers (at least one is required).

The action is to transfer control (GOTO) one of the statement numbers specified depending on the value of e which is evaluated, and should be rounded to an integer.

When this integer has value 1 control passes to the first (left-hand) statement s_1, when the integer is 2 control passes to s_2, and so on.

If the integer is out of range (which is 1 to N), control is transferred to the statement following the ON–GOTO statement.

A simple illustration is:

```
10   REM ON-GO TO DEMO
20   K=-1
30   PRINT "K=";K;"AND LINE";
40   ON K GOTO 70,90,110
50     PRINT "50 EXECUTED"
60     GO TO 120
70     PRINT "70 EXECUTED"
80     GO TO 120
90     PRINT "90 EXECUTED"
100    GO TO 120
110    PRINT "110 EXECUTED"
120  K=K+1
130  IF K<=4 THEN 30
```

136

```
140   END
RUN
K=-1 AND LINE 50 EXECUTED
K=0 AND LINE 50 EXECUTED
K=1 AND LINE 70 EXECUTED
K=2 AND LINE 90 EXECUTED
K=3 AND LINE 110 EXECUTED
K=4 AND LINE 50 EXECUTED
END AT LINE 140
```

Each alternative must end with a GOTO 'end of groups' to avoid execution continuing into the next one. If the expression is out of the range of the number of values in the GOTO list, then execution continues with the next statement after the ON–GOTO, which is line 50 above.

The full conversion program is:

```
10    REM CONVERSION FROM DECIMAL TO ROMAN
      NUMERALS
20    REM VALID FOR INPUT FROM 0 TO 3999
30    DIM R$(3,3)
40    REM SET VALUES INTO ARRAY
50    R$(0,1)="I"
60    R$(0,2)="V"
70    R$(0,3)="X"
80    R$(1,1)="X"
90    R$(1,2)="L"
100   R$(1,3)="C"
110   R$(2,1)="C"
120   R$(2,2)="D"
130   R$(2,3)="M"
140   R$(3,1)="M"
150   REM
160   INPUT N
```

```
170    PRINT "DECIMAL";N;"ROMAN";
180    N$=""
190    FOR J=3 TO 0 STEP −1
200      T=10↑J
210      S=INT(N/T)
220      N=N−S*T
230      ON S+1 GOTO 430,260,260,260,310,340,340,340,340,410
240    REM DEFAULT DROP THROUGH
250      GOTO 430
260    REM S IS 1,2,3
270      FOR K=1 TO S
280        N$=N$+R$(J,1)
290      NEXT K
300      GO TO 430
310    REM S IS 4
320      N$=N$+R$(J,1)+R$(J,2)
330      GO TO 430
340    REM S IS 5,6,7,8
350      N$=N$+R$(J,2)
360      S=S−5
370      FOR K=1 TO S
380        N$=N$+R$(J,1)
390      NEXT K
400      GO TO 430
410    REM S IS 9
420      N$=N$+R$(J,1)+R$(J,3)
430    REM END OF ON−GOTO
440    NEXT J
450    PRINT N$
460    END
```

Resist the urge to make use of the symmetry of actions for the values 1 to 4 and 5 to 9 by means of messy GOTO statements. The complications involved are not worth the effort. A later chapter will describe how subroutines and functions can be used in this context.

Here is an exercise based on the above program. After line 17Ø proceed to convert N to a string value (call it M$), then between lines 2ØØ and 22Ø extract each digit from the string M$ as a character, but remember to convert these to numbers for the ON–GOTO statement in line 23Ø. The results should be the same before the changes were made.

The general form of the case statement is not available in BASIC but is illustrated in the symbol below:

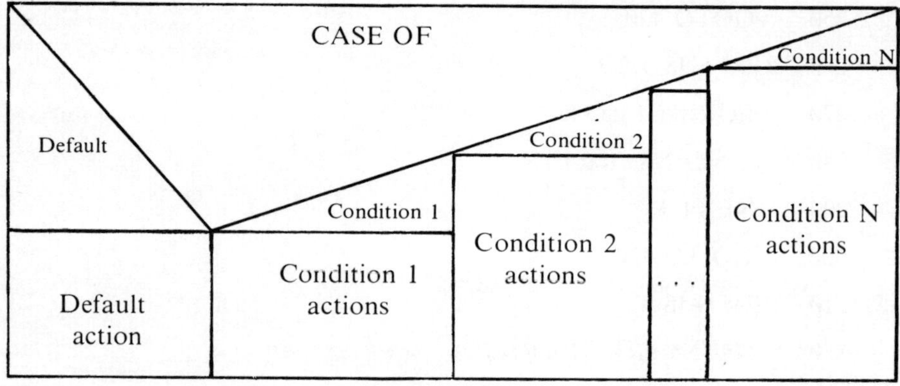

At least BASIC allows a simplified form of this to be used by the careful combination of ON–GOTO and GOTOs at the end of each alternative. One drawback to this symbol is that it is bulky and leaves unequal amounts of space to write in the action boxes. With some loss of immediate visual meaning you could use:

	CASE OF		
Default	Condition 1		Condition N
Default actions	Condition 1 actions	. . .	Condition N actions

but this still spreads across the page, so is sometimes used as:

<table>
<tr><td colspan="2">CASE OF</td></tr>
<tr><td>Default</td><td>Default actions</td></tr>
<tr><td>Condition 1</td><td>Condition 1 actions</td></tr>
<tr><td></td><td>.
.
.</td></tr>
<tr><td>Condition N</td><td>Condition N actions</td></tr>
</table>

which is rather misleading, as the actions in one process box do not lead onto the next, as is the rule in the normal diagram. These forms for the case symbols are not used in this book.

4.4 READ AND DATA STATEMENTS

The DATA statement provides a means of storing a limited amount of data with the program itself, and has certain advantages over assigning the values as constants in LET statements. The data are obtained from the DATA statements by means of a READ statement, as the following program demonstrates:

```
10   REM READ-DATA DEMO
20   READ A,B,C
30   PRINT A,B,C
40   REM
50   DATA 3,-2,45
60   END
RUN
3           -2           45
END AT LINE 60
```

The value of A is read as the first item in the DATA statement, the value of B from the second, and the value of C from the third. DATA statements can appear anywhere in the program. When execution passes over them there is no action whatsoever. They act only to retain a list of values for the READ statement. The above program would be the same if line 5Ø were deleted, and the DATA statement placed elsewhere, say line 5.

It is good practice to group DATA statements together, preferably at the end or beginning of a program, because multiple DATA statements are allowed.

4.4.1 Using DATA statements

Imagine there is a pointer at the beginning of the DATA statement. In the example above the READ assigns the first number in the DATA list 3 to the variable A, and moves the pointer to the next number (–2).

Each READ action assigns a value to a variable from the current position of the pointer. Thus, the pointer is at –2 and the variable is B, so B is given the value –2, and the pointer moves on.

If the pointer reaches the end of the DATA statement and more data are required, then it moves to the beginning of the next DATA statement, or is given an error message if there are not enough data. For example:

```
10   READ A,B,C,D,E,F,G,H,I

20   DATA 14,32,96,78,3,11

30   DATA 3Ø3,411,9999
```

Although DATA statements can appear anywhere in the program they should be grouped together, as they are linked in the sense that when a READ has finished with one it will carry on with data from the next DATA statement with a higher line number. A very common error is a mismatch between the number of values required by the one or more READ statements and the number of values given on the many DATA statements. Such an error is more easily identified if the DATA statements appear together.

READ and DATA are useful for storing data in the program which do not vary from one run to another. They are also very useful in assigning initial values to variables or arrays. Refer to the conversion program in Section 4.3.1; lines 5Ø to 14Ø could be replaced by a loop with READ and DATA statements:

```
50   FOR K=Ø TO 3

60     FOR L=1 TO 3

70       READ R$(K,L)

80     NEXT L

90   NEXT K
```

with the DATA statements:

```
100   DATA I,V,X,X,L,C,C
```

110   DATA D,M,M,,,

Note that, as with INPUT, the double quotes are optional for strings in DATA statements, so:

50   DATA "FRED","JIM"

has the same effect as:

50   DATA FRED, JIM

Only if a comma is required in the string are the double quotes usually used. Thus:

50   DATA "FRED,JIM"

is regarded as the single string FRED,JIM.

<table>
<tr><td colspan="2" align="center">READ and DATA statements</td></tr>
<tr><td>General form</td><td>READ item 1, item 2, . . .</td></tr>
<tr><td colspan="2">The READ statement assigns the next available values in the DATA statement successively to the variables items 1 and 2 in the READ list.</td></tr>
<tr><td>General form</td><td>DATA item 1, item 2, . . .</td></tr>
<tr><td colspan="2">The DATA statement contains the constants, both numeric and string, as items separated by commas which are assigned to variables by the READ statement.</td></tr>
</table>

4.4.2 The RESTORE statement

At any point in a program it is possible to re-set the imaginary DATA pointer back to the beginning of the first DATA statement of the program by using a RESTORE statement. Its effect can be observed by modifying the example program given at the start of Section 4.4, by adding lines 12, 25, 28, and modifying line 30 to give:

```
10   REM   READ-DATA   DEMO
12   REM      AND RESTORE
20   READ A,B,C
25      RESTORE
28      READ D,E,F
```

```
30   PRINT A,B,C,D,E,F
40   REM
50   DATA 3,-2,45
60   END
RUN
```

3	-2	45	3
-2	45		

```
END AT LINE 60
```

The RESTORE statement allows the new READ statement on line 28 to re-read the DATA on line 50 from the beginning again.

The following program illustrates the use of READ, DATA, and RESTORE in a practical application; the program stores names and addresses and prints out an address corresponding to an input enquiry name. Notice the 'repeat until' symbol used in the structogram; a similar form was used in the program in Section 4.2.5. There are two possibilities to be covered, either the end of the list of names and addresses in the DATA statement is reached or the required match is found. In the latter case the variable F is set to one, and the loop terminates.

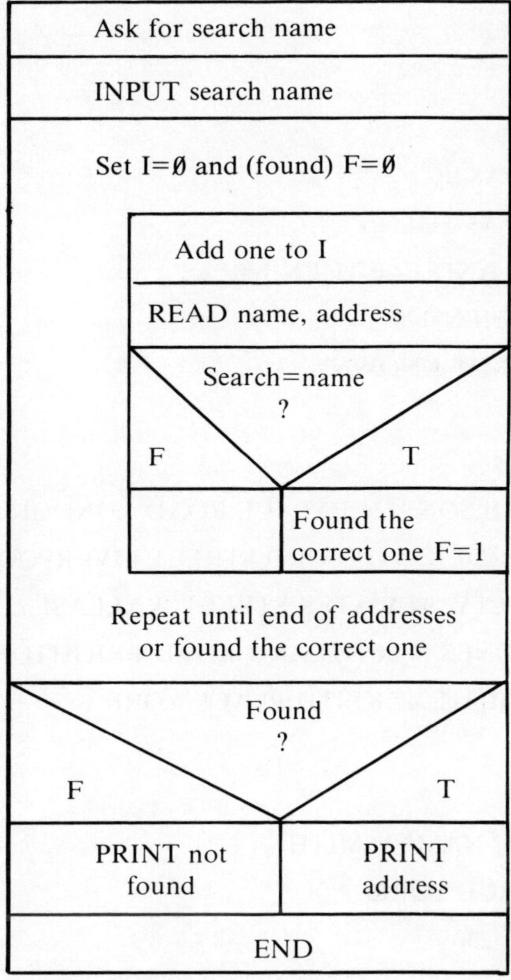

Notice that the DATA statements do not appear in the diagram which refers only to action statements. The program is:

```
10   REM ENQUIRY PROGRAM FOR NAMES & ADDRESSES
20   REM LIMITED NUMBER ONLY
30   REM   P IS SET TO CONTAIN THE NUMBER OF NAMES &
          ADDRESSES
40   REM
50   P=5
60   PRINT "GIVE SEARCH NAME";
70   INPUT N$
```

144

```
 80   I=0
 90   F=0
100      I=I+1
110      READ A$,B$
120      IF N$=A$ THEN F=1
130      IF I<P AND F=0 THEN 100
140   IF F=1 THEN 170
150   PRINT "NOT KNOWN"
160   STOP
170   PRINT B$
180   DATA WILSON, 126 PALACE ROAD LONDON
190   DATA ARDEN, 5 OXFORD STREET LIVERPOOL
200   DATA ALTY, 94 WATER STREET WALLASEY
210   DATA JONES, 2 SCOTLAND ROAD BRIGHTON
220   DATA SMITH, 42 KEITH PLACE YORK
230   END
RUN
GIVE SEARCH NAME? SMITH
42 KEITH PLACE YORK
END AT LINE 230
RUN
GIVE SEARCH NAME? WALTON
NOT KNOWN
END AT LINE 230
```

Each name and address was put in a separate DATA statement for clarity, but is not strictly necessary. The search method is the most elementary one possible since there is no ordering of the names and addresses. It does not matter with small amounts of data (less than 100 items) since the time taken to scan the complete list will be very short.

Re-running the program for each enquiry is tedious. It is better to design a loop as shown in the diagram below:

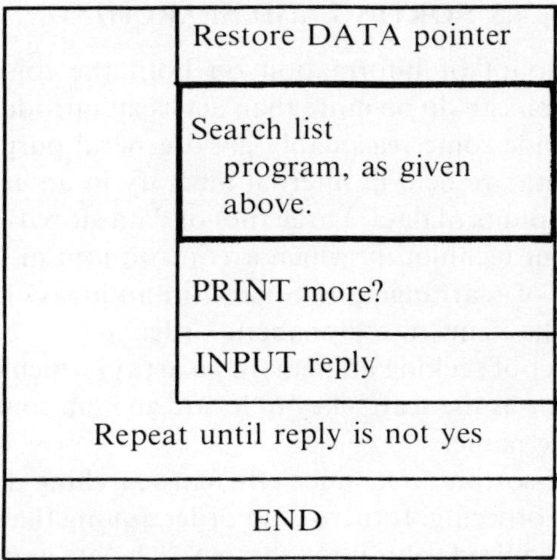

The program in the inner box is exactly the one listed above, with slight modifications to remove the STOP and END statements. The alterations are:

```
  5   RESTORE
160   GO TO 230
230   REM END OF SEARCH
240   PRINT "MORE";
250   INPUT A1$
260   IF A1$="YES" THEN 5
270   END
```

The action of RESTORE is to bring the imaginary data pointer to the beginning of the first DATA statement for the start of each search. The relationship between READ–DATA statements and the use of data files is very close. To convert to sequential data file use, very little change need be made to the program apart from a few instructions or commands to link the files and program together. In the ICL 2903/4 BASIC system, for example, certain sequential file statements with special options may be used as READ, DATA, and RESTORE, with the same effects.

Thus READ–DATA usage acts as an introduction to files. Some programming languages, for example PASCAL, regard files as another type of 'object' available to the program, with certain statements available for its manipulations. Files are described fully in Chapter 8, and these comments conclude the review of the 'objects' available to the programmer in BASIC.

4.5 SORTING AND SEARCHING

There is a vast amount of information on both the topics of sorting and searching. This section can do no more than act as an introduction, set out some guidelines, and provide some reasonably good general purpose examples. It is assumed that the data are held in internal memory in an array, which implies small or medium amounts of data. Large files of data stored on magnetic tape or discs require different techniques, which are introduced in Chapter 8.

Sorting is the act of rearranging the items (in an array) into some specified order; e.g. putting the items into alphabetic order.

Searching is the act of seeking an item (in an array) which matches the search key; e.g. using a name as the search key to locate an item containing the address corresponding to the name.

We shall consider sorting first, since efficient searching depends on the data having some type of ordering. If there is no order among the data items the only way of obtaining a required value is to examine each data item in turn, as demonstrated in the example in Section 4.4.1.

The general problem of sorting data in an array may be reduced to a choice of techniques, each of which takes a different amount of time and uses a different amount of temporary extra storage. For an array of a given size, there is a trade-off between time and extra storage—either a longer time and little storage or a shorter time and larger amount of storage.

4.5.1 The bubble sort

This is a simple technique; it uses no temporary storage, but is quite slow. However, it is easily understood and is the ideal general purpose technique, particularly when the computer store is limited and time is not so important.

The basis of this technique is to inspect pairs of adjacent data items and swap them if they are in the wrong order. To do this you need an extra variable to hold one of the results during the swapping. If A and B contain values which need swapping, then:

```
10   T=A

20   A=B

30   B=T
```

using the variable T (for temporary), does the swap. Similarly for string variables.

Consider sorting numeric values into descending order. Figure 4.2 shows the application of the technique to an array of size 4:

(a)   Move through the array from the first element to the last element·taking adjacent pairs of values. Swap the values if the left one is smaller than the right one.

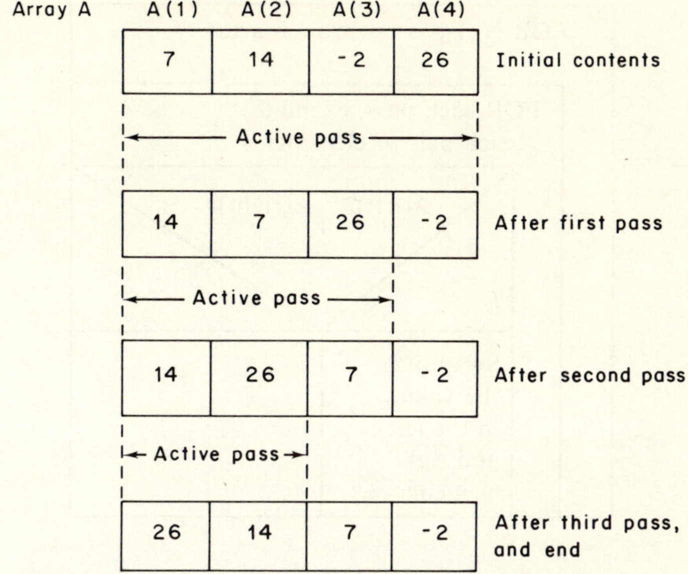

Figure 4.2 Stages in bubble sorting an array of four values

This guarantees that the smallest value ends up in the last element, although the other elements are not necessarily in order. Concentrate on the remaining values between the first and the element next to the last one.

(b)   Apply (a) to the shorter set of unsorted values between the first and the element next to the last.

As with the first pass, this guarantees that the smallest value in the set of elements ends up at the final position, next to last.

(c)   Look at the remaining values, and continue in like manner.

Thus, as the method proceeds, each pass becomes shorter and the values accumulate, in order, from the last element backwards. Each pass ensures that the smallest value ends up at the top of that portion of the array, i.e. it is 'bubbled' up to the correct position.

The structogram for the technique is given below, followed by the program fragment:

148

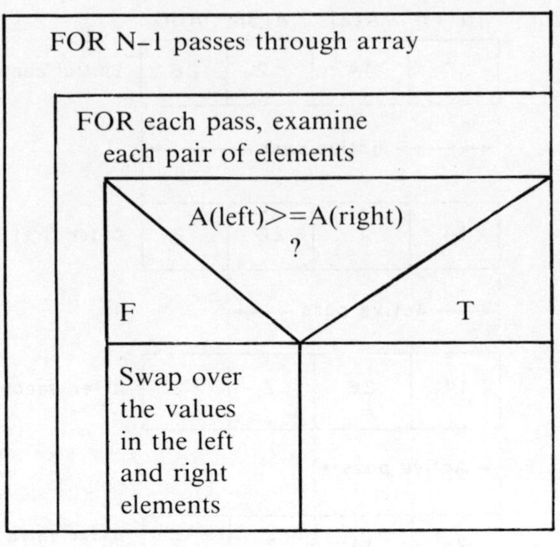


```
1000   REM BUBBLE SORT FRAGMENT
1010   REM ASSUMES ARRAY A(1). . . .A(N)
1020   REM HOLDS THE VALUES
1030   REM SORTS INTO DESCENDING ORDER
1040   FOR I=N TO 2 STEP –1
1050     FOR J=1 TO I–1
1060       IF A(J)>=A(J+1) THEN 1100
1070       T=A(J)
1080       A(J)=A(J+1)
1090       A(J+1)=T
1100     NEXT J
1110   NEXT I
1120   REM END OF SORT
```

To sort the data into ascending order simply change the condition on line 1060 to be <=. String data can be sorted in a string array A$ using a temporary variable T$.

Sometimes there are several variables associated with each logical data item, such as a name in A$ and an address in B$; for example:

```
10   DIM A$(95),B$(95)
```

The sort, on names in A\$, proceeds as described above, but with the addition of B\$ which just follows all the moves in A\$. Thus lines 1060 to 1090 become:

```
1060   IF A$(J)>=A$(J+1) THEN 1100

1065      T$=A$(J)

1070      A$(J)=A$(J+1)

1075      A$(J+1)=T$

1080      T$=B$(J)

1085      B$(J)=B$(J+1)

1090      B$(J+1)=T$
```

If only the first few characters of each name are required for sorting, then this selection and comparison could be achieved on line 1060. For example, taking three characters and the Microsoft string function

```
1060   IF LEFT$(A$(J),3)>=LEFT$(A$(J+1),3) THEN 1100
```

To estimate the speed of the algorithm, consider the action of comparing values. The first pass compares $(N-1)$ pairs, the second $(N-2)$ pairs, down to the last 1 pair of values. The total number of comparisons is:

$$1+2+3+\ldots+(N-2)+(N-1) = \frac{N-1}{2}[(N-1)+1]$$

$$= \frac{N}{2}(N-1) \simeq \frac{N^2}{2}$$

If some proportion, say a half, of these comparisons lead to swapping values, then the number of swaps is approximately $N^2/4$. Thus the time taken for a complete sort is proportional to N^2, where N is the number of data items sorted.

4.5.2 Other sorts

There is not sufficient space to describe other sorting methods in the detail given to the bubble sort above, but rather than omit them altogether they are given with a brief comment on their actions. For a full description of the methods see one of the many books available on computer algorithms; one that is very good is *Concise Survey of Computer Methods* by Peter Naur (Studentlitteratur, Lund, Sweden, 1974).

The Shell sort is faster than the bubble sort and goes as $N\log_2(N)$, where N is the number of data items to be sorted. It uses as a basis the technique of the bubble sort, but instead of comparing adjacent values of data it starts with widely

150

spaced pairs on the order of N/2 apart and sorts all these before reducing the spacing. In the last pass the distance is 1, so it is essentially a bubble sort pass. The method devised by D.A. Shell is based on the Algol 60 procedure by J. Boothroyd.

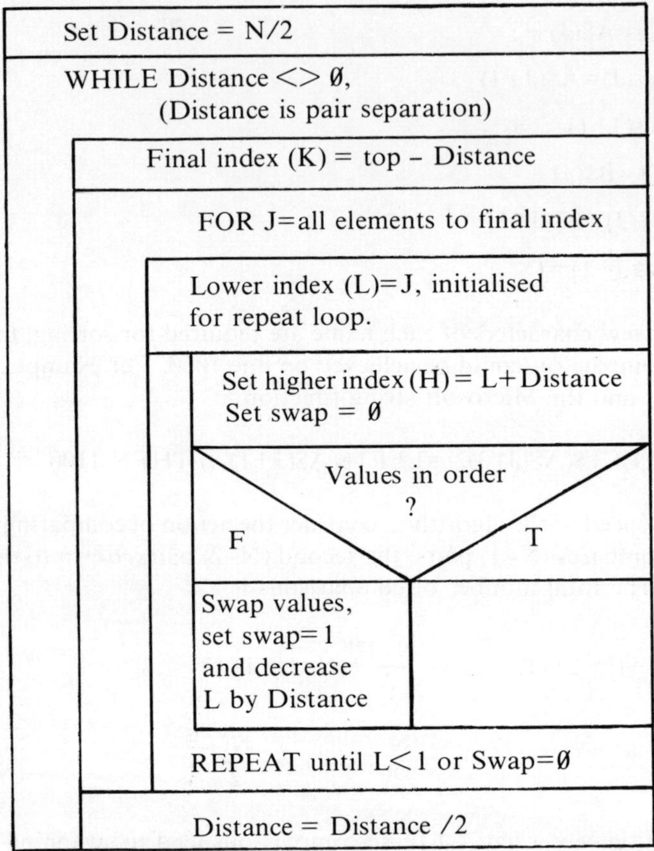

The program fragment is:

```
1000    REM   SHELL SORT
1010    REM   ASSUMES ARRAY A$(1)...A$(N)
1020    REM   HOLDS STRING VALUES
1030    REM   SORTS INTO ALPHABETICAL ORDER
1040    D=N/2
1050    REM
1060    IF D=0 THEN 1210
1070        K=N-D
1080        FOR J=1 TO K
```

```
1090        L=J
1100        H=L+D
1110        S=0
1120     IF A$(L)>=A$(H) THEN 1180
1130        T$=A$(L)
1140        A$(L)=A$(H)
1150        A$(H)=T$
1160        L=L-D
1170        S=1
1180      IF L=1 AND S=1 THEN 1100
1190     NEXT J
1195     D=INT(D/2)
1200   GOTO 1060
1210   REM EXIT WITH SORTED VALUES
```

If you wish to compare the bubble sort with the Shell sort choose some sets of data varying in length between 10 and 100 elements. You should find that the Shell sort is much faster with the larger number of elements. A trial on one computer with the programs above gave the Shell sort as five times faster than the bubble sort on 100 elements.

Of the many other sorting algorithms one of the best is Quicksort, devised by C.A.R. Hoare. Although it has a worst case performance proportional to N^2 (like the bubble sort) it has an average performance better than $N\log_2 N$ (like the Shell sort). However, it requires additional temporary storage space. A full analysis of the algorithm is given in *Fundamentals of Data Structures* by E. Horowitz and S. Sahi (Pitman Publishing Ltd, London, 1977) and a good implementation in BASIC is given in *Introduction to Computer Applications using BASIC* by R.M. Jones (Allyn and Bacon, U.S.A., 1981).

4.5.3 Sorting with an index

The swapping in any sort process may be quite time consuming on some computers if strings are involved, or there may be multiple arrays involved which are regarded as one logical item. Rather than rearrange all the values during the sorting process, one alternative is to build an index which gives the positions of the values in the array. During the sort the values remain where they are but the index is changed. At the end of the sort the index can be used to copy the original values into a new array in the proper order or retained to be used with the original array.

If we have an array A(1ØØ) for sorting, we choose an index I(ØØ), preferably an integer one if the facility is available as this saves store space, and set:

```
FOR L=Ø TO 1ØØ
   I(L)=L
NEXT L
```

The index is taken to mean:

I(original position)=new position

so at the start of the sort I(1)=1, I(2)=2, etc. During each sorting pass compare values in array A as determined with I( ), but switch values of the index in I( ). For example, the bubble sort in Section 4.5.1 becomes:

```
 9ØØ   REM INDEXED SORTING
 91Ø   FOR L=1 TO N
 92Ø      I(L)=L
 93Ø   NEXT L
1ØØØ   REM BUBBLE SORT FRAGMENT
1Ø1Ø   REM
1Ø2Ø   REM
1Ø3Ø   REM
1Ø4Ø   FOR I=N TO 2 STEP -1
1Ø5Ø      FOR J=1 TO I-1
1Ø52         I1=I(J)
1Ø54         I2=I(J+1)
1Ø6Ø         IF A(I1)>=A(I2) THEN 11ØØ
1Ø7Ø            I(J)=I2
1Ø8Ø            I(J+1)=I1
11ØØ      NEXT J
111Ø   NEXT I
112Ø   REM END OF INDEXED SORT
```

Printing:

```
FOR L=1 TO N

   PRINT A(L);

NEXT L
```

will produce the original, unchanged, set of values, but:

```
FOR L=1 TO N

   I1=I(L)

   PRINT A(I1);

NEXT L
```

will produce the required sorted set of values.

An index is of great advantage where the data values are spread over several arrays. Say in A(1Ø), B(9), C(27) then an index I(46) may be created, where the first 1Ø elements refer to A, the next 9 to B, and the final 27 refer to C. Of course, the algorithm needs to be modified to switch comparisons between A, B, and C.

Other sorts can, with care, be modified in the same way. In addition, separate techniques may be devised which take advantage of the index to speed up the sorting process.

4.5.4 Searching

Searching for a given value in an array is a very frequent operation. There is a *search key* which is to be matched against the *record key* of each of the data values to locate the *victim*. If the data are in unknown order there is no more efficient process than the simple search, described earlier, in which each data value record key is compared with the search key in some regular manner. The number of comparisons made is, on average, N/2 for an array of N values.

Only when some ordering has been arranged in the data is it possible to devise faster techniques to search it. For example, the fact that entries in a telephone directory are in alphabetic order enables us to locate a name and telephone number very quickly.

The binary search is a general purpose, fast technique for searching an ordered data set. For an array of N values, the average number of comparisons made is proportional to $\log_2 N$. Compare this to the simple search which is proportional to N.

N	$\log_2 N$
1Ø	3.3
1ØØ	6.6
1ØØØ	9.9

Obviously the extra effort required to order a data set more than pays for itself using this method of searching.

The technique works by successively dividing the data into two equal parts—hence the name binary search. Initially the whole file is considered as active, and the centre record key is obtained and compared with the search key. There is a chance that they will be equal, in which case the search is successful, but if not, then the search key will be greater or less than the record key. Depending on the ordering of the file the first or second half will be selected as the new active part of the data, and the centre record key of that active part is obtained and compared to the search key. The process is repeated until success or failure. This successive division of the file works surprisingly well. Figure 4.3 shows a string array ordered alphabetically by the first few characters in each string (the record key) in the process of the first cycle.

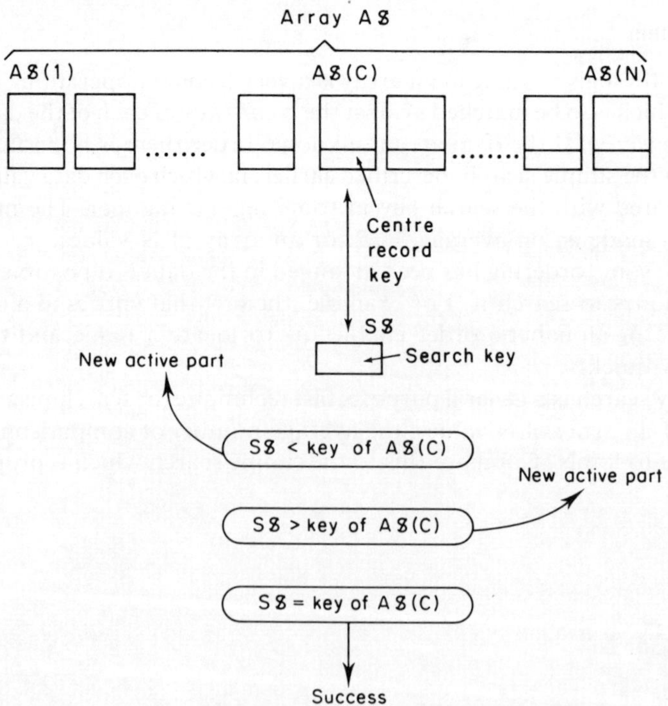

Figure 4.3 Array A$ is ordered alphabetically. First cycle in binary search with search key S$

The form of the algorithm below follows a form suggested by P. Naur which starts the lower and upper subscript limits of the data array at virtual values −1 and N+1, where the array runs from Ø to N. In this algorithm the first M characters of each string are taken as the record key and the strings are arranged in alphabetic order on these keys. The strings could be names followed by addresses or other information, and thus the search could be part of an enquiry system. The structogram is:

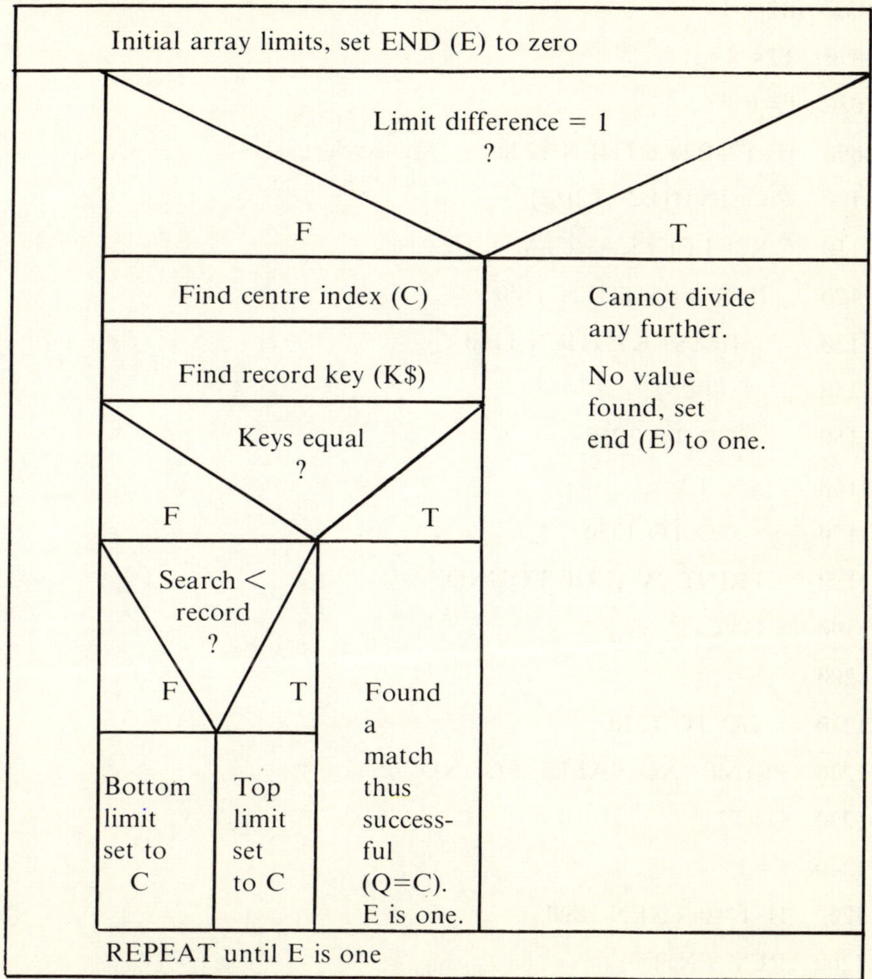

The program fragment is entered with an array A$(Ø)…A$(N), the value for N, the value for M which is the record key length, and a search key in S$. It returns the index of the required array item in Q, which is set to N+1 if no value is found.

```
1ØØØ  REM BINARY SEARCH
```

156

```
1010    REM ASSUMES ARRAY A$(0)...A$(N)
1020    REM CONTAINS VALUES SORTED ALPHABETICALLY
1030    REM ON RECORD KEY IN FIRST M CHRS.
1040    REM RETURNS SUBSCRIPT IN Q OF
1050    REM FOUND VALUE, ELSE N+1
1060    B2=-1
1070    T2=N+1
1080    E=0
1090    IF T2-B2=1 THEN 1220
1100      C=INT((B2+T2)/2)
1110      K$=LEFT$(A$(C),M)
1120      IF S$=K$ THEN 1180
1130        IF S$<K$ THEN 1160
1140          B2=C
1150        GO TO 1250
1160          T2=C
1170        GO TO 1250
1180      PRINT "VALUE FOUND"
1190      Q=C
1200      E=1
1210      GO TO 1250
1220    PRINT "NO VALUE FOUND"
1230    Q=T2
1240    E=1
1250    IF E=0 THEN 1090
1260    REM EXIT
```

The variable E is introduced to cover the various conditions needed for exit from the repeat loop. Arbitrary jumps out of this loop cannot be represented by the structogram symbols so their use encourages good programming style.

The fragment may be tested with the following:

```
10    REM TEST BINARY SEARCH
```

```
20    DIM   A$(20)

30    N=15

40    M=1

50    INPUT "GIVE A SEARCH KEY";S$

60    FOR I=0 TO N

70       READ A$(I)

80    NEXT I

90    DATA   ABBA,BRIAN,COLIN,FRED

100   DATA   GERRY,HUGH,JIM,LEN

110   DATA   MIKE,NICK,OLIVER,PETER

120   DATA   RUPERT,STAN,TIM,WILLIAM
```

and:

```
1300     PRINT Q,A$(Q)

1310   END
```

Running this program to find all the names in the list and recording the number of comparisons gave an average of 3.4 comparisons per successful search ($\log_2 16$ is 4); this ranged between a worst case of 5 comparisons and a best case of 1 comparison.

Exercises

4.1   Write a program to read ten numbers from a DATA statement and print out the largest and smallest numbers.

4.2   Write a program to record and display examination marks for a class. The names of the pupils are stored in a number of DATA statements in the program. In use, the program prompts with the name for each mark to be input at the terminal. After the average mark is displayed, a list of names and corresponding marks is output. (Try using an array to store the marks.)

4.3   Write a program which acts as a register of attendance for a class of pupils. The data are presented as a list of ones and zeros: one for present and zero for absent. For eight pupils the register for one day may look like:

1, 1, Ø, 1, 1, 1, Ø, Ø

which could be put into a DATA statement, or input at the terminal.

Design the program to read a week's attendance data (5 days) and print out the total number present each day and the number of days each pupil is present. (Arrays will be needed.)

4.4 Develop a program for the following string handling:

(a) Set two string variables to your surname and christian name, add them, and print out the result.

(b) Use string functions to pick out and print your initials.

(c) Set a string variable to your title (MR, MS, etc.) and another to your address, and print out your name and address in the usual format.

4.5 A group of six workmen are engaged on a building site. Each week two of them are responsible for brewing the tea. Design and write a program to print pairs of names for the job over a complete rota of 15 weeks, during which each man will have done the job for 5 weeks. Try using a DATA statement and string array for the names.

Your program may produce a rota which is fair for all the men, but leaves some of them doing a number of consecutive weeks making the tea. So the extra restriction is added that no man may be on the rota for more than two consecutive weeks. Develop a second program which incorporates this restriction.

4.6 Design and write a program to analyse the word lengths in a sentence. The program must accept a range of sentences containing all the usual punctuation. It should calculate the maximum, minimum, and average number of characters per word in the sentence and print the results.

4.7 Design and write a program to analyse text. It accepts a block of text as sentences and calculates the frequency of occurrence of the different words which are present. Thus, as it processes the text, if a new word is encountered it is stored in a table with the frequency value of one; if it is not new then it is located in the table and its frequency value is increased by one.

Sort the results and display the words with their frequency counts in alphabetic order.

4.8 Write a program to help you recall information, which may be stored in DATA statements. The data have the form 'keyword' followed by other information. Given an input word the program should locate and print out the information required.

For example, use part of the index of this book, where the topic is the keyword and the other information is the page number. Given a specific topic as input the program should respond with the page number.

Any other information, such as parliamentary constituencies as keyword with the current member of parliament and the vote as the information, may be used. (Ideally the information should be in a file, see Chapter 8.)

5
Modular programming

The preceding chapters have introduced programming and most of the features provided by the BASIC programming language required to design and produce simple programs. Chapter 3 introduced structograms, which are excellent as a way of appreciating the effects of combining small groups of BASIC statements. Structograms may also be a useful design aid when combined with the stepwise refinement technique introduced in Section 3.6.

One problem which has not yet been discussed is the task of designing a complete program to solve a quite complex task. Just trying to develop the program directly at a VDU becomes more or less impossible once the number of program lines exceeds the display capacity of the screen (2Ø to 4Ø lines), as we tend to forget what has been written and lose control of the complexities as they develop.

The method of stepwise refinement tries to dissect the problem into small and relatively independent parts which can be developed separately. Do these parts, or modules, have a parallel in other programming languages? Yes they do—as *functions* and *subroutines* which can be defined by the programmer. Unfortunately BASIC does not quite implement all the features needed to fit in with the requirements of full modularity, although it does allow reasonable modular programming. Some extensions to BASIC do go some way to rectifying the shortcomings mentioned here, and these are described together with the standard function and subroutine features in the following sections.

5.1 USER DEFINED FUNCTIONS

The major facility required for good design is the ability to group program statements together in a block. Such a block of statements may be independent of the main program and perform one specific task. For example, the built-in SQR function provides the square root of a number. Thus:

```
2Ø   Y=5
3Ø   Z=SQR (Y*Y+2*Y)
```

or

```
1Ø   PRINT SQR (981+Z)
```

Earlier chapters discussed the range of standard functions, both string and numeric, which automatically calculate frequently used features such as the square root. Without this facility you would have to devise a set of instructions to calculate the square root and include them with the program when required.

When analysing the parts involved in a problem it is not unusual to find some actions occurring several times. Functions and subroutines allow you to write out the program instructions for these actions only once, but use them in several places in the program.

Both functions and subroutines provide modules which perform one or more separate actions for the program as a whole. The function returns a *single value*, numeric or string, which is assigned to the function name. The subroutine does not return a value, but may change *any* or *all* of the variables available throughout the program. It does not have a name.

5.1.1 DEF FN statement

If a repeated calculation can be expressed as a single BASIC statement, giving a single value for the result such as the square root, then you should define a function to express it.

Standard BASIC allows only one-line functions which are usually located at the beginning of a program since they must be defined before they can be used, except for the BBC system where functions and procedures must not be defined in the body of a program and are best placed after the program END statement.

Consider the problem of calculating the nett pay of a person with a tax allowance of £1200 and a basic tax rate of 35 pence in the pound:

```
10   REM SIMPLE TAX PROBLEM
20   REM   G=GROSS INCOME
30   REM   N=NETT INCOME AFTER TAX DEDUCTIONS
40   DEF FNT (A)=A−(A−1200)*35/100
50   REM
60   INPUT "GIVE GROSS INCOME";G
70   IF G<=1200 THEN 100
80      PRINT "GROSS PAY=";G;"NETT PAY=";FNT(G)
90   STOP
100     PRINT "NO DEDUCTIONS, PAY=";G
110  END
RUN
GIVE GROSS INCOME? 4500
GROSS PAY=4500 NETT PAY=3345
END AT LINE 90
```

162

Whenever the function FNT(G) is referred to in line 8Ø then the expression in the DEF FNT statement in line 4Ø is used with the current value of G. The value of G is not changed as a result of the function evaluation.

The variable A which appears on line 4Ø in the above program in the definition of the function FNT between the brackets following the name is called a *formal parameter*. When the function is used on line 8Ø the variable G acts as an *actual parameter* which provides the input value to the function.

DEF FN statement

General form   DEF FNx = expression

or

DEF FN$x(y)$ = expression

where

> x is the function name, usually limited to a single letter.
> y is a single variable called a parameter, or a parameter list of variables separated by commas. The parameters are local to the function definition (explanation below).
>
> 'expression' may be a constant or any combination of variables from the parameter list and any others in the program.

The function can be defined for string or numeric use and the appropriate type indications ($,%,#) included after the function and variable names.

Notes

Some systems such as Sinclair ZX81 do not support user defined functions; others restrict functions to numeric values only.

Many systems which allow long variable names such as Microsoft and BBC also allow long names for functions.

The complete function definition must appear on one line, for block functions see Section 5.1.2.

Examples of one-line functions:

DEF FNP   = 3.14159

DEF FNA(S)   = S*S+4

DEF FNP(Q)   = 3*B+Z*Q

DEF FNZ(Q)   = SQR(13.7*Q+A)

DEF FNA(A,B,C)   = (A+B+C)/3

In the definition any variable name which appears in the parameter list is local to the function. This means it is distinct from a variable of the same name which appears elsewhere in the program. It carries the value passed to it at the time of the function call. Other variables appearing in the 'expression' are those generally available in the program and their current values at the time of the function call will be used. The following example demonstrates these features:

```
10   REM FN EXAMPLE
20   A=2
30   B=30
40   C=-21
50   REM
60   DEF FNX(A)=A*B+C
70   REM
80   PRINT "A=";A;"B=";B;"C=";C
90   PRINT "VALUE IS 6*B+C=";FNX(6)
100  PRINT "A=";A;"B=;B;"C=";C
110  END
```

The execution of line 60 causes no effect apart from recording the definition of the function, which is used in line 90 with the value 6. The variable A on line 60 is a local (dummy) variable and should be different from the A used externally, which should be printed out with the same values before and after the function call.

The expression in function definitions may include other functions, provided that other user functions used have already been defined; i.e. appeared earlier in the program or are built-in functions. Thus:

```
20   DEF FNR(X)=INT(X*RND(1)+1)
```

will give a random integer between 1 and X, so that the loop:

```
30   FOR I=1 TO 10
40     PRINT FNR (6);
50   NEXT I
```

will print out ten random values between 1 and 6.

This single-line function does not allow very much in the way of modularity as required by structured programming, but is of some help, particularly in replacing multiple uses of the same long expression.

164

5.1.2 Block functions

The ability to use a series of statements as a function is much closer to the generally accepted notion of a function than the single-line type allowed in most BASICs. Most other computer languages allow groups of statements to form the function body, but only a few extended BASICs have this 'advanced' feature.

Within function blocks, additional local variables may be declared which act in the same way as the parameter variables in that they are entirely separate from external variables with the same names.

The ICL 2903/4 BASIC system allows all types of statements to appear in a function block which is terminated by the new statement FNEND. Local variables appear declared after the closing brackets of the parameter list on the DEF FNx line. The following example illustrates a block function to calculate $N! \equiv N$ factorial, where:

$$N! \equiv N*(N–1)*(N–2)*.....*3*2*1$$

so:

$$3! = 3*2*1 \qquad 5! = 5*4*3*2*1$$

```
10   REM BLOCK FN EXAMPLE
20   DEF   FNF(N) T,I
30   T=1
40   FOR I=1 TO N
50       T=T*I
60   NEXT I
70   FNF=T
80   FNEND
90   REM
100   PRINT "3!=";FNF(3)
110   PRINT "2!=";FNF(2)
120   PRINT "5!=";FNF(5)
130   END
RUN
3!=6
2!=2
5!=120
END AT LINE 130
```

The function block extends from line 2Ø to line 8Ø and T and I are additional local variables.

It is possible in ICL BASIC to define a recursive function. Recursion means that the function calls itself. It is a useful but often overemphasized feature of a computer language. Great skill is needed in the construction of recursive functions, which in practice may turn out to be obscure and inefficient during execution of the program. The above factorial program could be written recursively as:

```
1Ø   REM RECURSIVE FN EXAMPLE
2Ø   DEF FNF (N)
3Ø   IF N=1 THEN 6Ø
4Ø     FNF=N*FNF (N-1)
5Ø     GOTO 7Ø
6Ø   FNF=1
7Ø   FNEND
```

The local variable N in this example forms a stack of values. Each time the function is called from within itself a new value is added to the top of the stack. A call of FNF (3) calls FNF with the first stack value of N set to 3. This becomes a call to FNF (2) on line 4Ø with 3 stored on the stack. FN (2) calls the function with N set to 2, and line 4Ø within this call causes 2 to be placed on the N stack and calls FNF (1). When FNF (1) is called the function returns the value FNF=1 only. All the calls can now be satisfied and at each the top value of N is removed from the stack and multiplies the FNF value. The return sequence is:

$$FNF=1 \quad \text{which gives } FNF(1)=1$$
$$\text{then } 2*FNF(1)=2*1 \text{ which gives } FNF(2)=2$$
$$\text{then } 3*FNF(2)=3*2 \text{ which gives } FNF(3)=6$$

The final result is the correct value of 3!

The BBC BASIC allows functions to be defined over one line or several lines, and include local variables by a LOCAL statement. It is terminated by an assignment (=) giving the function value, which may appear without a left-hand side in a block function extending over several statements. For the BBC system, one-line functions have the usual form as shown in the following two examples:

```
2Ø   DEF FNF(X)=X*X+3*X-2Ø
1Ø   DEF FNS(X)=SQRT(X+B-C)
```

The assignment (=) which gives a BBC function its value may appear once or several times in a function which extends over several statements. For example, the following function returns the result as the larger of the two input values:

```
100   DEF FNZ(Q,R)
110   IF Q>R THEN =Q ELSE =R
```

Thus the statement:

```
10   PRINT FNZ(2,3)
```

will produce the result 3. Repeating the factorial example:

```
10   REM BBC FN EXAMPLE
20   DEF FNFACT (N)
30   LOCAL T,I
40   T=1
50   FOR I=1 TO N
60     T=T*I
70   NEXT I
80   =T
```

Line 80 gives the termination indication and value to the function FNFACT( ).

BBC functions may be recursive, so that the recursive example above may be used with the = termination indication, and perhaps a fuller name. Using the BBC extended IF statement it is possible to write:

```
10   REM BBC RECURSIVE EXAMPLE
20   DEF FNFACTORIAL (N)
30   IF N=1 THEN =1 ELSE =N*FNFACTORIAL (N-1)
40   REM
```

where the function extends over lines 20 and 30 only. Note that in BBC BASIC, functions and procedures must not be defined in the main part of a BASIC program.

Side-effects in all function usage should be avoided. Functions should produce one result, which is delivered via the function name. All other changes are called side-effects; these include changing the values of generally available variables or producing some changes in other features such as file positions or input/output. If such effects are required a subroutine should be used.

5.2 SUBROUTINES

Whereas functions deliver only one value, via the function name, subroutines can deliver any number of values. They do this by being able to use and modify any of the variables and arrays available throughout the program. They are not allowed to have any local variables, and do not have parameter lists of dummy variables like functions.

There is considerable danger of accidental and unwanted changes to variables in this approach. Many other computer languages place a strict restriction on the use of general variables by subroutines and make local variables used inside subroutines quite independent of those used in other parts of the program. BASIC unfortunately does not do this, which causes BASIC to be considered, by some, as unsuitable as a good general programming language. Some extended BASICs overcome these criticisms by providing a procedure block which works in the correct way (see Chapter 6 for details).

Provided reasonable care is used, the subroutine feature can be used extensively with the refinement design method. However, it is the job of the programming language to take as much of the routine work away from the programmer as possible, so if BASIC had provided a sensible subroutine feature as standard this extra care would not be necessary.

5.2.1 GOSUB and RETURN statements

A subroutine is a collection of program statements which can be called using the GOSUB statement from any line of the program. When the statements have been executed and a RETURN statement is reached, execution control is automatically transferred back to the statement on the line immediately following the GOSUB. In Figure 5.1, lines 500 to 600 represent a subroutine which is first called from line 100 and returns control to line 110 after execution, and is then called from line 200 and returns control to line 210 after execution. Notice the STOP statement at the end of the main program. If absent, control would continue to line 500 and execution proceed to line 600 where an error would occur, with some error message such as RETURN STATEMENT FOUND WITHOUT A GOSUB.

The two statements involved with subroutines, GOSUB and RETURN, occur at different places in the program. There is no statement which indicates the start of a subroutine and you should *always* use a REM statement to indicate the start. The GOSUB followed by a statement number causes a jump to the subroutine which begins at the statement number specified. The RETURN, which is the last statement in a subroutine, causes a jump back to the statement immediately following the GOSUB call to the subroutine.

Actually the effect of a subroutine is the same as replacing each GOSUB by the complete set of statements from the subroutine. Consider the following few statements:

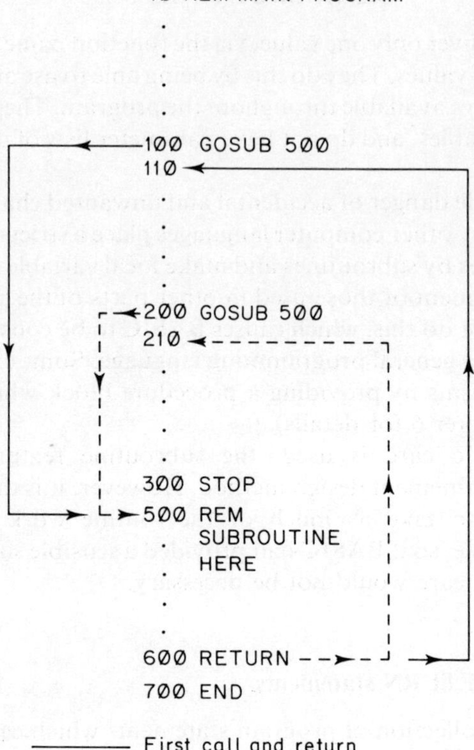

Figure 5.1 Execution paths for two calls to a subroutine

```
210   FOR L=1 TO N
220      PRINT "–";
230   NEXT L
240   PRINT
```

They produce a line made up of N minus (–) characters, and are used as a sub-routine in the following program:

```
10   REM MAIN PROGRAM
20   PRINT "THIS IS A LONG HEADING"
30   N=22
40   GOSUB 200
50   PRINT "AGAIN"
60   N=5
```

```
70    GOSUB 200
80    FOR I=1 TO 5
90       N=I
100      GOSUB 200
110   NEXT I
120   STOP
200   REM SUB FOR UNDERLINING WITH N CHRS.
210   FOR L=1 TO N
220      PRINT "-";
230   NEXT L
240   PRINT
250   RETURN
260   END
RUN
THIS IS A LONG HEADING
----------------------
AGAIN
------
-
- -
- - -
- - - -
- - - - -
END AT LINE 120
```

Statements 200 to 250 draw a line N characters long and are used in the example to underline the text printed from lines 20 and 50. Note the value of N is set before the GOSUB and is available (as are all variables) inside the subroutine. A triangular shape is formed by calling the subroutine from within the FOR loop on line 80. As L is used and altered in the subroutine it must not be used as the loop variable in the line 80 FOR statement.

The following subroutine may be useful. It can print out N repetitions of the character whose ASCII value is M:

```
200   REM PRINT SUBROUTINE
210   REM N REPETITIONS OF
220   REM ASCII CHARACTER M.
```

170

```
230     FOR L=1 TO N
240         PRINT CHR$(M);
250   NEXT L
260   PRINT
270   RETURN
```

<table>
<tr><td colspan="2" align="center">GOSUB and RETURN statements</td></tr>
<tr><td>General form</td><td align="right">GOSUB s</td></tr>
<tr><td colspan="2" align="center">s is a statement number</td></tr>
<tr><td>General form</td><td align="right">RETURN</td></tr>
<tr><td colspan="2">Control is transferred to the subroutine beginning at statement number s. Statements are then obeyed in order until a RETURN statement is reached. Then control is transferred to the line following the GOSUB call.</td></tr>
</table>

Some BASICs provide a multiple branch statement identical to the ON–GOTO statement discussed in Section 4.3.1 with the GOTO replaced by GOSUB. Any RETURN transfers back to the statement on the line following the ON–GOSUB.

Points to check when using BASIC subroutines:

(a)   Clearly identify the beginning and end of each subroutine. Distinguish it by indentation of the statements, if possible.

(b)   *Never* jump into, or out of, a subroutine using a GOTO statement. Each subroutine should be considered as an independent module and a complete whole.

(c)   Keep a written list of the global input variables and the output results for each subroutine. This is best kept as REM statements in the program.

(d)   Remember to check that variables used in the subroutine do not change any values in use externally, such as loop counters. If possible it is a good idea to use a different naming convention for these variables in each subroutine.

(e)   Unlike functions, subroutines do not appear in the program prior to use, so it is a good idea to group the subroutines together after the STOP statement at the end of the main program.

5.3 PROGRAM DESIGN

Although there are very many different design techniques available, none of them can cover the wide range of problems encountered in computing. However, it seems that two quite general methods are emerging which are complementary.

One is the stepwise refinement method introduced earlier and the other depends on data matching.

Data matching is a technique developed by M. Jackson and others and is very useful in data processing applications where large files of data are being compared and updated; e.g. invoicing systems, payroll systems, customer accounts, and product data storage systems. These systems are characterized by doing a small amount of processing (simple arithmetic and logical operations) on a large amount of data. The data dominates the problem and the design technique takes account of the structure of the data to give the structure of the program. Unfortunately, recognizing the data structures and using them to produce program structures requires more space to describe than is available here. Interested programmers should consult *Principles of Program Design* by M. A. Jackson (Academic Press, 1975), which is an excellent book on the subject.

5.3.1 Stepwise refinement

This technique is available in a number of slightly different forms and is known by various names such as top-down refinement, successive refinement, methodical programming, or even structured programming, although this applies to the whole process of design and program production.

Stepwise refinement can deal with a vast number of problems and turn them into computer programs, but since its basis is the development of processes to be applied to data, it tends to be most successful where the processes dominate and the input/output data are relatively simply organized. A parallel to writing down the stepwise refinement stages is to draw structograms, and while these are excellent at depicting processes they do not show any input/output data structures. Where the data structures dominate the problem investigate the data matching technique mentioned above.

The essential stages in the stepwise refinement method are as follows:

(a)   Level 1, start with a very general view of the whole program. Decide on the logical steps needed in the solution, even if you do not know how to solve them yet. The logical steps may reflect the different physical steps in the solution or may be convenient group names for things to be done which are still rather vague. Write down in English, or pseudo code (see Section 5.3.3), the series of steps required to solve the problem.

(b)   Level 2, proceed to take each of the steps detailed in (a) above and expand its description in general terms. For example, it may involve indicating a loop structure but leaving the operations within the loop still vague. Thus with complex operations only general outlines will be produced.

(c)   Level 3 and onwards, proceed as in (b) above in a series of cycles. In each cycle expand out the details left vague in the previous stages, and probably generate more undefined details. However, as the cycles proceed the undefined details become simpler and simpler so that at some stage they can be completely filled in.

172

(d) The design is complete. A written description, in modular form, of the required program has been produced. It should be a straightforward task to produce the BASIC program from this design.

(e) When a refinement module introduces details and variables which are irrelevant to the rest of the program or there is duplication of modules, then such a module is a very strong candidate for a subroutine or function. When this is the case the refinement statement becomes the subroutine or function call, and the module forms the body of the subroutine or function.

To produce a design capable of translation into a satisfactory program it is best to use certain programming structures only. These are discussed in detail in Section 5.3.2, while the rest of this section contains a simple example demonstrating the process given above.

A program is required which will receive as input a value for N which is the number of pupils in a class, together with the heights, ages, and weights of the pupils. It should produce average values of the three quantities. Apply (a) to the general problem.

Level 1

    Input number of pupils.
    Calculate average height.
    Calculate average age.
    Calculate average weight.

Now apply (b) to the steps above.

Refinement 1.1. Calculate average height.
    Input the values of height.
    Calculate the average in a loop.
    Print out results.

Refinements 1.2 and *1.3* are identical but apply to age and weight in place of height. The result is:

Level 2

    Number of pupils, INPUT N.
    (1.1) for height
    (1.2) for age
    (1.3) for weight

where each of the refinements is indicated. Continue the process and, since each of the refinements is essentially the same, consider only refinement 1.1. Expand the three actions in that description.

Refinement 2.1. Input the values of height.
PRINT a request for the values.
INPUT the values into an array using a loop or the MAT INPUT feature.

Refinement 2.2. Calculate the average in a loop.
Loop through the N values, accumulating the sum in S.
Divide S by N to obtain the average.

Refinement 2.3. Print out results.
PRINT the name of the feature (e.g. age) and the average value.

The same expansion applies to all three main parts of level 2, so it seems reasonable to introduce the above as general purpose subroutines with the name of the quantity—height, age, weight—carried in a string variable. Thus level 3 becomes:

Level 3

```
INPUT "No. of PUPILS";N
Set variable to "HEIGHT".
Call refinements (2.1), (2.2), and (2.3).
Set variable to "AGE".
Call refinements (2.1), (2.2), and (2.3).
Set variable to "WEIGHT".
Call refinements (2.1), (2.2), and (2.3).
END
```

With a little care the structure has emerged in true modular manner. Implicit in the above is the decision to input all the values into the same array, call it A( ), and carry the feature name in a string variable, call it A$. With these assumptions the refinements can be coded as subroutines:

```
(2.1)  500   REM INPUT VALUES SUB
       510   PRINT "INPUT";N;"VALUES OF";A$
       520   FOR I=1 TO N
       530      INPUT A(I),
       540   NEXT I
       550   RETURN
(2.2)  400   REM AVERAGE SUB
       410   S=0
       420   FOR I=1 TO N
       430      S=S+A(I)
```

```
        440   NEXT I
        450   S=S/N
        460   RETURN
(2.3)   700   REM PRINT OUT SUB
        710   PRINT "THE AVERAGE VALUE FOR ";A$;"IS";S
        720   RETURN
```

Since it is clear that the three actions are always involved in a sequence it would save repeating the calls by putting this into a subroutine also. Thus this is just a process subroutine:

```
        200   REM PROCESS SUB
        210   GOSUB 500
        220   GOSUB 400
        230   GOSUB 700
        240   RETURN
```

Note that this is essentially refinement 1.1. The main program is from level 3, and is written out as:

```
        10    REM MAIN PROGRAM
        20    DIM A(100)
        30    INPUT "NO. OF PUPILS";N
        40    A$="HEIGHT"
        50    GOSUB 200
        60    A$="AGE"
        70    GOSUB 200
        80    A$="WEIGHT"
        90    GOSUB 200
        100   STOP
```

A final statement 750 END, after the subroutines, may be needed. At each stage in the process of refinement the actions were expressed in a module, most of which eventually became subroutines. This was easy to do for this simple example, but the module could easily have remained as a group of statements within a subroutine or the main program.

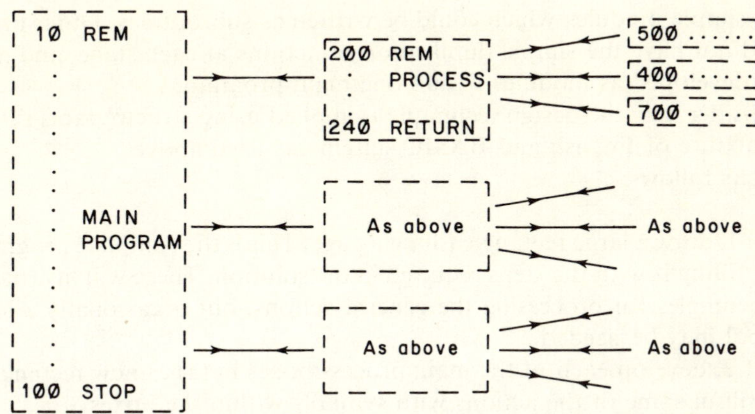

Figure 5.2 Module call and return structure for the example program of Section 5.3.1

Figure 5.2 shows the resulting structure of the program. Each GOSUB is indicated by a horizontal arrowed line going to the appropriate subroutine. The list of instructions for each box is omitted for clarity.

Turn the figure on its side to have the main program box at the top, and you will see that the main feature of the design method is to grow the structure downwards. The early ideas form the basis of the top modules while the lower ones perform simple specific actions. You can plan the structure of the program to some extent before you know exactly how the bottom modules will work. However, you do need to make some decisions as you proceed, which affect the structure of the bottom modules, and you need to know if it is possible to do these things in BASIC on your computer. For example, it is no use assuming that these modules can use MAT (matrix) functions if they are not provided. Thus the TOP-DOWN refinement method does need a sensible look-ahead to see what is feasible.

Each module has the form:

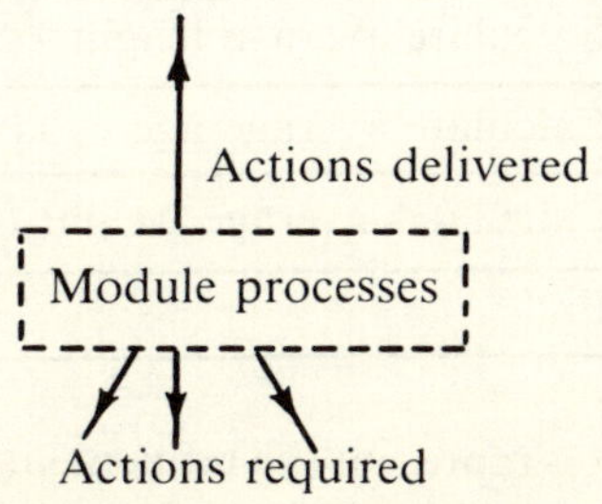

so the problem of designing a program becomes one of setting out the module specification. Once specified each module can, in theory at least, be written and debugged independently. This is not quite true in BASIC because of the global use of variables and the dangers of accidentally altering important values within subroutines.

It needs to be stressed that the above program example was chosen to break down into simple modules which could be written as subroutines. Other problems would not have the simple duplication of actions at each stage, and may have been developed as modules within one main program.

Now consider how the design technique is applied using structograms rather than the mixture of English and BASIC statements used above.

Proceed as follows:

(a)   Level 1, draw a large rectangle filling a page. This is the complete program. Start filling it with the steps required in the solution. These will invariably be rectangles for processing the general actions, but occasionally a loop symbol may be needed.

(b)   Level 2, develop each of the main process boxes in (a) as new rectangles, and fill in some of the actions with symbols within the boxes.

(c)   Level 3 and onwards, continue the elaboration of any rectangular process boxes until a final level of detail is attained. As the detail develops the nested iteration and decision symbols will get smaller and smaller, but remember that any rectangular symbol can be removed from the whole diagram and developed as a separate module, i.e. subroutine or function.

(d)   Examination of the complete design, whether all in a one-page box or over several boxes, will give a complete scheme for writing the BASIC program instructions. Replace suitable rectangular blocks by subroutines or functions using the criteria discussed in stage (e) of the earlier design specification.

Structograms are designed to keep you to the correct programming structures, whereas it is perhaps easier to stray away from proper structured programming with the purely verbal techniques. The first stage becomes:

Input number of pupils
Calculate average height   (1.1)
Calculate average age   (1.2)
Calculates average weight (1.3)
End

The numbers in the boxes represent the refinements. Taking a general 'calculate average' process and expanding it gives:

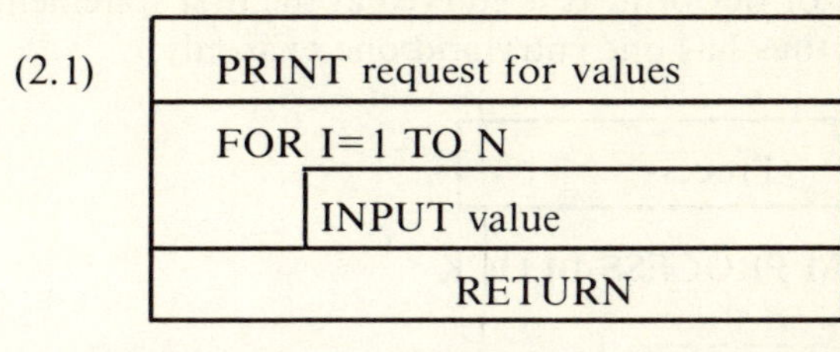

Certainly more detail could have been added at this stage if desired—even the iteration symbols for (2.1) and (2.2). These individual process expand to give:

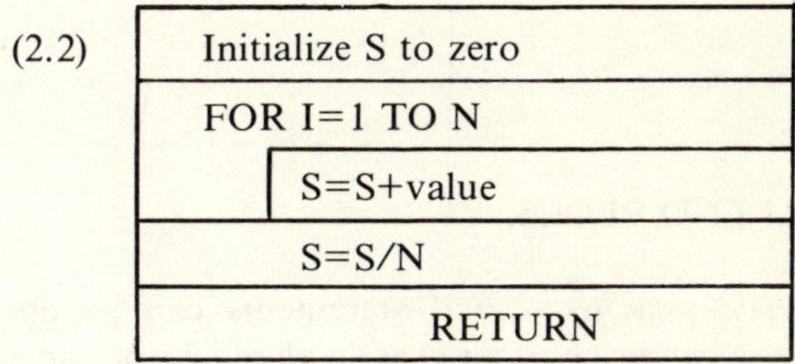

Most of this detail could have been sketched into the large initial chart, leaving the choice of subroutine boundaries to later in the development. Remember that any rectangular symbol is a possible candidate for a subroutine or function.

5.3.2 Detailed structures

Rather than use a mess of BASIC statements to construct a program, the aim of proper design is to achieve:

Correctness
Clarity
Simplicity

which can be achieved very easily by restricting the groups of BASIC statements used to these types. Development via structograms automatically produces these types only. Since BASIC is rather lacking in the appropriate programming statements you have to use a certain amount of care to build them up from more primitive statements, such as GOTO.

Here are the three types together with structograms, lines of standard (minimal) BASIC, and extended BASIC illustrating each one.

A *sequence*, or *concatenation*, of statements is a block of statements with no jumps into it or out of it. It is entered at the first statement and left at the last statement; it thus has one entry and one exit only:

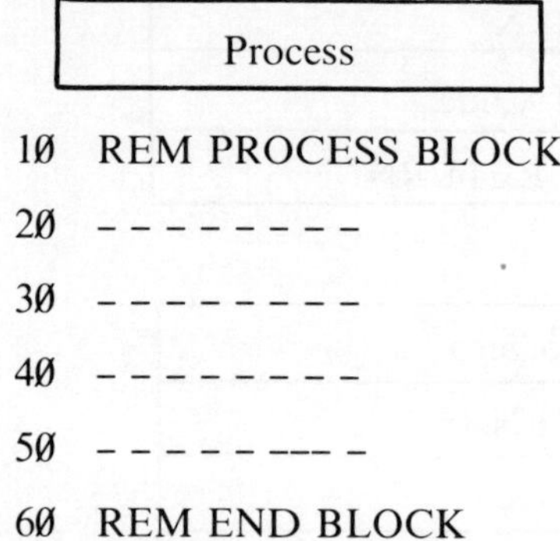


```
10   REM PROCESS BLOCK
20   - - - - - - - -
30   - - - - - - - -
40   - - - - - - - -
50   - - - - - --- -
60   REM END BLOCK
```

In some BASIC systems several statements can be put on one line with separators; these can be considered as small blocks provided there are no jumps out of the sequence.

Alternation is making a choice between two alternatives which may be single statements or sequences of statements. It is best thought of as:

'If condition is true then process 1, else process 2'

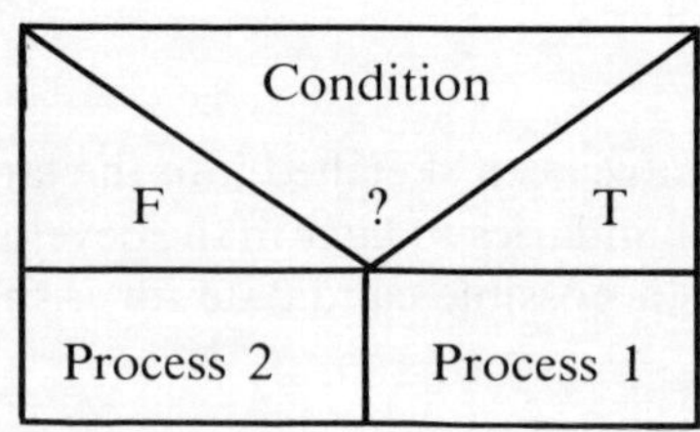

For example:

```
10   IF Y=1 THEN 100
20   X=2
30   L=X+6
```

$\left.\begin{array}{c}\\ \\ \end{array}\right\}$ Process 2

```
 40   GO TO 150
100   X=1
110   L=Y-X
150   - - - - - - - - -
```
} Process 1

which is very cumbersome. It may be made slightly clearer if the processes are subroutines:

```
10   IF Y=1 THEN GOSUB 500
20   IF NOT (Y=1) THEN GOSUB 400
```

which is not elegant, but at least follows the form of the alternation reasonably well. Many BASICs provide an extended IF statement (see Chapter 6) which should be used when possible:

```
10   IF Y=1 THEN X=1: L=Y-X ELSE X=2: L=X+6
```

but it is usually restricted to one line; hence the use of colons to provide a sequence of statements for each alternative.

Of course, it sometimes happens that process 2 is null, so that we have:

'If condition is true then process 1'

and examples are:

```
10   IF Y=1 THEN X=10
```

or

```
10   IF Y=1 THEN GOSUB 200
```

In this case it helps to save space in the structogram by skewing it so the null part of the alternative does not take up too much space. Thus:

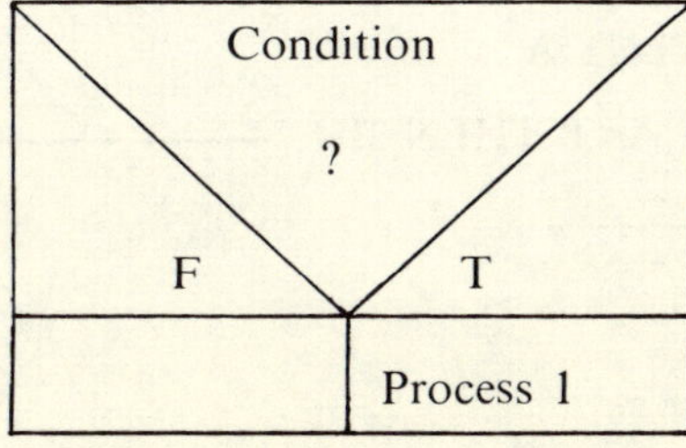

becomes

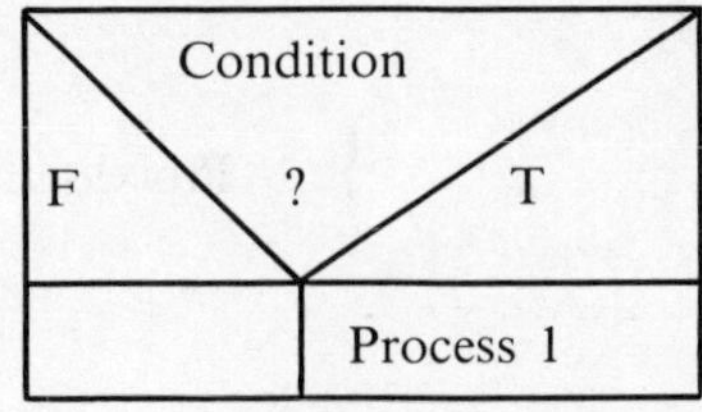

Iteration is the repetition of a sequence of statements involving some form of looping. The basic form is:

'while condition is true do process'

which implies a check on the condition at the beginning of each loop. Standard BASIC does not supply such a general looping statement, but does provide the FOR–NEXT statements which is a special case of the 'while . . . do' form with the simple condition that the loop variable value lies inside the allowed range of values. For example:

```
10   FOR I=1 TO 6 STEP 2
20      S=S+I
30   NEXT I
```

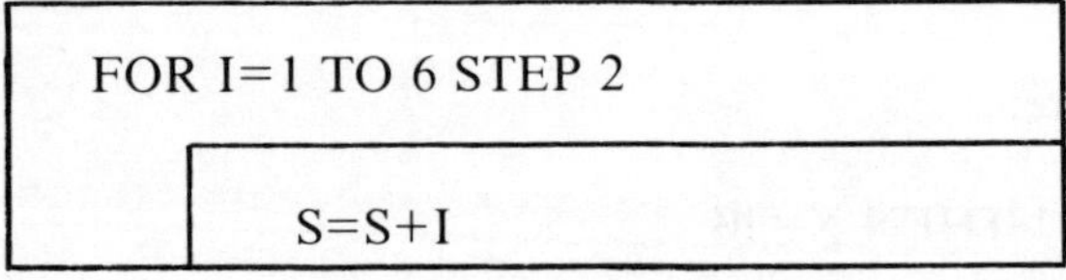

When there is a complex condition standard BASIC provides no help and the loop must be constructed out of IF and GO TO statements. Remember, the conditional test forms the first part of the loop.

In the following example the loop is required to read data and continue until a negative value is reached:

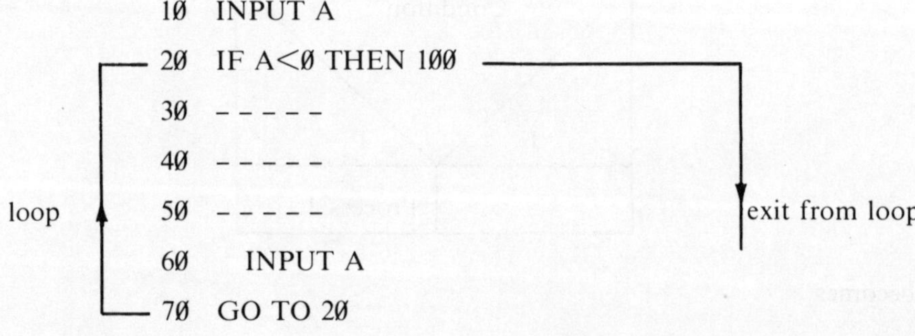

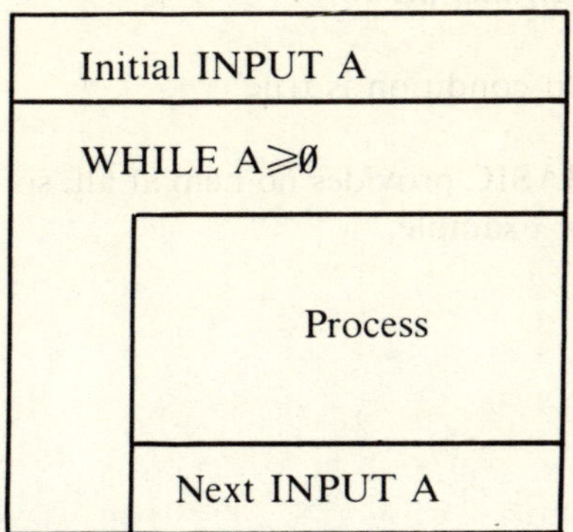

Note that the condition on line 20 is the negation of the WHILE condition. It is possible to program this structogram as:

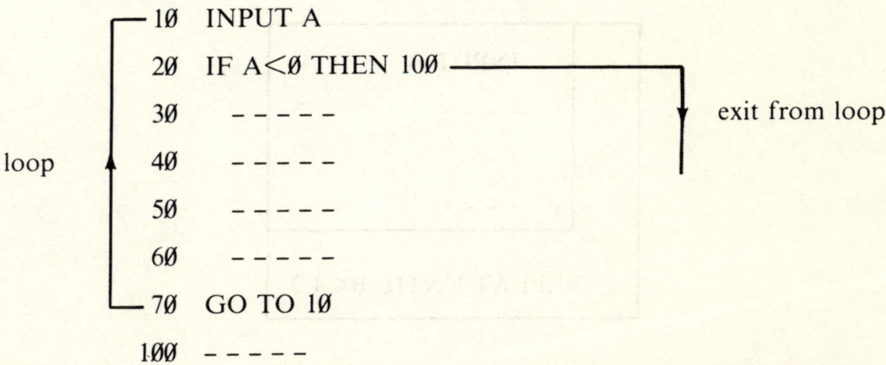

to save a duplicate INPUT A. However, the end of the loop is not now the statement on line 70, but the statement on line 10. Line 10 is also the initial statement prior to entering the loop, and the loop has wrapped round to include this statement. Although it seems to save a statement this form is obscure and not recommended. Thus the general form of this looping feature is:

Only a few BASICs have a WHILE loop statement (see Chapter 6).

The other variant of iteration is the case where the conditional test occurs at the end of the loop, which has the form:

'Repeat process until condition is true'

For this case standard BASIC provides no help at all, so IF and GO TO statements must be used. For example:

```
1Ø      INPUT B
2Ø      - - - -
3Ø      - - - -
4Ø      - - - -
5Ø   IF B>4.2 THEN 1Ø
6Ø   - - - - - -
```

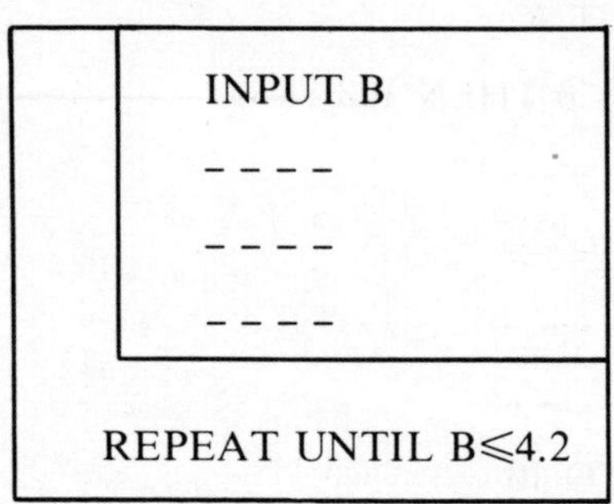

Note the negation of the condition in the structogram of the IF statement. Structograms are designed so that the horizontal bar part of the loop symbol indicates the position of the conditional test.

Very few BASICs have a REPEAT statement (see Chapter 6).

5.3.3 Pseudo code

Pseudo code is really the verbal analogue of structograms. It comprises the set phrases for the groups of statements: sequence, alternation, and iteration considered above, together with descriptions in English. Pseudo code is not rigidly fixed; make your own from:

Comments

Formulae

Descriptions of actions and processes

Sequences

Alternation—'if . . . then . . . else . . .'

Iteration   —'While . . . do . . .'

              —'Repeat . . . until . . .'

The descriptions of processes can contain BASIC statements such as INPUT, PRINT, READ, and assignments, but no jumps or other BASIC control features which should be developed from the three approved types as the final stage of the design process.

It is best appreciated by considering an example. The problem is to read a set of data, find the maximum value, and output the data divided by the maximum value. For example, if the data comprised:

4, 2.51, 10.0, –5.0, 7.5

the output would be:

0.40, 0.251, 1.00, –0.5, 0.75

The first level is clearly:

Level 1

Data input.

Find maximum.

Data output.

Refinement 1.1. Data input can be expanded in pseudo code as:

Obtain the number of data items.
While still items left
   read and store item.
endwhile.

This may be immediately translated into BASIC:

100   INPUT "GIVE NO. OF ITEMS";N

110   FOR I=1 TO N

120   INPUT A(I);

130   NEXT I

Refinement 1.2. Find maximum can be detailed as:

184

Choose a data item as the maximum value.
Scan through the data and swap if any value exceeds the current maximum.

Refinement 1.3. Data output can be detailed as:

While still items left
   PRINT item/maximum.
endwhile.

This may be immediately translated into BASIC:

```
300   FOR I=1 TO N
310     PRINT A(I)/M
320   NEXT I
```

Level 2

This includes the three parts expanded above. The only one requiring more attention is (1.2), which may be expanded in pseudo code as:

Let M=first data item.
While still items left
   if M$<$current item, then M=current item.
endwhile.

and translated into BASIC as:

```
200   M=A(1)
210   FOR I=2 TO N
220     IF M<A(I) THEN M=A(I)
230   NEXT I
```

Since the above modules are only used once and are very simple they may be put together to form a single program, rather than made into subroutines. Thus:

```
 10   REM EXAMPLE FROM PSEUDO CODE
 20   DIM A(20)
100   INPUT "GIVE NO. OF ITEMS";N
110   FOR I=1 TO N
120     INPUT A(I);
130   NEXT I
```

```
200   M=A(1)
210   FOR I=1 TO N
220      IF M<A(I) THEN M=A(I)
230   NEXT I
300   FOR I=1 TO N
310      PRINT A(I)/M;
320   NEXT I
500   END
RUN
GIVE NO. OF ITEMS ? 5
? 4, 2.51, 10.0, -5.0, 7.5
0.40 0.251 1.00 -0.5 0.75
END AT LINE 500
```

In a realistic problem many levels may be required using pseudo code until all the modules are ready for programming.

5.3.4 Summary

(a) TOP–DOWN design. Develop the problem down into modules, which are self-contained groups of actions. During the initial stages if you find that you cannot go any further, you may well have started off with incorrect features. Perhaps you did not understand the problem fully. Attempts at a solution are often part of a learning process for the problem. Start again with a different approach, perhaps different control structures and a different order of evaluation of actions.

It is sometimes difficult to get started with some problems; one approach which is sometimes helpful is to get a large sheet of paper, such as blank computer printout, and write down in groups spread across the paper various actions, properties of the solution, formulae, and possible computing structures such as arrays—in fact, anything at all which may be helpful. Keep at it, and gradually some coherent ideas on the solution will begin to emerge and the formal design process can start.

(b) Expand the actions in each module, either in a form of English leading to pseudo code or via a diagrammatic form using structograms. Individual programmers will find one of the ways, diagrammatic or verbal, more suitable for their way of thinking. If structograms seem harder to use it may be due to the tight control they force the programmer to use over the control structures in the program. In either case always avoid arbitrary jumps in program control.

(c) Finally, translate the design given by the pseudo code or structograms into BASIC. You may use GO TO statements at this stage but only as part of the correct control structures. Try to use meaningful names for variables and functions. Use sufficient REM statements to indicate the program actions and try to lay out the program in a tidy way. The modules specified in the design process may be subroutines or functions, or just blocks within another subroutine, function, or the main program.

(d) Keep the paper you used to rough out the design and if necessary make a final copy to keep with the program listing. In this way you will have some documentation of the complete program.

Avoid the temptation to sit down at the VDU and write programs directly by typing in a few statements, then running them, and correcting the errors and re-running them, and so on. By all means use this method to try out computational techniques to see if they work, but retire from the computer at some point and calmly design the program on paper.

5.4 DESIGN EXAMPLE

Artificial intelligence work has had a number of attempts at getting the computer to produce coherent text and write stories or even novels. It has proved impossible up to the present, but here is a short program which attempts to produce a few hundred words as a story. The results are certainly amusing and the sentences are guaranteed to be grammatically correct from the way they are constructed.

The basis of the story will be randomly chosen sentence patterns containing randomly chosen words. The sentence patterns are contained in strings giving keywords, which are names of the parts of speech, to be replaced by actual words. Thus:

"PERSON VT POSSESSIVE ADJ NOUN"

and the actual words are contained in strings following their keyword type:

"NOUN: JAGUAR, ROVER 3500, COAT, CAT, TROUSERS"

Any other general words and punctuation will also appear in the sentence patterns, thus:

"PERHAPS PERSON WILL VI PREP THE NOUN"

The parts of speech used are:

Nouns	NOUN
Possessive adjectives	POSSESSIVE
People	PERSON

Transitive verbs (past tense)   VT

Intransitive verbs (present tense) VI

Prepositions   PREP

Adjectives   ADJ

Adverbs   ADV

The program works in the following general way. A sentence pattern is selected and it is scanned for the keywords NOUN, POSSESSIVE, PERSON, etc. When a keyword is identified the appropriate list of actual words is obtained, and one is selected at random to replace the keyword.

The design is based on developing as many self-contained modules as possible and would be ideal with the procedure blocks which some systems such as the BBC provide. In fact, the original program was composed entirely of block functions, but as these are not widely available the design is altered slightly to produce subroutine blocks.

Level 1

    Initialize variables and functions required.
    Set the sentence patterns and word lists into the appropriate string arrays.
    Select the number of sentences N to be produced.
    Generate and print N sentences.

The part which does the work is the last item above. It will be developed as a subroutine.

Refinement 1.1. Generate and print N sentences.
    While sentences required.
        Select a sentence pattern at random.
        Construct a sentence to the pattern selected.
        Print it.
    endwhile.

Level 2

    Together the level 1 expansion and refinement 1.1 give the level 2 description. Taking the major item yet to be elaborated, which is in refinement 1.1, and expanding it as a subroutine gives:

Refinement 2.1. Construct a sentence to the pattern selected.
    While there are still word lists (rules).
        Scan sentence and replace all occurrences of a keyword by one of the
            actual words from the list.
    endwhile.

Level 3

Level 2 plus refinement 2.1 gives level 3 with reasonable clarity apart from the 'Scan sentence…' operation. Expand this as a subroutine:

Refinement 3.1. Scan sentence and replace all occurrences of keyword by one of
    the actual words from the list.
    Obtain word type from beginning of the word list (rule).
    Find the number of occurrences of this keyword (word type) in the sentence.
    While still occurrences left,
        Obtain an actual word at random.
        Replace the occurrence by the actual word.
    endwhile.

Level 4

There is sufficient detail in most of the above for level 4 to be completed. Perhaps the only item which needs elaboration is 'Obtain an actual word at random'.

Refinement 4.1. Obtain an actual word at random.
    Find the number of actual words in the word list (rule).
    Obtain a random number.
    Extract the appropriate word using this number.

Level 5

Thus level 5 is reached. At this stage most of the actions required are reasonably close to the final programming statements. This enables a direct transition to BASIC statements after one more iteration, in which some concrete decisions will be made on the string functions required and the names and uses of the important variables.

One very useful modification may be included before proceeding. Back in refinement 1.1, after the sentence is generated there is an instruction 'Print it' which would become a simple PRINT statement. However, this simple printing will cause a break-up of words at the end of each display line on the VDU and a continuation of the part words to the next line. This may be acceptable, but for a nicely formatted output this statement can be developed as another subroutine.

Refinement 1.2. Print it.
    Use a string variable as a buffer, add the sentence to this buffer.
    If the length of characters in the buffer is less than the VDU display width
        then return from subroutine.
    else print a line up to a convenient word end and delete the printed
        characters from the buffer.

Thus two refinements, 1.1 and 1.2, would go forward to level 2. The new one still requires some elaboration.

Refinement 2.2. Print it.
    Add sentence to buffer.
    If number of characters in buffer $<$ line length then return.
      else set 'length' = line length.
    While character not a space at position 'length' decrease 'length' by one.
    endwhile.
    Print 'length' number of characters from buffer.
    Delete printed characters from the buffer and any, what are now, leading
      spaces.

Return to level 1 for the start of level 6 and expand the statements of the main program. One feature which will be required on most systems is a random number generator to return values in the range 1 to N.

Level 6

    Define random number function, range 1 to N.
    Define string arrays required.
    Assign the sentence patterns to array S\$( ).
    Assign the word lists (rules) to array R\$( ).
    Generate N in range 15 to 25 as the number of sentences in a paragraph.
    Call refinement (1.1) to produce N sentences.
    Stop.

    (Refinement (1.1) subroutine)
      Empty buffer B\$( ).
      For J is 1 to N
        Get S\$ (random number) as sentence, put into T\$.
        Call refinement (2.1) to convert T\$ into an actual sentence.
        Call refinement (2.2) to output T\$ nicely.
      Next.
    Return.

    (Refinement (2.1) subroutine)
      For I=1 to R (number of rules).
        Set B1\$ equal to rule R\$(I).
        Call refinement (3.1) to replace any keyword by an actual word.
    Next.
    Return.

    (Refinement (3.1) subroutine)
    Find position of (:) in B1\$.
    Left of the (:), the rule keyword goes to W\$.
    Right of the (:), the list of actual words goes to S\$.
    Find the number (N1) of occurrences of the keyword W\$ in the
      sentence T\$.
      For I1=1 to N1.

  Call refinement (4.1) to give a random word in B1$.
  Replace the occurrence in T$ by actual word in B1$.
Next.
Return.

(Refinement (4.1) subroutine)
Count the number of words (N1) in list S$ by counting the commas.
Get a random number between 1 and N1.
Find position, by commas, of the appropriate word.
Set B1$ to contain this word.
Return.

(Refinement 2.2 subroutine)
Add sentence T$ to buffer B$.
L is the number of characters in B$.
If L < line length (4Ø) then return
 else L=L1.
 While B$ character at L is not 'space'
  L=L–1
 endwhile.
 Print B$ from 1 to L characters.
 While B$ character at L is a space
  L=L+1
 endwhile.
 Shift buffer B$ by deleting L left characters.
Return.
END

One of the reasons that so much string processing is required is the variable layout of both the sentence patterns and the rules, so that commas and spaces need to be counted and positions established for selection and replacement. You could make the program simpler if you stored each of these items in a separate string array element, using, for example, two-dimensional arrays for S$(I,J) and R$(I,J). However, it becomes a little more difficult to alter the sentence patterns and word lists if this approach is used, and one of the good features of this program is the ability to experiment easily with different word lists and sentences.

Note that the subroutine refinement (2.2) has many uses outside this example, as a word processing output routine. In fact, the whole program could be used for other purposes as it just puts objects into patterns. For example, the objects could be graphic items; instead of words, a list of cursor control directions which draw something could be used. The sentences would then be patterns which draw pictures for the whole or part of the screen to give computer art. Likewise, if a sound generator is available the system could be designed to produce computer music.

Using Microsoft string functions the full program derived from the level 6 routine is given below:

```
10    REM COMPUTER TEXT COMPOSITION
20    REM FNA GENERATES A RANDOM NUMBER 1 TO N
30    DEF FNA (N)=INT(N*RND+1)
40    REM
50    DIM S$(5), R$(10), P1(20)
60    S=5
70    S$(1)="PERSON VT POSSESSIVE ADJ NOUN."
80    S$(2)="PERHAPS PERSON WILL VI PREP THE NOUN."
90    S$(3)="ADV, PERSON VT THE NOUN."
100   S$(4)="PREP THE ADJ NOUN PERSON VT."
110   S$(5)="VI THAT, PERSON WILL ADV VI THE ADJ NOUN."
120   REM
130   R=8
140   R$(1) "NOUN: BLACK HOLE, STARSHIP, PLANET, MOON,
      SUN"
150   R$(2) "POSSESSIVE: HIS, HER, THEIR"
160   R$(3) "PERSON: THE GALACTIC LORD, THE DARK ONE,
      HE, SHE"
170   R$(4) "VT: HIT, TURNED, WENT, FLEW, STOPPED, LEFT"
180   R$(5) "VI: LOOK, STOP, LEAVE, NOTICE, RUN, DESTROY"
190   R$(6) "PREP: UNDER, THROUGH, ROUND, ON, NEAR,
      CLOSE TO"
200   R$(7) "ADJ: BRIGHT, PULSING, LONELY, FEEBLE"
210   R$(8) "ADV: SLOWLY, QUIETLY, SWIFTLY, SUDDENLY"
220   REM
230   N=15+FNA(10)
240   GOSUB 270
250   STOP
260   REM
270   REM SUB: PRINTS OUT N SENTENCES
280   PRINT
290   B$=""
```

```
300    FOR J=1 TO N
310      T$=S$ (FNA(S))
320      GOSUB 390
330      GOSUB 720
240    NEXT J
350    PRINT B$
360    PRINT
370    RETURN
380    REM
390    REM SUB: REPLACES WORDS IN T$ ACCORDING TO
       RULES R$( ).
400    REM INPUT T$ AS SENTENCE PATTERN, OUTPUT T$
       COMPLETED.
410    FOR I=1 TO R
420      B1$=R$(I)
430      GOSUB 470
440    NEXT I
450    RETURN
460    REM
470    REM SUB: USES PRESCRIPTION IN B1$ TO REPLACE
       WORDS IN T$.
480    REM INPUT T$,B1$, OUTPUT T$ WITH SOME WORDS
       REPLACED.
490    C=INSTR (B1$,":")
500    W$=LEFT $(B1$, C-1)
510    S$=RIGHT $(B1$,LEN(B1$)-C)
520    REM W$ HAS KEYWORD (PART OF SPEECH), S$ LIST OF
       WORDS
530    Y$=T$
540    X$=W$
550    GOSUB 900
560    FOR I1=1 TO O
```

```
570     GOSUB 630

580     P=INSTR (T$,W$)

590     T$=LEFT$ (T$,P–1)+B1$+RIGHT$ (T$,LEN(T$)–P–LEN
        (W$)+1)

600   NEXT I1

610   RETURN

620   REM

630   REM SUB: MAKES RANDOM CHOICE FROM LIST OF
      WORDS

640   REM INPUT S$, OUTPUT B1$ THE WORD

650   Y$= ","+S$+","

660   X$= ","

670   GOSUB 900

680   I2=FNA (O–1)

690   B1$=MID$(Y$,P1(I2)+2,P1(I2+1)–P1(I2)–2)

700   RETURN

710   REM

720   REM SUB: NICE PRINTING FOR TEXT

730   REM APPENDS A SENTENCE IN T$ TO BUFFER B$

740   REM FOR PRINTING OVER SEVERAL LINES WITHOUT
      SPLIT WORDS

750   REM INPUT IS T$ CONTAINING COMPLETED SENTENCE

760   B$=B$+" "+T$

770   L=LEN(B$)+1

780   IF L<=41 THEN RETURN

790   L=41

800   IF MID$(B$,L,1)=" " THEN 830

810     L=L–1

820     GOTO 800

830   PRINT LEFT $ (B$,L–1)

840   IF MID$ (B$,L,1)<>" "THEN

850     L=L+1
```

```
860     GOTO 840
870   B$=RIGHT $ (B$,LEN(B$)-L+1)
880   RETURN
890   REM
900   REM SUB: OCCURRENCES ROUTINE FOR MICROSOFT
910   REM INPUT STRING Y$,CHARACTERS IN X$ TO BE
      MATCHED IN Y$
920   REM OUTPUT O CONTAINS NO. OCCURRENCES
930   REM ARRAY P1( ) CONTAINS POSITIONS OF MATCHES
940   O=0
950   I3=1
960   J3=LEN (Y$)
970   K3=LEN (X$)
980   M3=0
990   P3=INSTR (I3,Y$,X$)
1000  IF P3<>0 THEN 1030
1010    M3=1
1020     GOTO 1070
1030  O=O+1
1040  P1(O)=P3
1050  I3=P3+K3
1060  IF (I3+K3)>J3 THEN M3=1
1070  IF M3 <> 1 THEN 990
1080  RETURN
1090  END
```

The last subroutine on lines 900 to 1080 is a slight development of the program described in Section 4.2.5 and is added as Microsoft has no function which returns the number of occurrences of a substring (X$) in another string (Y$). The positions of the occurrences are recorded in the array P1( ) for later use. Calls to this routine are made between lines 530 to 550, and 650 to 670. Some systems provide comprehensive functions which return occurrences and matching positions in a single call, so the final details of the implementation depend on the functions available on your system.

Returning to the original purpose of the program, you will see an amusing but not entirely coherent story produced when you RUN it. The reason is simple, the computer keeps to the rules of grammar and manipulates the words, but a story requires a framework round the ideas which may or may not be manipulated fairly randomly. The words are merely the surface appearance of the deeper ideas. If it were possible to get the computer to manipulate the ideas rather than the words, then the results would be quite startling.

Exercises

5.1   Design and write a program to convert Centigrade temperatures to Fahrenheit by defining a function to perform the conversion. Assume that a list of Centigrade temperatures input will be terminated by a zero value.

5.2   Design and write a program to produce a standard letter from you to a number of people. Each letter will be the same apart from the name and address, so use a subroutine to print the letters using the variable information from the main program.

This type of letter is often sent out by companies describing their products or by pressure groups to all Members of Parliament asking them to vote for a particular bill.

The program should produce a series of letters using information stored in DATA statements. Display the results on the VDU in the usual way if you do not have a printer.

5.3   Design and write a program to produce a list of people in an order based on their ages, from youngest to oldest. The data format for each person is:

name, age

For example: B.E. JONES, 24

Invent ten people and store their data, not sorted in any way, in DATA statements. Use subroutines for output and sorting.

PART III
Advanced

A section for experienced programmers only. In addition to advanced programming topics several specialist areas are covered.

6
BASIC plus

This chapter explores some of the extra facilities which many BASICs offer. It covers a number of fairly standard features, e.g. PRINT USING and logical operators, together with extensions of BASIC, e.g. control structures such as REPEAT loops, different variable types, and semi-graphic display facilities.

Some extensions of BASIC have grown into separate languages, such as COMAL, and this is described to illustrate the direction that BASIC may take in the future.

6.1 EXPRESSIONS

Section 1.2.5 discussed in detail the requirement for a convention of evaluation for arithmetic expressions; this section considers all types of operators and their position in the order of evaluation.

Figure 6.1 shows the relative priority of all the operators available in most BASICs. The highest is the parentheses, so in nested expressions the innermost groups of parentheses are evaluated first. Thus:

$$D+X*(C+X*(B+X))$$

involves only two multiplications, and yet is exactly the same as:

$$D+C*X+B*X*X+X*X*X$$

When there is more than one operator at the same priority level then they are evaluated from left to right. For example, Figure 6.1 shows that multiply and divide have the same priority, so that:

$$A/B*C \quad \text{is} \quad \frac{A\times C}{B}$$

but:

$$A/(B*C) \quad \text{is} \quad \frac{A}{B\times C}$$

	Standard operators	Additional operators
High priority		
Parentheses	( )	(BBC only: – NOT)
Raising to a power	↑ or **	(BBC only: ↑)
Negation	–	
Multiply, divide	* /	(BBC only: MOD DIV)
Integer divide		(Microsoft only: \ MOD)
Addition, subtraction	+ –	
	= <>	
Relational operators	< >	
	<= >=	
	NOT	
	AND	
	OR	
	XOR	(BBC use EOR)
	IMP	(some systems)
	EQV	(some systems)
Low priority		

Figure 6.1 The order of precedence of operations. The highest priority operations are performed first; those of equal precedence are done left to right

Negation is an operator which changes the sign of the contents of a variable. If A contains 37.21 then –A will be –37.21. It should always be possible to write:

    B=C*–A

as the negation has a higher priority than multiply, but some systems object and require:

    B=C*(–A)

which is clearer for the programmer to understand as well as the system.

Some systems supply an integer division operator which is the backslash (\) or the word DIV. It may be used between real or integer variables (see Section 6.2) but before division the operands are rounded to integers, and thus should be in the allowed range –32,768 to 32,767 for most micros. It is slightly faster than real division. Examples are:

    17\4 gives 4

    17 DIV 4 gives 4

and

    3.142\2 gives 1

The MOD function also works with integer division, but gives the integer value which is the remainder of the division. Thus:

    17 MOD 4 gives 1

Both MOD and DIV can be used with real values and systems round up to the next integer before the operation as:

    3.142\1.7 gives 1

and

    3.142 MOD 1.7 gives 1

because it is evaluated as 3/2 (by the rounding action) to give 1 and remainder 1.
    Other systems (like the BBC) truncate to give:

    3.142 DIV 1.7 gives 3

and

    3.142 MOD 1.7 gives 0

which is the evaluation of 3/1.
    The relational operators all have the same priority, which is below all the arithmetic operations. The operators act between pairs of arithmetic expressions and cannot appear in sequence:

    A>=B   is valid

    A>=B=C   is invalid

Complicated expressions such as the last one will have to be constructed using the logical operators discussed in the next section. Relational operators are designed to form a logical result from two arithmetic expressions. This logical result is either *true* or *false* and is used as a conditional (or boolean) expression wherever this is required in BASIC, e.g.:

IF A>=B+C THEN 2ØØ

or in an extended control structure such as:

REPEAT

— — — — — —

— — — — — —

UNTIL A>=B

Table 6.1 The values used by the relational and logical operators

	Results of relational operators	
	When 'true'	When 'false'
Sinclair ZX81	1	Ø
ICL 2904	1	Ø
Microsoft	–1	Ø
PET	–1	Ø
BBC	–1	Ø

In general, for all systems:

'True' is≠Ø

'False' is=Ø

How are the values 'true' and 'false' represented in the computer? In BASIC they are represented as binary integer values so that:

Zero is 'false'

Non-zero is 'true'

Since the relational operators form logical expressions they must produce the above values for 'true' and 'false'. They do in general, but rather than choose some arbitary non-zero value for 'true' they are set to either +1 or –1 depending upon the system. Table 6.1 gives values for some systems. Thus for the 'true' is –1 system:

    PRINT (5>3) produces −1

    PRINT (5>7) produces Ø

and

    A=(5>=2)

gives A the value −1. Although the parentheses are not strictly required some systems flag an error if they are not used. Variables may be used also, as in:

    C=(A>B)

and longer expressions:

    C=((A>B) AND (Z<=Y))

The usage is obscure and is not recommended for general programming, but may prove useful where there is a requirement for special binary patterns to be built up using integer variables, or switch values required from logical expressions as above.

6.1.1 Logical operators

The logical operators are NOT, AND, OR and must be used with logical expressions which are either 'true' or 'false'. The results produced by these operators are also either 'true' or 'false'. Thus:

    IF A<B AND B>=C THEN 5ØØ

has as its basis the comparison of two logical values on either side of the AND operator. Such expressions make sense when read out in English and are readily accepted, but for completeness the following table is given where T is 'true' and F is 'false':

Conditional 1	Conditional 2	Conditional 1 AND conditional 2	Conditional 1 OR conditional 2
T	T	T	T
T	F	F	T
F	T	F	T
F	F	F	F

The NOT operator has a higher precedence than the other logical operators and changes T to F, and vice versa. Notice that the AND operation is only 'true' when both the conditionals are 'true', while the OR operation is 'true' in all cases except where both conditionals are 'false'. What follows is a partial summary of the rules of logic; the letters a, b, and c represent logical values ('true' or 'false'):

    (a AND b) AND c=a AND (b AND c)

    (a OR b) OR c= a OR (b OR c)

    a AND b=b AND a

    a OR b=b OR a

and

    a OR (b AND c)=(a OR b) AND (a OR c)

    a AND (b OR c)=(a AND b) OR (a AND c)

with the action of NOT as:

    NOT (a AND b)=(NOT a) OR (NOT b)

    NOT (a OR b) =(NOT a) AND (NOT b)

The latter are useful in practice for simplifying obscure expressions, so that:

    IF NOT (A>B AND B<=C) THEN 500

may be written as:

    IF (A<=B OR B>C) THEN 500

To complete the set of operators for full symbolic logic manipulations some BASIC systems add the three extra operations XOR (written EOR in BBC), IMP, and EQV shown in the table below:

Conditional 1	Conditional 2	Conditional 1 XOR conditional 2	Conditional 1 IMP conditional 2	Conditional 1 EQV conditional 2
T	T	F	T	T
T	F	T	F	F
F	T	T	T	F
F	F	F	T	T

The standard OR means 'or' and 'and' with the conditions being 'true', but the exclusive XOR means only 'or'. Thus the case when both conditions are 'true' does not give 'true' using XOR. It is used more frequently than the other operators in this group and if not available may be constructed out of the standard operators by:

a XOR b≡(a OR b) AND (NOT(a AND b))

IMP is short for implication, sometimes called condition, and means the logical compound preposition 'if a then b'. Examination of the truth table above shows that this preposition is 'false' only if a false conclusion b is drawn from a true antecedent a.

EQV is short for equivalence, sometimes called double condition, and is the two-way implication which means 'a if and only if b'. It can be derived from the one-way implication by:

a EQV b≡(a IMP b) AND (b IMP a)

6.1.2 Bit manipulation

Logical operators act in the same way as relational operators, with the values for 'true' and 'false' being explicitly used by the program. The following program fragment illustrates this usage for a 'true' is 1 minicomputer (not a micro which may act differently, see below):

```
10   REM LOGICAL OPS: NOT FOR MICROS DEMO.
20   INPUT "GIVE A,B",A,B
30   PRINT "NOT A IS"; (NOT (A))
40   PRINT "NOT B IS"; (NOT (B))
50   PRINT "A AND B="; ((A) AND (B))
60   PRINT "A OR B="; ((A) OR (B))
70   STOP
80   END
RUN
GIVE A, B? 4,0
NOT A IS 0
NOT B IS 1
A AND B=0
A OR B=1
END AT LINE 80
```

    RUN
    GIVE A, B? 12, 13
    NOT A IS Ø
    NOT B IS Ø
    A AND B=1
    A OR B=1
    END AT LINE 80
    RUN
    GIVE A, B? -67, 90
    NOT A IS Ø
    NOT B IS Ø
    A AND B=1
    A OR B=1
    END AT LINE 80

The results are in line with the general convention in BASIC that 'false' is a zero value and 'true' is a non-zero value. In this case, on an ICL 2904 system, the results of applying an operator yield the appropriate system choice for 'true' (here it is +1) and not an arbitrary non-zero value (see Table 6.1). It is possible to write:

    IF (B) THEN 5ØØ

where B contains a value which is interpreted as 'true' or 'false'. But beware of casual use of this type of feature because:

    IF (A) OR (B>C) THEN 5ØØ

does not mean what it appears to say if read as an English condition.

Most micros work slightly differently in the way they apply the logical operators to arbitrary values. However, note that if they are given the values Ø and –1 (or +1 in some systems) as 'true' and 'false' they will return similar values as results. Given arbitrary values for input. these operators work in a bitwise fashion. This means they take the corresponding bits of each of the operands and compare them according to the required operation, giving a bit result. The table below effectively duplicates earlier tables, but indicates the behaviour of individual bits (Ø or 1 only) with the logical operators:

Bit a	Bit b	Bit a AND bit b	Bit a OR bit b	Bit a XOR bit b	Bit a IMP bit b	Bit a EQV bit b
1	1	1	1	Ø	1	1
1	Ø	Ø	1	1	Ø	Ø
Ø	1	Ø	1	1	1	Ø
Ø	Ø	Ø	Ø	Ø	1	1

Most micro systems first convert the input numbers to 16-bit two's complement integers in the range –32,768 to 32,767 before making the bitwise comparison, so numbers outside this range will cause an error.

Thus, running the previous program on most micros would produce the following results:

```
10   REM LOGICAL OPS: MICRO DEMO
20   INPUT "GIVE A,B",A,B
30   PRINT "NOT A IS"; (NOT (A))
40   PRINT "NOT B IS"; (NOT (B))
50   PRINT "A AND B="; (A AND B)
60   PRINT "A OR B="; (A OR B)
70   END
RUN
GIVE A,B? 63, 16
NOT A IS –64
NOT B IS –17
A AND B=16
A OR B=63
END AT LINE 70
RUN
GIVE A,B? –1, 8
NOT A IS Ø
NOT B IS –9
A AND B=8
```

A OR B=-1

END AT LINE 70

<u>RUN</u>

GIVE A,B? <u>-1, -2</u>

NOT A IS 0

NOT B IS 1

A AND B=-2

A OR B=-1

END AT LINE 70

To make sense of the above use the tables given for the bit by bit operation and remember that the numbers are represented in the two's complement form. For example:

63	is	0000	0000	0011	1111
-64	is	1111	1111	1100	0000
16	is	0000	0000	0001	0000
-17	is	1111	1111	1110	1111
-1	is	1111	1111	1111	1111
0	is	0000	0000	0000	0000
8	is	0000	0000	0000	1000
-9	is	1111	1111	1111	0111
-2	is	1111	1111	1111	1110
1	is	0000	0000	0000	0001

These are all in 16-bit two's complement form. The binary bits have been set out in groups of four only for readability. The logical operators can be used to create or 'mask' certain bits of a byte which may be manipulated by the BASIC program through the PEEK and POKE instructions, or in connection with an input/ output operation such as checking the status of various bits which occur in a status byte produced by a disc controller action.

6.2 VARIABLE TYPES

All BASICs provide one type of variable which is designed for storing real numbers. It is also used for storing integer values since numbers like 127 can be stored in the real variable as 127.0. The main problem with any variable type is its precision, since only a limited amount of space is set aside in the computer store for each variable. The more bits allowed per variable the greater its precision, but any arithmetic operation generates rounding errors and eventually these errors become quite noticeable. Even in trivial cases errors can arise, if, for example, A=1 and B=2 then it is possible that A*B is not 2 but 1.999999, so a test to see if A*B is equal to 2 would fail! Actually the above is not very likely to occur as certain rounding actions usually take place automatically in the arithmetic. However, one way to avoid this problem is to use integer variables for any areas which are particularly sensitive to exact values such as loop control and conditional tests. Some BASICs provide special integer variables (see Table 6.2) for this purpose and usually designate them as such by a % sign following the variable name. Thus:

A%

TOP%

COUNTERS%

are valid integer names.

Table 6.2 The availability of different variable types

System	Integers	Reals	
		Single precision	Double precision
Microsoft	Yes	Yes (7 significant figures)	Yes (16 significant figures)
BBC	Yes	Yes (9 to 10 significant figures)	No
CBM PET	Yes	Yes (9 significant figures)	No
Sinclair	No	Yes (9 to 10 significant figures)	No
ICL 2904	No	Yes (11 to 12 significant figures)	No

Where the usual precision for real variables is insufficient some systems provide a double precision real variable which has approximately double the number of significant figures. It is designated by the # sign. So:

210

    DIVISOR#

    T#

    SUM#

are valid double precision variables. Of course, such variables take up nearly double the amount of store space that a single precision (ordinary real) variable occupies. The amount of time taken to multiply or divide double precision variables is also much more than for single precision variables.

Whenever the system allows integer or double precision variables it also allows the same types of arrays. The following description of integer and double precision variable usage will thus apply to the appropriate type of the array elements.

6.2.1 Integer variables

These variables are often limited to two bytes of store, which means that they can contain only whole numbers in the range –32,768 through Ø to +32,767. However, this is quite adequate for most of their uses such as loop counters:

    FOR COUNT%=1 TO 5ØØ

or array index values:

    B(I%)=A(L%)+1Ø.6

or case statements:

    ON SELECT% GOSUB 1ØØ, 2ØØ, 4ØØ, 9ØØ

or in conditional expressions:

    IF T%=99 THEN GOSUB 293

The special integer division operator should be used in integer arithmetic as it is faster than real division. The operator, mentioned in Section 6.1, is the backslash (\) or the word DIV.

Conversion of type from real to integer is done automatically in an assignment statement and the result may be rounded, as in:

    1Ø   A%=9.8

    2Ø   PRINT A%

    RUN

    1Ø

or it may be truncated, as in:

    1Ø   A%=9.8
    2Ø   PRINT A%
    RUN
    9

Determine how your system operates before using this feature. Programs which are to be moved to other systems can guarantee the same effects only if they do their own rounding; for example:

    A%=INT (B+Ø.5)

which ensures that positive values in B ending in Ø.5 and upwards are put to the higher integer, while those ending in values below Ø.5 are set to the lower integer. Table 6.3 gives the functions which produce integer values. The function FIX may be obtained by the following expression if it is not available on your system:

    SGN(X)*INT(ABS(X))

Integers should be used whenever possible in programming as they have the advantage of occupying less store, having faster arithmetic operations than reals, and providing unambiguous values for control statements.

Table 6.3 Functions giving integer results

Function	Action	Examples
INT(X)	Largest integer $<=X$	INT(21.8) gives 21 INT(–21.8) gives –22
Microsoft only		
CINT(X)	Rounds X	CINT(21.8) gives 22
FIX(X)	Truncates X	FIX(21.8) gives 21
		FIX(–21.8) gives –21

BBC integer variables are only one byte shorter than real variables, and occupy four bytes with allowed values between ± 2 thousand million. The variables A% through Z% are regarded as special in that they keep values between CHAINed programs and also have a use with assembly procedures.

6.2.2 Double precision variables

Most real variables of BASIC systems give results correct to 6 or 7 significant figures; others are correct to 11 or 12 significant figures. There is sometimes a function like EPS provided, such that EPS is the smallest value which satisfies

$$1-EPS<1<1+EPS$$

If you do not have such a function, you can obtain the precision of standard real variables by running the program shown below:

```
10   E=1
20    E=E/2
30   IF (1 –E)<1 AND 1<(1+E) THEN 20
40   PRINT "THE PRECISION IS GIVEN BY";E
50   END
RUN
THE PRECISION IS GIVEN BY 3.63798E–12
END AT LINE 50
```

This indicates that the precision is 11 to 12 figures. Line 30 may be changed to 'IF (1–E)<1 THEN 20' if your computer does not support the AND operator. The result when this program is run on a BBC computer is 1.16E–10. The program may be repeated with E# in place of E (above) to determine the precision of double precision variables if these are available on your system.

Double protection variables should be used sparingly as their arithmetic is slow and they take up more store than ordinary reals. Some numerical calculations do need them, but usually in a few crucial parts of the program. These are the inner loops where arithmetic expressions are evaluated many times or areas where the result depends on differences between large numbers. Double precision arrays should be avoided whenever possible, as their use changes program run times from seconds into minutes.

Type conversion to double precision is automatic in assignment statements, but be clear what is happening in the arithmetic. Thus:

```
D#=A/B*C
```

gives no greater precision than:

```
D=A/B*C
```

because the variables and hence the arithmetic on the right-hand side is all done in single precision; only on assignment is the result padded out to fill a double precision variable (in the first example). The general rule is that all operands in an arithmetic expression are converted to the same degree of precision before evaluation. Thus:

D#=A#/B*C

should result in all double precision arithmetic and results, while

D=A#/B*C

should also perform the arithmetic in double precision but reduce the results to single precision on assignment. This may in fact be quite satisfactory, as it could happen that the cause of numerical error was within a single arithmetic expression only. Some systems allow the designation to be attached to constants indicating double precision arithmetic. If this is the case 6.45#/7.12 is evaluated in double precision, whereas 6.45/7.12 is evaluated in single precision.

Table 6.4 Microsoft functions for double precision

Function	Action	Example
CDBL(X)	Converts the single precision value X into double precision.	CDBL(454.67) gives 454.6700134277
CSNG(Y)	Converts the double precision value Y into single precision.	CSNG(1.234567890) gives 1.2345678

Table 6.4 gives two functions for explicitly performing the conversion between real numbers in single and double precisions. When investigating numerical stability it is often useful to have a general purpose subroutine or function to reduce the number of digits in a variable in order to investigate the effect of reducing precision. There are two different ways this may be done. Firstly, simply round off any value to D decimal places:

```
100   REM SUB: ROUNDS X TO D DECIMAL PLACES
110   X=INT(X*10**D+SGN(X)*.5)/10**D
120   RETURN
```

This simple rounding is not appropriate in many cases where the values vary in magnitude. This is the case when the words 'significant figures' are used. It means

214

that a certain number of figures which carry the information are to be kept regardless of the magnitude, so to three significant figures:

1.2345E+5 is 1.23E+5

and

1.2345E-1Ø is 1.23E-1Ø

The technique above may be used when the value has been scaled down to the range 1 to Ø.1; thus:

```
100    REM SUB: GIVES N SIGNIFICANT FIGURES IN X
110    IF X=Ø THEN RETURN
120    S=1.Ø
130    IF ABS(X)<1 THEN
140       X=X*.1
150       S=S*1Ø
160       GO TO 13Ø
170    IF ABS(X)>.1 THEN
180       X=X*1Ø
190       S=S*.1
200       GO TO 17Ø
210    X=INT(X*1Ø**N+SGN(X)*.5)*S/1Ø**N
220    RETURN
```

If a $\log_{10}$ function is available it can be used to determine the magnitude of X in place of the two loops above. Another way to perform the reduction is to convert X to a string and process it as a series of characters.

Ensure the above subroutine is used correctly when acting to limit the number of significant figures in the arithmetic. For example, the expression:

```
5Ø    Y(I)=(B(I)-T)/A(I,J)
```

should be expanded to:

```
5Ø    X=B(I)-T
6Ø    GOSUB 1ØØ
7Ø    X=X/A(I,J)
```

```
80   GOSUB 100

90   Y(I)=X
```

6.2.3 Setting general types

A few BASICs, e.g. Microsoft, provide a statement to declare that all variable names which begin with a particular string of letters will be of a specified type. Thus:

```
10   DEFINT I,K,L
```

will automatically set the type of all variables which begin with either I or K or L to be integers. The usual default type in all BASICs is type real, but the statements DEFINT, DEFSNG, DEFDBL, and DEFSTR will reset the type for the variables specified to be integer, real, double precision, and string respectively. A hyphen (-) may be used to indicate a range of letters.

```
10   DEFDBL A-E
```

is the same as:

```
10   DEFDBL A,B,C,D,E
```

Explicit type setting of variables using #,$,%, and ! overcomes the DEF type setting. Thus:

```
10   DEFDBL A,B,C

20   B!=4.2

30   C%=6
```

will take the C% as an integer and B! as an ordinary real. (In Microsoft BASIC the ! can be optionally used to indicate a single precision variable.)

To avoid confusion it is best to set out a personal convention when using these statements—perhaps reserve I for integers, S for strings, and D for double precision variables.

6.3 PRINT USING STATEMENT

The PRINT USING statement allows very precise layout of numbers and strings right down to where each individual numeric may appear. Although the automatic layout provided by the standard PRINT statement is very flexible there are certain cases where it is a disadvantage. These occur in producing financial reports, account ledgers, printing cheques, and tabular output.

This statement is one of the most complicated in BASIC and has a great

number of variations between computers. In what follows the features common
to most usages are described.

6.3.1 Formats

Every PRINT USING statement contains, or refers to, a format which is a
picture or image of the layout of the output value, string, or number. The basic
constituent of this format is the hash (#) character which indicates that a digit or
character should be printed. The effect of this is shown in the example below
which also illustrates the differences between the two PRINT statements:

```
10    REM PRINT USING DEMO
20    FOR I=1 TO 6
30       READ A
40       PRINT A
50    NEXT I
60    PRINT
70    RESTORE
80    FOR I=1 TO 6
90       READ A
100       PRINT USING "-####.##";A
110    NEXT I
120    DATA 2.2,1000,47.345,-6.25,.037,1
130    END
RUN
2.2
1000
47.345
-6.25
3.7E-2
1
    2.20
1000.00
    47.35
```

    −6.25

    Ø.Ø4

    1.ØØ

END AT LINE 13Ø

The latter group of figures is nicely lined up, rounding has taken place at the second decimal place, and trailing zeros have been added.

The format image is the string following the word USING. Every format is given as a string. The positions of the output digits are strictly determined by the positions of the # characters. The decimal point is printed as it appears four characters from the start of the format and the numbers are adjusted to it. The decimal point can appear anywhere, or not at all, in the format image.

Table 6.5 Format specification characters commonly used. Two different systems for strings are indicated; these are called 'A' and 'B' here

Format specification	Action for numbers	Action for strings
#	Prints one digit or zero or blank.	Prints one character, in the 'A' system. See comments below.
.	Prints decimal point.	
,	Prints a comma at every third position to the left of the decimal point.	
$ or £	Prints $ or £ at the position specified.	
$$ or ££	Floating $ or £. Only one of the characters is printed immediately before the number.	
+	May appear before or after the #s. The signs (+,−) of the output values are printed.	
−	As with + above, but only the negative sign of the output values are printed.	
↑↑↑↑ or ∧∧∧∧ or !!!!	Indicates that the exponent field is to be printed.	

*	Prints *s in all unused spaces to the left of the decimal point.

< and >	Introduces a character string field designated by #s. < means left justify, > means right justify. (The 'A' system for strings.)
\\ \\	Two backslash characters with N spaces between cause printing of N+2 leftmost characters. (The 'B' system for strings.)
!	Prints the one leftmost character in a string. (The 'B' system for strings.)
&	Prints the full string. (The 'B' system for strings.)

Table 6.5 gives a selection of the commonly used format description characters. There seems to be a reasonable amount of agreement about numeric formats but there are several different systems operating for string output. Looking first at numeric output, Table 6.6 gives some idea of the effect of the different formats. Note that these would normally appear within string quotes in the PRINT USING statement.

Table 6.6 Examples of numeric formats

Format field	Numeric to be printed	Result
##	12	12
###	12	12
###.##	12	12.00
###.##	123	123.00
###.##	.123	0.12
####,.	12	12.
####,.	1234	1,234.
$##.##	1.2	$ 1.20
$$##.##	1.2	$1.20
**####.##	123	*123.00

**####.##	1	***1.ØØ
*$###.##	1	**$1.ØØ
+####	123	+123
+####	–123	–123
–####	123	123
–####	–123	–123
##.##↑↑↑↑	123	1.23E+Ø2
##.##↑↑↑↑	.Ø12	1.2ØE–Ø2

Normally leading zeros are suppressed, but zeros trailing after the decimal point are printed. The exception is a number less than one which has the zero immediately before the decimal point printed.

Security printing for cheques and credit vouchers is aided by the floating $ or £, when both appear doubled on the format description, and by the double * which fills in as many places as necessary with *s. The combination *$ or *£ gives both features of field fill and floating money sign. When the money sign is floated some systems prohibit the printing of the plus and minus signs. If negative values are to be printed the sign indication should be placed after (to the right of) the numeric field.

The scientific number format using the exponential form requires all four carats (arrows) to include the full specification E+nn. One of the leading digit positions is kept for the sign so that "##.#↑↑↑↑" has the same effect as "–#.#↑↑↑↑".

The comma, if it appears, can appear anywhere in the numeric format. It is used to separate the digits in groups of three before the decimal point.

String formats are quite simple but there are several different systems, two of which are indicated in Table 6.5. The system called 'A' here specifies a field as "<###" which would print up to three characters left justified in the field or ">###" which would right justify them in the field. Table 6.7 illustrates this system.

Table 6.7 String formats in the 'A' system

Format field	String to be printed	Result
<###	AB	AB
<###	ABC	ABC
<###	ABCD	ABC
>###	AB	AB
>###	ABC	ABC
>###	ABCD	ABC

220

The other system for string printing, called 'B' here, uses a pair of backslash characters to specify the string field. Two backslash characters together print two string characters. Two backslash plus a space print three string characters, and so on. The & on its own indicates a variable string field and the full string is output, although the use of this feature tends to destroy the regular printing in columns which is the main feature of PRINT USING. Table 6.8 illustrates this system.

Table 6.8 String formats in the 'B' system

Format field	String to be printed	Result
!	ABCD	A
\ \	ABCD	AB
\ \	ABCD	ABCD
\ \	AB	AB
&	ABCDE	ABCDE
&	A	A

Some systems use a field such as LLLL to print up to four left justified string characters and RRR to print up to three right justified string characters.

Many large computer systems use the 'A' system, while microcomputers which supply PRINT USING, such as Microsoft BASIC, use the 'B' system.

If a number is too large for the numeric field it is often printed in full but preceded by a % sign to indicate the error. Strings are truncated if they are too large for the field.

6.3.2 Format Printing

The format description can be contained in the PRINT USING statement as:

    1ØØ   PRINT USING "##.#";A;B,C

or in a string variable as:

    5Ø   S$="##.#"

        .

        .

        .

        .

    1ØØ   PRINT USING S$;A;B,C

with the same effect. This flexibility allows you to input the format description with the data, if required, so that different data sets can be correctly displayed from one program.

One system, a large computer, requires that if the format is not with the PRINT USING it must be given like a constant, without the string quotes but preceded by a colon (:) on a new line. The line number of this format must appear after USING as:

    90   PRINT USING 200,A;B,C

              .

              .

              .

              .

    200   :##.#

The main purpose of this feature seems to be to avoid trying to fit both a long format description and a list of variables into the restricted line length which each BASIC statement must use.

PRINT USING statement

General form   PRINT USING format description, output list

where:

    format description is either a set of format characters enclosed in quotes, or a string variable which contains the format characters.

    output list is the usual output list of variables and separators used in PRINT statements.

Note that the separator between the format description and output list varies between systems, the usual forms are:

      format description, output list

      format description; output list

      format description: output list

    Details of the format description characters are given in Table 6.5. The values of the output list are printed in order using the format fields specified in the format description.

    If there are more format fields than output values the extra fields are ignored. If there are less format fields than output values the format is used from the beginning again until all the output values have been printed.

222

The following program illustrates some of the features of the PRINT USING statement:

```
10   REM PRINT USING DEMO
20   FOR I=1 TO 6
30      READ A$,A
40      PRINT USING "THE COST OF A\    \=£+##.##";A$,A
50   NEXT I
60   DATA COAT,89.95,DRESS,25.50
70   DATA PEN,1.99,INK,.65
80   DATA WATCH,7.99,SHOES,20
90   END
RUN
THE COST OF A COAT   =£+89.95
THE COST OF A DRESS  =£+25.50
THE COST OF A PEN    =£ +1.99
THE COST OF A INK    =£ +0.65
THE COST OF A WATCH=£ +7.99
THE COST OF A SHOES  =£+20.00
END AT LINE 90
```

6.4 CONTROL STRUCTURES

This section looks at the facilities which help to provide a neat, efficient, and ordered control in BASIC programs. The forms of control examined here approximate most closely to those recommended in structured programming.

Having discussed problems of significant figures in earlier sections of this chapter, consider the type of statement which forms the conditional expression in control structures such as IF, WHILE, UNTIL:

IF A=B THEN...

When a lot of computing has been done on the variables A and B in the conditional (A=B) these variables are unlikely to have the correct values for equality in all expected cases. Thus the test may or may not be true in situations where the programmer has assumed that there is equality. To correct this use integer quantities:

IF A%=B% THEN

or set a limit appropriate to the number of significant figures expected for that type of variable. If six to seven significant figures are expected then:

IF ABS(A–B)<=1.ØE–6 THEN

is a safer test.

6.4.1 Multiple statements

A number of BASICs allow several statements to be typed on the same (physical) line provided they are separated by a special character, usually a colon (:), sometimes a backslash (\). Thus:

```
1Ø   PRINT "THIS": PRINT "AND": PRINT "THIS."
2Ø   PRINT "NEXT"
```

would produce:

```
RUN
THIS
AND
THIS.
NEXT
```

Statements separated by colons do not have statement numbers and cannot be jumped into via a GOTO. They are executed in order, left to right, after the labelled statement is executed.

This feature can be used merely to save typing and produces programs which look like a solid mass of characters with no discernible structure. Or it can be used to enhance readability and illustrate program structure. Remark statements can be added at appropriate places:

```
2ØØ   FOR I=1 TO N1           :REM WORK ACROSS COLUMNS
21Ø      GOSUB 75Ø            :REM SELECT PIVOT
22Ø      I1=I+1
23Ø      FOR J=I1 TO N        :REM ELIMINATE IN COL. I
       .    .
       .    .
       .    .
```

Most importantly, sequences or blocks of statements can be constructed which cannot be jumped into:

    200   A=0: B=6: I=I+1: PRINT Z(I);

and form the rectangular process structogram:

<table>
<tr><td>A=0</td></tr>
<tr><td>B=6</td></tr>
<tr><td>I=I+1</td></tr>
<tr><td>PRINT Z(I);</td></tr>
</table>

While it would be nicer if such a block could extend over many physical lines, at least small blocks can be constructed on one line.

The above applies particularly to IF–THEN statements:

    100   IF A>=B THEN PRINT "GREATER": Z=A: GOSUB 500

When the condition is true the statements following the THEN are executed in order. Consider:

    100   IF A>=B THEN PRINT "GREATER": GOSUB 500: Z=A

The problem is that Z=A is never executed because the return from the GOSUB will go to the next line with a statement number, not the next statement. Similarly if GOSUB is replaced with GOTO.

Small FOR–NEXT loops on one line may be used as a time delay feature:

    100   REM TIME DELAY, VALUE DEPENDS ON COMPUTER

    110   FOR I=1 TO 10000: NEXT I

or to initialize array values:

    100   FOR I=1 TO 200: A(I)=0: NEXT I

or for many other simple processes.

6.4.2 Extended lines

A few systems, for example Microsoft, offer a means of extending a logical line over several physical lines. Instead of pressing <return> at the end of a line press <line feed>, or <control & J> for Microsoft, and continue with the statement on the next physical line:

```
10    A=10*B+                          <control & J>

         Z*(C+2*B)                     <return>

20    PRINT A                          <return>
```

A logical line may thus be extended over several physical lines by means of special control keys. There is usually a limit to the number of characters allowed in a logical line, typically 255 characters. In BBC BASIC just continue typing and the cursor will wrap round to a new line on the screen. Press <return> only when the extended line is complete.

Lengthy single statements such as PRINT USING and IF statements will find this feature an advantage. It may also be combined with the multiple statement per line feature to allow larger blocks of statements (see Section 6.4.1).

6.4.3 IF–THEN–ELSE statements

The IF–THEN–ELSE statement provides one of the basic building blocks of structured programming. The statement:

$$\text{IF } A>2 \text{ AND } B<0 \text{ THEN } Z=1 \text{ ELSE } Z=2$$

will set Z to one if the conditional expression is true, and if it is not true it will set Z to two. It exactly corresponds to the structogram:

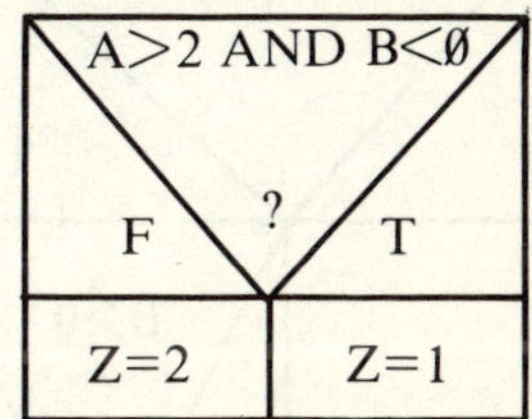

By means of statement separators the alternatives may be small blocks:

$$\text{IF } A>0 \text{ THEN } T=S+L: I=I+1 \text{ ELSE } S=0: I=J$$

which is:

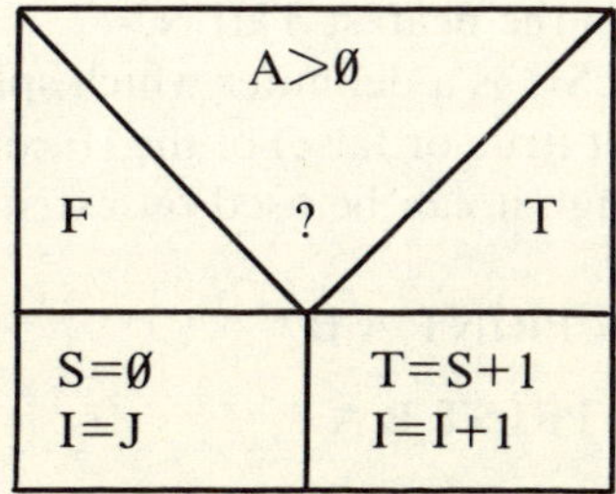

However, the whole statement must appear on one line, which is rather restrictive. Only if extended logical lines are permitted is it possible to include more actions within each block and allow a readable layout, for example, in Microsoft BASIC:

```
210   IF A>0 THEN REM ADD TO SUM:         <control & J>
         S=S+A : I=I+1                    <control & J>
      ELSE REM EXIT WITH VALUE:           <control & J>
         T=S*S                            <return>
```

In theory, IF–THEN–ELSE statements may be nested, but the comment about restricted line lengths applies even more strongly in this case. It is virtually impossible to get a meaningful nested set of IF statements on one line. Take care with nested IF statements, because

```
IF A>B THEN IF B>0 THEN Z=1 ELSE Z=2
```

means in Microsoft BASIC:

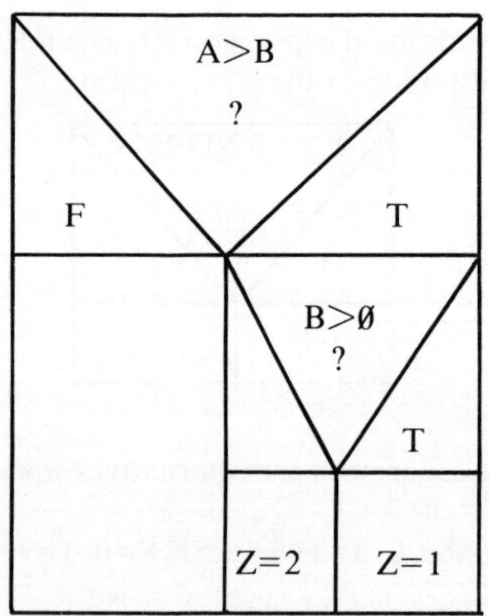

as the ELSE is attached to the nearest THEN.

BBC BASIC regards ELSE as a delimiter which splits the line into two parts corresponding to the result (true or false) of the IF condition. This implies only one ELSE per line, although it can be used on extended lines, for example:

```
100   IF A>B THEN PRINT A,B
         ELSE PRINT B,A                   <return>
```

But it is allowed to be appended to the ON–GOTO and ON–GOSUB statements to provide default execution paths. Thus:

ON I+J GOTO 100,200,300,400 : ELSE GO TO 1000

and

ON I+J GOSUB 100,900,200 : ELSE PRINT "ERROR" : STOP

6.4.4 Iteration

The only forms of looping control statements provided by standard BASIC is FOR–NEXT and a combination of IF–THEN and GOTO. However, there are two general forms of looping control, which are:

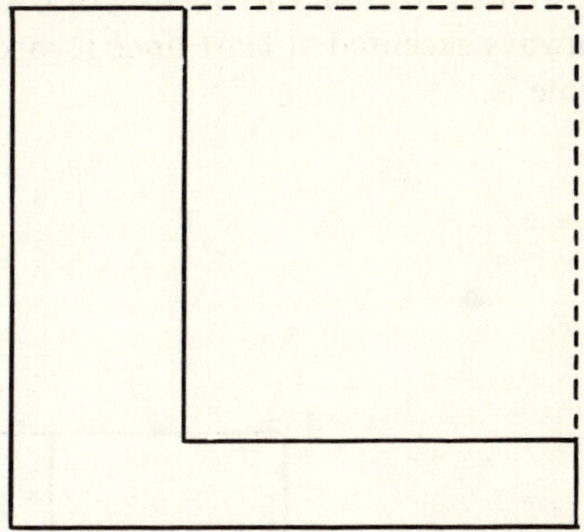

REPEAT–UNTIL condition

where the test is at the end of the loop, and:

WHILE condition

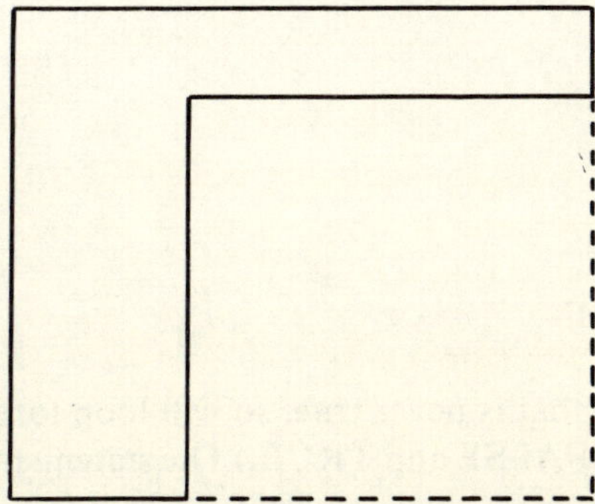

where the test is at the beginning of the loop. The pseudo code descriptions would be:

REPEAT statements UNTIL condition.

and

WHILE condition DO statements.

The principle difference is that a REPEAT–UNTIL loop is always performed at least once, but the WHILE loop may not be performed at all if the condition is not satisfied.

The FOR–NEXT loop should be a special case of WHILE, using the condition that the loop counter should lie in a certain range. When this is not true the looping ceases. However, a few systems such as the BBC test at the end of FOR–NEXT, so the implementation is a special case of REPEAT–UNTIL. In fact, the only general iteration structure provided by the BBC BASIC is the REPEAT–UNTIL one, so it seems that this version of BASIC tests loops at the end. That is, they are always executed at least once regardless of the condition involved. A BBC example is:

```
10   REPEAT
20      I=I+1
30      T=T+A
40   UNTIL I>N
```

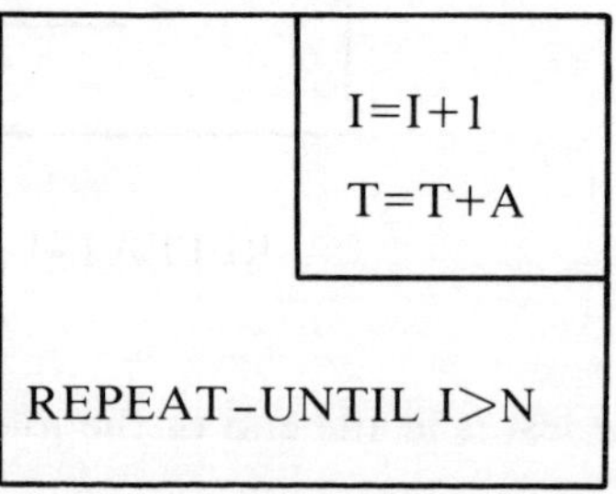

also:

```
10   REPEAT
20      ......
30      ......
40      ......
50   UNTIL FALSE
```

which gives a condition that is never true, so will loop forever. (Note that BBC provides two functions, FALSE and TRUE.) The statements may appear on one line:

10　REPEAT INPUT A : SUM=SUM+A : UNTIL A<0

The Microsoft version of BASIC gives examples of the second iteration structure, WHILE. This system tests both the FOR–NEXT and WHILE loops at the beginning, and does not provide a REPEAT–UNTIL statement. The Micro-soft loop start statement is:

WHILE condition

followed by a group of statements terminated by:

WEND

Here is an example derived from the bubble sort program of Section 4.5.1. That program may do unnecessary checking of array elements if they are fully ordered before the N–1 outer passes are complete.

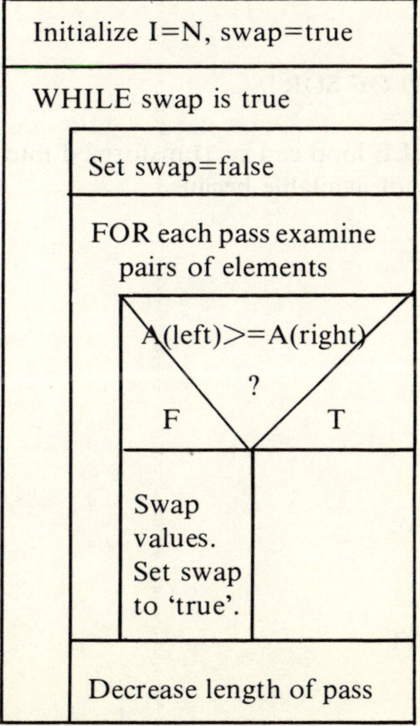

1000　REM BUBBLE SORT FRAGMENT

1010　REM ASSUMES ARRAY A(1)......A(N)

1020　REM HOLDS THE VALUES

1030　REM SORTS INTO DESCENDING ORDER

```
1034  I=N
1038  SWAP=1                              :REM TRUE IS NOT ZERO
1040  WHILE SWAP
1045    SWAP=0
1050    FOR J=1 TO I-1
1060      FOR A(J)>=A(J+1) THEN 1100
1070        TEMP=A(J)
1080        A(J)=A(J+1)
1090        A(J+1)=TEMP
1095        SWAP=1
1100    NEXT J
1105    I=I-1
1110  WEND
1120  REM END OF SORT
```

The logic of the WHILE loop can be transformed into a REPEAT loop if the WHILE construct is not available because:

```
WHILE condition
    .
    .
    .
WEND
```

is exactly equivalent to:

```
IF condition
    THEN REPEAT
        .
        .
        .
    UNTIL NOT condition
```

or:

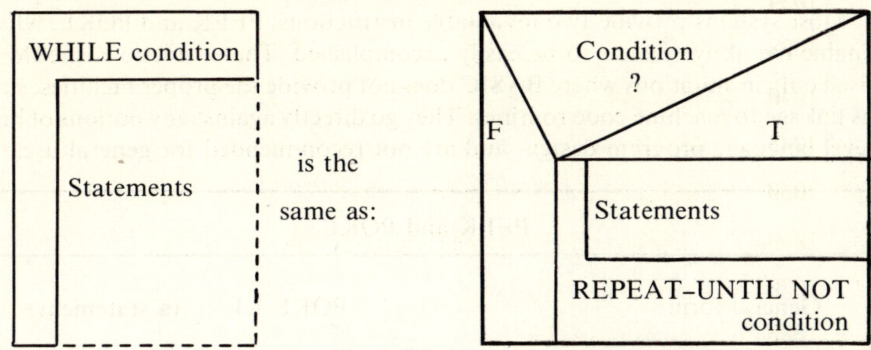

The transformation is quite tortuous and both the iteration statements are better mimicked by suitable combinations of IF–THEN and GOTO if they are not available.

Some authors recommend the use of an 'IF condition THEN EXIT' type of pseudo code statement within loops. The effect of this is to terminate the loop prematurely if the condition is satisfied. It is nothing but a jump out of the loop to the next statement following it. Thus it is uncertain on reaching this statement whether the loop has been completed and its conditions have been satisfied, or the alternative condition if the IF statement has been satisfied. Uncertainty is not part of good design, and this action can cause difficulties with theoretical proofs of correctness. So this type of pseudo code statement is not recommended, even though it seems a tempting feature to use in practice. There is also no satisfactory way of representing it in structograms. It is always preferable to set various logical flags or switches as a composite looping condition and alter these within the loop to cause termination.

6.5 ROUTINES AND PROCEDURES

Not many systems venture so far as to provide proper procedures, which are bodies of instructions similar in some ways to block functions, although most microprocessor-based BASICs do provide some instruction to call and execute machine code routines from BASIC.

6.5.1 Using machine code

Using machine code routines from a BASIC program is not in theory very difficult as many systems provide at least one way of calling up a machine code routine. However, in practice, there are a number of very minor details such as store addresses and lists of numeric values to be correctly placed whenever such a call is made. This is only to be expected, as machine code deals with the physical reality of the computer so actual store addresses must be found and used, arithmetic registers loaded with values, and stack pointers checked and changed.

Most systems provide two invaluable instructions, PEEK and POKE, which enable the above details to be easily accomplished. These functions should be used only in situations where BASIC does not provide the proper facilities, such as linkage to machine code routines. They go directly against any notions of high level language program design, and are not recommended for general use.

PEEK and POKE

General form   POKE I,J   (a statement)

                  and

                      Variable=PEEK(I)   (a function)

where:

    I contains in decimal (or hexadecimal with appropriate indication character) the address of a byte in the computer store, between Ø and 65,535.

    J contains a decimal (or hexadecimal) byte value, to be placed in the byte at address I. The value of J is between Ø and 255.

Note that BBC BASIC does not have these functions.

Thus:

    10   POKE 16251,22

will place the value 22 in the byte at location 16251 in the store. Variables can be used; if they are not integers they will be rounded to an integer:

    100   A=62ØØØ

    110   B=33

    120   POKE A,B

Some systems allow the use of hexadecimal values, which are indicated by preceding the value with & or &H. For example, &FF is the hexadecimal for 255, &1A is the hexadecimal for 26. Thus:

    10   POKE &5AØØ,&FF

puts 255 into address 23Ø4Ø.

A PEEK instruction shows you the byte (8 bit) values of each store location. The following program illustrates its use:

```
10    REM EXAMINE STORE
20    INPUT "GIVE STARTING ADDRESS";I%
30    INPUT "GIVE NUMBER OF BYTES";B%
40    FOR N%=1 TO B%
50       PRINT " ";PEEK(I%+N%);
60    NEXT N%
70    PRINT
80    END
```

Given a starting address and the number of bytes required the program will display in decimal (between Ø and 255) the contents of bytes in the store. Using PRINT " "; CHR$(PEEK(I%+N%)); will display the character representation of each byte. Microsoft provides a function HEX$(X) which returns the hexadecimal value of decimal X, and this can be used in place of CHR$. Thus store values can be displayed in decimal, character, and hex representations fairly easily.

The converse of looking at blocks of bytes in store is to actually write new values to a region of store using POKE. This is a convenient way of loading small machine code instructions with a BASIC program. For example:

```
10    REM POKE DEMO
20    DATA 31,167,2Ø8,165,179,166
30    DATA 18Ø,133,18Ø,134,179,162
40    DATA    Ø,161,179,168,138,76
50    DATA 12Ø,210
60    FOR I%=1 TO 20
70       READ N%
80       POKE I%+825,N%
90    NEXT I%
100   END
```

would put a complete machine code routine in store addresses 826 to 845 for later use from BASIC.

Many BASICs provide two ways of calling the machine code routine. The most general way is to use the CALL instruction which has the form:

CALL address, optional values for input.

as in:

    10   CALL &FF10

and in a slightly different form for a Microsoft 6502 routine:

    10   START=&FF10
    20   CALL %START(10,20,30)

Execution passes out of BASIC to the machine code routine which starts at the given address. If there are values, these may be loaded into some of the registers, or pointed at by registers, or a block of store pointed at by one register pair. The details depend on the exact microprocessor in your system. If necessary your machine code routine will have to save the current values of registers and stack pointers as its first action. Just before returning the routine should restore these values, so that BASIC can resume where it left off.

The second means of calling a machine code routine is to use it like a simple function, with one value only as input and one as output. The call is via the USR(X) function.

    10   A=USR(2*B+3)

The input value X is sometimes restricted to be an integer and, if real, is rounded to an integer. The result may also be restricted to be an integer on some systems. There is no mention of where the routine is located, so before it is used the starting address must be POKEd somewhere. Exactly where depends on your system, thus:

    100   POKE 1,58

    110   POKE 2,4

    120   A=USR(B)

When POKEing addresses there is a split of the 16 bit address into two 8 bit bytes and the lower part is normally put into the first byte. In the example above:

    Byte number 1 gets 58 which is 3*16+10=3A hex

    Byte number 2 gets   4 which is 4=4 hex

1	2
Hex values 3A	4

give address:

$$4*256+3*16+10=1082$$

The routine executed from this address by USR picks up the value (from the variable B in the above example) from some area of store pointed at by a register pair. Microsoft additionally provides a simple means of passing an address; if:

```
10   DEF USRØ=2400
```

then whenever USRØ(X) is used the decimal address set in DEF USRØ is used. USR may be followed by a simple digit, as ten different routines may be used.

The BBC system does provide a USR function, but this takes its address from the input value on the USR statement; e.g.:

```
20   A=USR (Z%)
```

and

```
50   PRINT USR (&1000)
```

Values stored at the time of the call in the special variable A%,X%,Y%, and C% are copied to the microprocessor's A,X,Y registers and C carry flag (1 bit) for use within the routine. The CALL statement has a similar format to that described earlier with the added availability of the registers and carry flag as with USR. See the BBC manual for details of value passing.

Note that the BBC system does not provide PEEK and POKE, but it does provide the very useful facility of embedding assembly code in normal BASIC statements. An opening square bracket ([) anywhere before or after a BASIC statement is followed by one or more lines of code. A closing square bracket (]) ends the assembly code. For example:

```
120   INPUT SUM
130   [.SHIFT ROR A
140      INY
150      CPY 8
160      BNE SHIFT ]
170   PRINT SUM
```

The BBC indirection operators (?, ! and $) are more versatile than PEEK and POKE but work in a similar way. Thus:

```
A=?B is equivalent to A=PEEK (B)
?A=B is equivalent to POKE A,B
```

The ? operator acts on a single byte, the ! operator acts on a single word containing four bytes and the $ operator acts on a string.

6.5.2 Procedures

Subroutines using GOSUB and RETURN work exclusively on global variables, i.e. variables available throughout the program. The correct variables must contain the appropriate values on entry to the subroutine.

Single-line functions can accept values through their parameter list and use any global variables. The dummy variables in the parameter list are actually local to the function and separate from global variables of the same name. Block functions extend this local feature by allowing the declaration of a set of local variables which act in the same way. But the line function returns one and only one value to the calling position, and in theory so may the block function also, though it can access and thereby modify global variables if it wants to return several values.

Procedures are available on several large computer BASIC systems, but among micros only on the BBC system, which is taken as the example here. The procedure is called by giving its name:

```
100   PROCPICTURE (9,27.6,BIG)
```

and takes any number of parameters as input. The corresponding (in type and number) dummy parameters are local to it, and other variables may be declared LOCAL. Global variables are also available, but should be used with care to retain the essential independence of the procedure. The values in the parameter list are copied to the local parameters for use. The procedure has the form:

```
500   DEF PROCPICTURE(A,B,C$)

510   LOCAL I%,S

520   PRINT B,C$

530   FOR I%=A TO B

        .

        .

        .

800   ENDPROC
```

It is introduced by the statement DEF PROC name and terminated by the ENDPROC statement. Procedure may be recursive, like block functions.

Procedures provide an ideal mechanism by which the modular programming advocated in this and other books may be implemented. They should be preferred over subroutines. Like BBC functions they should be placed after the end of the main program.

The procedure parameters may be used to pass values into it; any values required as a result of the procedure must be passed to global variables (i.e. those used in the main part of the program). If a single result is required then use a block function instead of a procedure. The following example shows a procedure PROCNUM which computes two values, the sum and largest input value, and returns them via the global variables C and D respectively:

```
10   INPUT A,B
20   PROCNUM(A,B)
30   PRINT C,D
40   END
50   DEF PROCNUM(X,Y)
60      C=X+Y                    :REM USING C TO RETURN VALUE
70      IF X>Y THEN D=X ELSE D=Y        :REM AND D ALSO
80   ENDPROC
```

Here is another procedure example which waits until the key whose symbol is given in A$ is pressed.

```
250   DEF PROCWAIT(A$)
260   PRINT "Press the ";A$;" key to continue."
270   REPEAT UNTIL GET$=A$
280   ENDPROC
```

6.6 SEMI-GRAPHICS

Semi-graphics is the ability to display text characters and partial characters anywhere on the VDU screen. At least all the ASCII characters and some cursor control movements should be programmable in a BASIC program, but preferably some other shapes or dots should also be available.

Such semi-graphics facilities are available using the PRINT statement on many systems. The effect is to program the cursor control functions and display any character at any chosen point on the screen. The Commodore PET has a very good set of graphics characters so this technique can produce reasonable quality pictures.

Other systems have moved towards more sophisticated graphics and allow tiny areas or dots or small line segments to be switched on or off, in a variety of colours, all over the VDU area. Statements such as PLOT are provided in these systems.

6.6.1 Using PRINT

Systems which provide graphics using the unmodified PRINT statement (like the PET computer) allow it to display any character, many of which will be

238

unprintable and will be the same as pressing the keys on the keyboard. So, clear screen, cursor home, cursor left and right and up and down, insert, and delete are all features which can be produced by PRINT, usually via the CHR$( ) function which will produce the character code given the ASCII number for the key function. Try:

```
10   FOR I=0 TO 255
20      PRINT CHR$(I);
30   NEXT I
40   END
```

and all sorts of strange things should happen to the display if your system supports this feature, because it is going through the complete repertoire of key actions. Each system has its own codes for many of the key actions so just one system, that of the PET, will be used to illustrate this feature. Table 6.9 summarizes the control actions for the PET, and the description which follows applies to the PET but gives a general idea of how such systems work. Remember

Table 6.9 Commodore PET screen control functions

Action	ASCII code
Cursor up	145
Cursor down	17
Cursor left	157
Cursor right	29
Clear screen	147
Home cursor	19
Insert character	148
Delete character	20

that in this PRINT-oriented system the print position advances by one (or more depending on commas or semicolons) after printing each character. To draw a horizontal line in the normal way from left to right we use:

```
10   FOR I=1 TO 10
20      PRINT "-";
30   NEXT I
```

Try drawing a vertical line with:

```
10   FOR I=1 TO 10
20      PRINT "1";CHR$(17);
30   NEXT I
```

and the result will be angled across the page as:

```
1
  1
   1
    1
     1
      1
       1
        1
         1
          1
```

So the cursor left must always be used in this case:

```
10   FOR I=1 TO 10
20      PRINT "1";CHR$(157);CHR$(17);
30   NEXT I
```

which will produce a vertical line as required. Only character positions can be accessed using the PRINT statement, which produces output at the line and character position at which the cursor appears. The screen is not addressed in any way, so movements from one position to another must be achieved through loops such as:

```
100   FOR I=1 TO N: PRINT : NEXT I
```

which moves down N lines and use the TAB function to move within a line. Either move up using CHR$(148) or home to the top left and move down M lines:

```
200   PRINT CHR$(19);: FOR I=1 TO M : PRINT : NEXT I
```

The following program draws a box of side K and L:

```
10   REM DRAWS A BOX OF THE PET
```

```
20    INPUT "GIVE SIDES K AND L";K,L
30    PRINT CHR$(147)                    :REM CLEARS SCREEN
40    PRINT "⌐";
50    FOR I=1 TO K : PRINT "–"; : NEXT I
60    A$=CHR$(157)+CHR$(17)              :REM LEFT,DOWN
70    PRINT "⌐";A$;
80    FOR I=1 TO L : PRINT "1";A$; : NEXT I
90    A$=CHR$(157)+CHR$(157)             :REM LEFT, LEFT
100   PRINT "⌐";A$;
110   FOR I=1 TO K : PRINT "–";A$; : NEXT I
120   A$=CHR$(157)+CHR$(148)             :REM LEFT,UP
130   PRINT "L";A$;
140   FOR I=1 TO L : PRINT "1";A$; : NEXT I
150   END
```

It does look a rather solid program and illustrates the disadvantage of packing too much on each line. Here it has been done to give each line a logical function. Line 40 prints the top left corner, line 50 prints the top of the box, line 70 prints the top right corner, and line 80 prints the right vertical side.

The PET has a special feature which allows these cursor functions to be visually put into a character string. Thus:

PRINT "–■ I■ I";

is the same as

PRINT "–";CHR$(157);CHR$(157);

because ■ I is the representation, within a string only, of pressing the cursor left key, which is the same as CHR$(157). PET users will no doubt be aware of this feature as these strange characters appear quite unexpectedly when trying to correct errors in a string.

Systems which enhance the PRINT statement either provide:

PRINT AT line, column; output list

where line and column are numbers or expressions which locate any character position on the screen, or:

PRINT @ N, output list

where N is a number or expression giving a screen location. In the latter case these locations are usually character positions numbered consecutively from top left to bottom right. The following example applies to the Sinclair ZX81 which uses the PRINT AT format and draws a box as in the above program:

```
10    REM SINCLAIR DEMO BOX
20    PRINT "GIVE SIDES OF BOX K AND L"
30    INPUT K
40    INPUT L
50    CLS
60    PRINT AT 2,10;CHR$(135)
70    PRINT AT 2,11+K;CHR$(4)
80    FOR I=1 TO K
90        PRINT AT 2,10+I;CHR$(131)
100       PRINT AT 3+L,10+I;CHR$(3)
110   NEXT I
120   PRINT AT 3+L,11+K;CHR$(1)
130   PRINT AT 3+L,10 ;CHR$(2)
140   FOR I=1 TO L
150       PRINT AT 2+I,11+K;CHR$(5)
160       PRINT AT 2+I,10 ;CHR$(133)
170   NEXT I
180   REM PUT IN A FLASHING SIGN AT BOX CENTRE
190   LET X=2+K/2
200   LET Y=10+L/2
210   PRINT AT X,Y;"OK"
220   GOSUB 260
230   PRINT AT X,Y;CHR$(180);CHR$(176)
240   GOSUB 260
250   GOTO 210
260   REM SUBROUTINE FOR DELAY
270   FOR I=1 TO 10
```

```
280   NEXT I
290   RETURN
300   END
```

The bottom and top of the box are drawn in the same loop between lines 80 and 110, as are the sides of the box from the loop between lines 140 and 170, and the bottom corners are set on lines 120 and 130. Added to the box drawing, based on the top left corner located at line 2 column 10, is the flashing sign at the centre of the box. This uses the inverse video characters for OK which are CHR$(180) and CAR$(176) in the Sinclair system. The subroutine regulates the flashing speed. With care, reasonable animation is possible.

Once quite complicated objects are drawn or moved around the screen it is vital to use some sort of easy way of referring to them. The pure PRINT system (without AT or @) allows a complete object such as an outline of a chess piece to be described in a single string using cursor control via CHR$( ) functions. Thus construct strings containing complete objects, and during the program place the cursor in the execution position and merely PRINT the string to obtain the object. A similar string can be constructed to delete an object, so that moving an object becomes the matter of a few PRINT statements. The PRINT AT system is quite different and approximates to the PLOT system in many ways. A series of PRINT AT instructions will be needed to define an object, so these are best grouped together as a function or subroutine with some general input parameters to give the position of the object.

Thus in the spirit of program modularity distance yourself from the messy details of drawing objects by packaging them in strings or program blocks. They can then be used in a very convenient high level manner which is reflected in a clean program design.

Some microprocessor computers map the VDU display in a direct manner to an area of the computer store so that each byte of store is one character position on the VDU. A change in any of these bytes of store immediately alters the corresponding character on the screen. For example, the PET screen consists of 25 rows of 40 columns, a total of 1000 character positions which map onto store locations 32768 to 33767. The transportation from rows and columns to store location is:

$$\text{Store address} = 32768 + (\text{column} - 1) + 40 * (\text{row} - 1)$$

The following program will thus produce a character of value X at position C column and R row:

```
10   INPUT C,R,X
20   POKE (32768+C-1+40*(R-1)),X
```

POKEing the screen display in this way is much faster than PRINTing to it, but should be used with care. See the comment in the introduction to PEEK and POKE in Section 6.5.1.

6.6.2 Plotting

The plotting features provided in BASIC are still some way short of a full graphics package, but have similar characteristics. Plotting is provided by functions such as PLOT, MOVE, DRAW, and similar, which operate at a better definition than character level and allow fractional parts of a character, or tiny portions (dots), on the screen to be switched on or off. Colour may also be available.

Plotting has underlying it the concept of a pen moving over a surface and making a mark on it. So if the current position has cartesian coordinates (XØ,YØ) then a call to DRAW X1,Y1 will move the 'pen' to the new position (X1,Y1) while drawing a straight line. The essential 'primitives' of plotting are:

(a) Make a mark (dot) at the current position.
(b) Move without making any marks to position X,Y.
(c) Move while drawing a straight line to position X,Y.
(d) Draw some special symbol at X,Y.

The last action (d) is not essential, but (a), (b), and (c) are required for a complete system. However, if necessary, you can manage with (a) and (b) and use repeated application of (a) to draw a straight line. It is not as easy as it seems to draw an inclined line using a series of dots or shapes. A quite complicated algorithm is required to give the best approximation to a straight line, which is perhaps why this feature is absent from some systems.

The alternative is to consider drawing as a 'brick building' action, which equates it to the same actions as described for PRINT in Section 6.6.1. This sees diagrams as built up from a series of dots or symbols in an arbitrary manner. There is no concept of a smoothly drawn line or a 'pen' moving. In this case build up subroutines or functions to define graphic objects and use them as described in that PRINT section.

The Sinclair ZX81 is an example of a system which provides the simplest features for plotting and can be used in either manner as described below. Each usual VDU screen character position is regarded as a square which is divided into quarters, as:

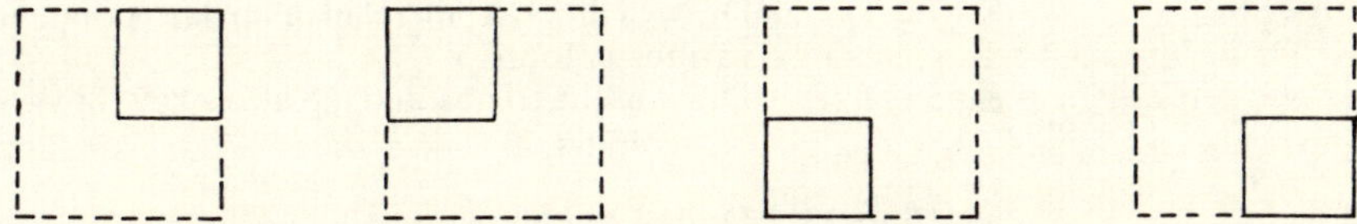

which may be switched on separately by a call to:

PLOT X,Y

and switched off by a call to:

UNPLOT X,Y

Since there are 22 lines of 32 columns of characters the plotting range of Y (up from base) is Ø to 43, and the range of X (across from left) is Ø to 63. Subroutines to provide the move and draw actions may be defined from the basic PLOT and UNPLOT statements.

The BBC system is an example of one which provides a whole range of proper plotting facilities. There are five different graphic modes that can be selected which differ in definition and colours available, but all are based on a cartesian coordinate system with origin at the bottom left and 128Ø units wide (the X coordinate) by 1Ø24 units high (the Y coordinate). Table 6.10 gives the actions of the various statements and functions.

Table 6.1Ø BBC BASIC graphic features

Graphic statement or function	Action
MODE N	Sets one of eight possible screen modes for N=Ø to 7, but only N=Ø,1,2,4,5 provides graphics.
VDU list of values	Complex control over graphics, colours display area, cursor control, e.g. VDU 22,N is equivalent to MODE N.
GCOL N,M	Sets graphics foreground colours or background colours and actions. When N=Ø the value of M is the plotting colour: M is Ø to 15 foreground colour. M is 128 to 143 background colour.
CLG	Clears graphics area of the screen to current background colour and homes cursor to (Ø,Ø).
PLOT K,X,Y	Can function in many ways depending on the value of K: K=Ø Move (X,Y) relative to last point. K=4 Move to absolute position X,Y. K=1,2,3 Draw a line (X,Y) relative to last point, in various colours. K=5,6,7 Draw a line to absolute position X,Y, in various colours. K=16 to 23 Dotted line drawn. K=64 to 71 One point is plotted. K=8Ø to 87 A triangle is drawn between (X,Y) and last two points used.

DRAW X,Y	Action as PLOT 5,X,Y.
MOVE X,Y	Action as PLOT 4,X,Y

The BBC system provides three types of statement. Set up facilities using MODE or the more complex VDU, basic colour and screen initialization using GCOL and CLG, and full plotting via PLOT of which DRAW and MOVE may be regarded as special cases. Future extensions to PLOT may include curve drawing.

The BBC commands COLOUR and CLS are equivalent to GCOL and CLG, but act in the text mode only.

The following simple program draws a triangle to illustrate the use of these instructions:

```
10    REM BBC PLOT TRIANGLES

20    REM INITIALIZE VALUES

30    ANGLE=2.094395              :REM 120 DEGREES

40    CENTREX=640                 :REM TRIANGLE CENTRE

50    CENTREY=512

60    R=400                       :REM RADIUS CIRCUM-
                                        SCRIBED CIRCLE

70    REM PLOT INITIALIZE

80    MODE 5

90    GCOL 0,129                  :REM RED BACKGROUND

100   GCOL 0,2                    :REM YELLOW LINES

110   CLG                         :REM CLEAR SCREEN

120   REM

130   FOR THETA=0 TO 2 STEP .1 :REM ROTATE TRIANGLE

140     X0=CENTREX+R*COS(THETA)

150     Y0=CENTREY+R*SIN(THETA)

160     MOVE X0,Y0

170     X=CENTREX+R*COS(THETA+ANGLE)

180     Y=CENTREY+R*SIN(THETA+ANGLE)

190     DRAW X,Y

200     X=CENTREX+R*COS(THETA+2*ANGLE)
```

246

```
21Ø     Y=CENTREY+R*SIN(THETA+2*ANGLE)

22Ø     DRAW X,Y

23Ø     DRAW XØ,YØ

24Ø   NEXT THETA

25Ø   END
```

6.7 WHITHER BASIC

Not all BASICs have the extensions described in the earlier parts of this chapter. What seems to happen is that as new computer systems appear on the market the corresponding BASIC system is slightly more extended than its rivals. So, over a period of years the language has grown because the early extensions have been accepted by most compiler writers as standard to the language. While many of these extensions have identical aims their notation varies considerably. There is in fact a MINIMAL BASIC standard drafted by the American National Standards Institute in 1976 and adopted in 1978 as Standard ECMA–55 by the European Computer Manufacturers Association and a recent (1982) ANSI standard which covers advanced features.

Extensions to BASIC seem to be produced in an erratic manner. Thus Microsoft BASIC has only WHILE–WEND loops and BBC BASIC has only REPEAT–UNTIL loops. The compiler writers really should speak to some users of their systems and they would find a demand for both types of loop structure. Putting in both types of loop would only cost a few more bytes of store for the compiler/interpreter and make it run slightly slower. Microsoft have evidently decided on WHILE–WEND because, like their FOR–NEXT loop, it tests at the beginning and is thus a very similar structure for the compiler/interpreter to handle; similarly, BBC test their FOR–NEXT loop at the end so REPEAT–UNTIL fits in conveniently.

COMAL strikes a welcome note of reason in the developments of BASIC. It was designed in 1974 as an extension to BASIC by B. Christensen and B. Lofstedt of Denmark. A standard, COMAL 8Ø, is now being finalized. The extensions to BASIC were many and were designed to reflect up-to-date ideas in programming languages and structured design methods. It is an excellent development and some of its features are sketched out in the following section. However, in recent years a number of good computer languages have been produced which are now little used—not because of any inbuilt faults, but merely because they were not taken up by the large computer manufacturers. It is to be hoped that COMAL does not suffer this fate. Consult *Structured Programming with COMAL* by Roy Atherton (Ellis Horwood, 1982) for further details of this excellent language.

6.7.1 General features

COMAL developed as a set of extensions to a standard BASIC. It includes the standard control structures found in Algol-like languages such as PASCAL, but is modified to simple forms to fit in with BASIC's style of layout.

Program action statements like most of those in BASIC must be contained on one line, but this does not include the control structures IF, CASE, FOR, WHILE, REPEAT, and procedure blocks. This frees the programmer from the irksome problems encountered in BASIC.

The distinction in COMAL is clear and easy to learn; simple statements such as assignment must be completely on one line, while the extended statements may be on several lines. Program layout may be designed to visually demonstrate its structure and system forced indenting is a great help towards this aim.

All the usual statements familiar in BASIC with essentially the same actions are present: INPUT, READ, DATA, RESTORE, PRINT, PRINT USING, IF–THEN, DIM, STOP, END. But the GOTO statement takes a label that is a name, rather than a statement number. The program statements are given line numbers to indicate execution order and to assist in editing the program, but these line numbers do not mean that these statements can be 'jumped to' as in BASIC. Only labelled statements, hopefully few, may be 'jumped to' using the COMAL form of GOTO. Thus for most practical purposes the GOTO statement becomes irrelevant.

Taken as a whole COMAL provides an appearance of consistency, which is one attribute not possessed by any BASIC.

6.7.2 Control Structures

The familiar FOR–NEXT loop is included in its usual form but with the inclusion of the word DO to indicate the block nature of the loop. For example:

```
FOR LOOP=1 TO 1Ø STEP 2 DO


      . Statements
      .

NEXT LOOP
```

and also in a one-line version, without a NEXT:

```
FOR CNT=1 TO 1ØØ DO S=S+1Ø
```

There are both WHILE and REPEAT loops, examples being:

```
WHILE A>Ø DO
   .
   . Statements
   .

ENDWHILE
```

248

and

    REPEAT

      .

      . Statements

      .

    UNTIL A>BOTTOM

and there is a one-line version of the WHILE loop similar to the FOR:

    WHILE (NOT A=B) DO A=A+C

There is a proper CASE statement rather better formed than the ON–GOTO statement in BASIC; it allows a choice of statement to be selected on matching complicated expressions and includes an OTHERWISE option. In addition, to once again emphasize the block nature of this statement there is an ENDCASE terminating part.

The standard IF–THEN statement is provided together with an IF–THEN–ELSE version, which like all the other control statements has a proper terminator ENDIF. Thus:

    IF (A>B AND C=O) THEN

      .

      . Statements

      .

    ELSE

      .

      . Statements

      .

    ENDIF

which provides a clear and unambiguous form.

6.7.3 Procedures

Procedures have names and may take as input any number of parameters. The procedure may act as a subroutine or a function, the only difference being the way it is called, and when used as a function the name must be assigned a value inside the procedure. A subroutine call may be made using the word EXEC, thus:

    20   EXEC BUFFEROUT(A,B)

and as a function by using the name in an arithmetic expression in the usual way:

    100   DUMMY=LIMIT+MAX(A,B,C)

where MAX is a procedure returning a value. It could have a structure:

    200   PROC MAX(REF X,REF Y,REF Z)

    210   MAX=X

    220   IF Y>MAX THEN MAX=Y

    230   IF Z>MAX THEN MAX=Z

    240   ENDPROC MAX

Notice the REF indication with the formal parameters X,Y,Z; this indicates that the call is by reference to A,B,C. This means that the actual variables A,B,C are used when X,Y,Z are manipulated within the subroutine and that any changes made in X,Y,Z are automatically changes in A,B,C, which can thus be used both as input and output to the procedure if required. Arrays are called by reference also; only simple string or arithmetic expressions are called by value, which is an input only transfer of the value into a temporary variable in the procedure. There is no means of returning values in this case. (Programmers familiar with FORTRAN may protest that it manages to return values in a call-by-value setup for subroutines. It does, but in a peculiar way and at great risk of corruption to program constants and instructions, which is altogether quite unsatisfactory.)

COMAL thus provides very useful procedure blocks with a correct and strict approach to parameter matching (between real parameters and dummy parameters).

7
Matrix handling

This chapter deals with two-dimensional arrays known as *matrices*. Matrix algebra also deals with one-dimensional arrays which are known as *vectors*.

The dimensions of all vectors and matrices should be declared in a DIM statement before they are used (see Section 4.1.1). Consult also Section 4.1.2 on the base limits of arrays before proceeding, as the matrix functions work on array elements which have non-zero subscripts.

Many microcomputer BASICs do not provide the matrix functions described here, so the actions of these functions are also given in groups of BASIC statements. However, such operations will proceed very slowly when written explicitly in BASIC, especially for large matrices (greater than $10*10$ elements). Thus if speed is a problem you should write the appropriate instructions in machine language and use the CALL facility provided in many BASICs to enter the machine code procedure. It may be possible to purchase a set of these routines for your computer.

7.1 DIMENSIONING

DIM A(2) may be regarded as a vector:

$$(a_1 \ a_2 \ a_3) \quad \text{or} \quad \begin{pmatrix} a_1 \\ a_2 \\ a_3 \end{pmatrix}$$

It depends on how it is used in the matrix multiplication statement as to whether it is taken to be a row vector or a column vector. The system does not distinguish the two types of vector.

DIM B(3, 4) may be regarded as a $3*4$ matrix:

$$\begin{pmatrix} b_{11} & b_{12} & b_{13} & b_{14} \\ b_{21} & b_{22} & b_{23} & b_{24} \\ b_{31} & b_{32} & b_{33} & b_{34} \end{pmatrix}$$

The first index, 3 above, gives the number of rows and the second index, 4 above, gives the number of columns. The correspondence is taken as b_{IJ} in algebraic notation becomes B(I,J) in BASIC notation.

Some systems operate an automatic re-dimensioning system. Although the number of elements in a matrix cannot be changed once the matrix has been declared in a DIM statement the bounds may be altered. For example, B(3,4) above has 12 elements and could be used as B(2,5) which has 10 elements or

B(4,3) which has 12 elements. Either the matrix initialization statements allow the new bounds to be explicitly declared or the bounds are changed as a result of a matrix operation such as multiplication, addition, or inversion. Check in your system handbook to see if this re-dimensioning is operated.

7.2 MATRIX VALUES

7.2.1 Input and output for matrices

Section 4.1.6 discussed fully the use of the MAT INPUT and MAT PRINT statements as they are very useful outside the area of matrix algebra.

<table>
<tr><td colspan="2" align="center">MAT INPUT statement</td></tr>
<tr><td>General form</td><td>MAT INPUT matrix</td></tr>
<tr><td></td><td>where 'matrix' is the name (no brackets or subscripts) of a one-dimensional or two-dimensional array.</td></tr>
</table>

The system will give a prompt, like a ?, for the data which may be typed in separated by commas. If insufficient data have been given on one line further prompts will be given. Excess data are ignored. The usual convention for matrices is for data input to elements with the second subscript varying fastest, i.e. *INPUT BY ROWS*.

Some systems allow a list of matrices and vectors to be input with the names separated by commas. At least one system uses the word READ instead of INPUT for this statement.

The form of BASIC to imitate the MAT INPUT A is:

```
1Ø   DIM A(25)
2Ø   FOR I=1 TO 25
3Ø     INPUT A(I),          }  MAT INPUT A
4Ø   NEXT I
```

For the BBC system omit the comma on line 3Ø.

Some systems provide a MAT LINPUT for string matrices and vectors which works in the same way as LINPUT described in Section 4.2.4.

<table>
<tr><td colspan="2" align="center">MAT READ statement</td></tr>
<tr><td>General form</td><td>MAT READ matrix</td></tr>
<tr><td></td><td>where 'matrix' is the name of a one-dimensional or two-dimensional array.</td></tr>
<tr><td colspan="2">Action as with MAT INPUT, but this statement takes its values from DATA statements.</td></tr>
</table>

Refer to Section 4.4 for a description of the standard READ DATA statements.

<table>
<tr><td colspan="2" align="center">MAT PRINT statement</td></tr>
<tr><td>General form</td><td>MAT PRINT list of matrices</td></tr>
<tr><td></td><td>where 'list of matrices' is one or many matrices separated by commas or semi-colons.</td></tr>
<tr><td colspan="2">The matrices are printed out row by row; all the rows of one matrix are output before printing the next. A vector in the list or at the end of the list followed by a separator will be printed as a single row. If a vector at the end of the list is not followed by a separator the vector will be printed as a single column.</td></tr>
<tr><td colspan="2">If a semicolon is used as a separator instead of a comma then the elements of each row will be printed close together.</td></tr>
</table>

The printing control via separators works in the same way as in the standard PRINT statement. Here is the usual BASIC equivalent of MAT PRINT A,B :

```
10    DIM A(3,3), B(4)     ⎤
20    FOR I=1 TO 3         ⎥
30      FOR J=1 TO 3       ⎥
40        PRINT A(I,J),    ⎥
50      NEXT J             ⎥
60      PRINT              ⎬  MAT PRINT A,B
70    NEXT I               ⎥
80    FOR I=1 TO 4         ⎥
90      PRINT B(I)         ⎥
100   NEXT I               ⎥
110   PRINT                ⎦
```

7.2.2 Matrix initialization

Several statements are provided which set all the elements of the matrix to the same value, zero or one, or just the diagonal elements of a square matrix to one. By subsequent scaler multiplication (see Section 7.3.1) all the elements which have been set to unity can be given any desired value.

<table>
<tr><td colspan="2" align="center">Matrix initialization statements</td></tr>
<tr><td>General forms</td><td>MAT matrix = CON
MAT matrix = ZER
MAT matrix = IDN

where 'matrix' is the name of a matrix or vector. Note square matrix only in the case of IDN.</td></tr>
</table>

CON sets all the elements of the matrix or vector to one; ZER sets them all to zero. Square matrices may be initialized with IDN which sets the elements on the diagonal (from top left to bottom right) equal to one and the others equal to zero.

Some systems allow explicit re-dimensioning limits to be indicated in brackets after CON, ZER, and IDN. Thus:

$$MAT\ A = CON\ (6)$$

$$MAT\ B = ZER\ (4,3)$$

sets the matrix A to a vector of size 6, and the matrix B to size 4×3.

CON and ZER may be expanded in BASIC as nested FOR loops, e.g. MAT A=ZER is:

```
10   DIM A(4,3)
20   FOR I=1 TO 4
30     FOR J=1 TO 3           }  MAT A=ZER
40       A(I,J)=0
50     NEXT J
60   NEXT I
```

The IDN applies to square matrices as MAT A=IDN:

```
10   DIM A(6,6)

20   FOR I=1 TO 6

30      A(I,I)=1

40      FOR J=I+1 TO 6

50         A(I,J)=0

60         A(J,I)=0

70      NEXT J

80   NEXT I
```

MAT A=IDN

provided the FOR loop test is made at the start of the loop. If your BASIC does not do this, use a pair of nested loops as in the CON and ZER example above and add line 45 as:

```
45   IF I=J THEN A(I,I)=1
```

Note that the following is the 4×4 identity matrix:

$$
\begin{pmatrix}
1 & 0 & 0 & 0 \\
0 & 1 & 0 & 0 \\
0 & 0 & 1 & 0 \\
0 & 0 & 0 & 1
\end{pmatrix}
$$

7.3 MATRIX ALGEBRA

All the fundamental matrix operations are provided by the MAT statements.

7.3.1 Matrix arithmetic

Unlike ordinary arithmetic operations complicated expressions cannot be made up. Each line will contain one matrix on the left of the assignment ($=$) sign and either one or two matrices on the right of it, depending on the type of operation. Both matrices and vectors may be used in MAT statements. Table 7.1 summarizes the available forms of the arithmetic statements.

Statement	Action	Comment
MAT A=B	Copies elements of B to A.	A may be redimensioned to the size of B.
MAT A=B+C	Adds the elements of B and C and copies the results to A.	B and C must be the same size.

MAT A=B–C	Subtracts the elements of C from B and copies the results to A.	B and C must be the same size.
MAT A=(k)*B	Multiplies each element of B by the scaler value k and copies the results to A.	The brackets are usually mandatory.
MAT A=B*C	Multiplies the elements of B and C together according to the rules of matrix algebra.	The number of columns of B must equal the number of rows of C.

Table 7.1 Matrix arithmetic. A, B, and C may be vectors or matrices. k is a simple variable, expression, or constant

The copy, or replacement, statement MAT A=B assigns the values of the elements B(I,J) to the corresponding elements A(I,J). Some systems will alter the dimensions of A to match those of B. The equivalent program is:

```
10   DIM A(3,4),B(3,4)
20   FOR I=1 TO 3
30     FOR J=1 TO 4
40       A(I,J)=B(I,J)
50     NEXT J
60   NEXT I
```

MAT A=B

The addition and subtraction statements, MAT A=B+C and MAT A=B–C, require that B and C are the same size and set all the elements A(I,J) to B(I,J)+ C(I,J) and B(I,J)–C(I,J) respectively.

The program for addition is:

```
10   DIM A(4,3), B(4,3), C(4,3)
20   FOR I=1 TO 4
30     FOR J=1 TO 3
40       A(I,J)=B(I,J)+C(I,J)
50     NEXT J
60   NEXT I
```

MAT A=B+C

For all these arithmetic functions the assignment may cause the size of A to be adjusted.

By scaler multiplication each element of the matrix is multiplied by the scaler value. Thus:

MAT A=(22.5)*B

causes each element A(I,J) to be given the value 22.5*B(I,J). Some systems require the brackets round the scaler part; on others it is optional but recommended to avoid confusion with the matrix multiplication. Other examples of scaler multiplication are:

MAT A=(X)*B

MAT A=(SQR(T)+Y(Z))*B

An equivalent program to MAT A=(22.5)*B is:

```
10   DIM A(4,3),B(4,3)
20   FOR I=1 TO 4
30     FOR J=1 TO 3
40        A(I,J)=22.5*B(I,J)
50     NEXT J
60   NEXT I
```

$$\left.\right\}\quad \text{MAT A=(22.5)*B}$$

Matrix multiplication is more complicated. The expression for the elements of MAT A=B*C is:

A(I,J)=B(I,1)*C(1,J)+B(I,2)*C(2,J)+ . . . +B(I,M)*C(M,J)

$$= \sum_{K=1}^{M} B(I,K)*C(K,J)$$

= vector product of the Ith row of B with the Jth column of C

Matrices B and C need not be square matrices or even the same sizes as long as the number of columns of B is equal to the number of rows of C. This is expressed in the formula for sizes as:

$$\text{Sizes} \quad \begin{array}{ccccc} A & = & B & * & C \\ (L*N) & & (L*M) & & (M*N) \end{array}$$

B and C may be vectors or matrices and A will be given the appropriate result.
Thus:

$$\begin{pmatrix} 15 \\ 33 \end{pmatrix} = \begin{pmatrix} 1 & 2 & 3 \\ 4 & 5 & 6 \end{pmatrix} \begin{pmatrix} -1 \\ 5 \\ 2 \end{pmatrix}$$

Sizes   2*1   2*3   3*1

$$\begin{pmatrix} -4 & -2 & \emptyset \\ 33 & 45 & 57 \\ 13 & 23 & 33 \end{pmatrix} = \begin{pmatrix} 4 & -2 \\ 5 & 7 \\ 9 & 1 \end{pmatrix} \begin{pmatrix} 1 & 2 & 3 \\ 4 & 5 & 6 \end{pmatrix}$$

Sizes   3*3   3*2   2*3

The following indicates some valid combinations (values have been given to
the matrices prior to use):

```
10   DIM A(2,2), B(2,3), C(3,2), D(3), E(2)
         .
         .
         .
         .
100   MAT A=B*C
110   MAT E=B*D
120   MAT E=D*C
130   MAT D=E*B
140   MAT D=C*E
```

On line 110 vector D takes on size 3*1 which is a column vector and the result in
vector E is size 2*1 which is a column vector, but on line 120 vector D takes on
size 1*3 which is a row vector and the result in vector E is size 1*2 which is a row
vector. As remarked earlier, the system does not distinguish the two forms of
vector. The following program is an example of matrix multiplication:

```
 10   DIM A(3,5), B(3,8), C(8,5)
 20   FOR I=1 TO 3
 30     FOR J=1 TO 5
 40       S=0.0
 50       FOR K=1 TO 8
 60         S=S+B(I,K)*C(K,J)
 70       NEXT K
 80       A(I,J)=S
 90     NEXT J
100   NEXT I
```

MAT A=B*C

Complicated operations, such as:

```
10   MAT A=(3)*B+C-D
```

are invalid in one statement and need expansion to give a series of statements:

```
10   MAT A=(3)*B
20   MAT A=A+C
30   MAT A=A-D
```

Note that division of matrices is not defined; the appropriate action may be obtained by multiplying by the inverse.

The same matrix cannot appear on both sides of the = sign in a multiply or transpose operation, probably because of the extra temporary store space which would be needed. Thus:

```
MAT A=A*A
MAT A=A*B
MAT A=TRN(A)
```

are invalid, whereas the following are allowed:

```
MAT B=A*A
MAT C=C+A
MAT D=B-D
```

260

7.3.2 Matrix operations

The other matrix operations generally available are inversion and transposition. When the system provides automatic re-dimensioning it should provide some means of obtaining the current working limits of the arrays. For example, the ICL 2903/4 system provides two functions; ROW(A) gives the limit of the first index of A and COL(A) gives the limit of the second index of A.

The transpose of a matrix is a new matrix with the rows and columns of the original interchanged. If the original matrix A has size N*M then the transpose of A is called A$'$ and has size M*N. For all values of I and J the equality $a_{IJ} = a'_{JI}$ is true. In BASIC the statement:

$$\text{MAT A=TRN (B)}$$

causes the elements B(I,J) to be copied to A(J,I). Thus:

$$A = \begin{pmatrix} 1 & 4 \\ 2 & 5 \\ 3 & 6 \end{pmatrix} \text{ is the transpose of } B = \begin{pmatrix} 1 & 2 & 3 \\ 4 & 5 & 6 \end{pmatrix}$$

The BASIC program corresponding to MAT A=TRN(B) is:

```
10   DIM A(3,2), B(2,3)
20   FOR I=1 TO 2
30      FOR J=1 TO 3
40         A(J,I)=B(I,J)              MAT A=TRN (B)

50      NEXT J
60   NEXT I
```

Inversion can only be performed on square matrices. If A and B are square matrices and I is the identity matrix such that:

$$A*B=B*A=I$$

then B is the inverse of A and is written $B=A^{-1}$ and A is the inverse of B and is written $A=B^{-1}$. Thus:

$$\begin{pmatrix} 1 & 2 & 3 \\ 1 & 3 & 3 \\ 1 & 2 & 4 \end{pmatrix} \begin{pmatrix} 6 & -2 & -3 \\ -1 & 1 & 0 \\ -1 & 0 & 1 \end{pmatrix} = \begin{pmatrix} 1 & 0 & 0 \\ 0 & 1 & 0 \\ 0 & 0 & 1 \end{pmatrix}$$

Each matrix on the left-hand side is the inverse of the other. Not all square matrices have inverses; those which do not are called singular. In BASIC the statement:

    MAT A=INV (B)

will assign the inverse of B to A (i.e. $A=B^{-1}$).

The formal way of calculating the inverse is to take the adjoint matrix and divide it by the determinant of the matrix. This is not an acceptable practical method. Numerical errors generated mainly by the truncation of values due to the limited accuracy provided by BASIC (to six or seven significant figures) should always be a consideration when using matrices, as apparently simple operations such as inversion may involve many thousands of simple arithmetic operations each of which may contribute some error value. With this in mind the best method of obtaining the inverse X of a matrix A is to solve the set of linear equations:

    A*X=I

There are many methods for solving such sets of equations which are efficient, stable, and designed to minimize numerical errors. Use one of these methods if you wish to compute the inverse of a matrix but do not have the inversion statement. A simple method is presented in Section 7.5.

7.4 MATRIX EXAMPLES

The following program illustrates some of the simple MAT statements, particularly input, output, and arithmetic statements:

```
10    REM SIMPLE MATRIX EXAMPLE
20    DIM A(4,4), B(3,3), C(3,3)
30    REM
40    MAT INPUT B,C
50    PRINT "MATRIX B"
60    MAT PRINT B
70    PRINT "MATRIX C"
80    MAT PRINT C
90    REM
100   MAT A=B+C
110   PRINT "MATRIX A=B+C"
```

```
120   MAT PRINT A
130   REM
140   MAT A=B-C
150   PRINT "MATRIX A=B-C"
160   MAT PRINT A
170   END
RUN
? 1,2,3
? 4,5,6,7,8
? 9,10,11,12,13
? 14,15
? 16,17,18
```

MATRIX B

1	2	3
4	5	6
7	8	9

MATRIX C

10	11	12
13	14	15
16	17	18

MATRIX A=B+C

11	13	15
17	19	21
23	25	27

MATRIX A=B-C

-9	-9	-9
-9	-9	-9
-9	-9	-9

END AT LINE 170

There can be a tendency to regard matrices rather like ordinary variables, particularly when it comes to simple arithmetic. For example, the algebraic expansion of $(a-b)^2$ is $a^2-2ab+b^2$ where a and b are scaler quantities. It is *not* true in general that $(A-B)^2$ is $A^2-2AB+B^2$ where A and B are matrices. But in the special case of B being the identity matrix I, it is true that $(A-I)^2=A^2-2A+I$, where $AI=IA=A$ and $I^2=I$. The following program demonstrates this equality for specific examples of A:

```
10    REM ILLUSTRATES MATRIX MANIPULATION

20    REM COMPUTES (A-I)**2 AND COMPARES

30    REM IT WITH A**2-2*A+I

40    DIM A(20,20), B(20,20), C(20,20)

50    REM USE REDIMENSIONING (IF AVAILABLE)

60    REM READ IN SIZE OF MATRICES.

70    READ N

80    REM SET SIZE VIA ZER STATEMENT

90    MAT A=ZER (N,N)

100   REM READ IN A SIZE N*N MATRIX FROM DATA

110   MAT READ A

120   REM FORM IDN IN B, USE REDIMENSIONING

130   MAT B=IDN (N,N)

140   REM FORM (A-I), C GETS SIZE FROM A AND B

150   MAT C=A-B

160   REM FORM (A-I)**2

170   MAT B=C*C

180   PRINT "MATRIX (A-I)**2"

190   PRINT "- - - - - - - -"

200   MAT PRINT B;

210   PRINT

220   MAT B=IDN (N,N)

230   REM (REUSE C) FORM A*A IN C.

240   MAT C=A*A

250   REM FORM A**2+I IN C
```

```
260   MAT C=C+B
270   REM FORM 2*A IN A
280   MAT A=(2)*A
290   REM FORM A**2-2*A+I IN C
300   MAT C=C-A
310   PRINT "MATRIX A**2-2*A+I"
320   PRINT "- - - - - - - - -"
330   MAT PRINT C;
340   PRINT
350   DATA 4
360   DATA 1,3,7,3,1,4,1,5,5,2,6,1,3,4,9,1
370   END
RUN
```

MATRIX (A–I)**2

- - - - - - - - - -

47	35	65	22
23	34	60	19
30	35	71	30
49	39	70	38

MATRIX A**2-2A+I

- - - - - - - - - - - -

47	35	65	22
23	34	64	19
30	35	71	30
49	39	74	38

END AT LINE 370

If your system does not have the re-dimensioning facility, set the array sizes to (4,4) and omit lines 60, 70, 350 and modify lines 90, 130 to remove the (N,N) parts of the statements.

You could test the general nature of the expansion $(A+B)^2$ against $A^2+2AB+B^2$ by suitable modifications to the program.

7.5 LINEAR EQUATIONS

This section gives a complete program for the solution of the set of linear equations:

$$A\mathbf{x}=\mathbf{b}$$

that is:

$$
\begin{pmatrix}
a_{11} & a_{12} & a_{13} & \cdots & a_{1N} \\
a_{21} & a_{22} & & & \\
a_{31} & & & & \\
\vdots & & & & \\
a_{N1} & \cdots & \cdots & \cdots & a_{NN}
\end{pmatrix}
\begin{pmatrix}
x_1 \\ x_2 \\ \vdots \\ \vdots \\ x_N
\end{pmatrix}
=
\begin{pmatrix}
b_1 \\ b_2 \\ \vdots \\ \vdots \\ b_N
\end{pmatrix}
$$

by the method of Gauss with partial pivoting. This is a simple method, but the techniques of partial pivoting help to contain the numerical truncation errors and make it very useful as a general method. In addition, it provides an easy route to the calculation of the inverse of the matrix A and the calculation of the determinant of A.

If you have a specialized set of equations which are diagonally dominant, or are very numerous, or ill-conditioned, or have some special property, you should consult a book on numerical methods as there are many methods available for solving sets of linear equations.

7.5.1 Gaussian elimination

The outline of the method, which is followed by the computer program, is as follows:

(a)   Select the largest element in the first column of the matrix A.

(b)   Interchange the equation (row) containing this element with the first equation (row). This involves swapping two b elements as well as the two rows; since the order in which the equations are originally written is arbitrary this swap has no effect on the results. This action is the partial pivoting of the method. When columns are moved as well as rows the elimination is with full pivoting, but keeping track of the variables in such interchanges is difficult.

(c)   Subtract multiples of the first equation from all the other equations below it in turn to produce zeros everywhere in the first column except in the first position. The multipliers in this action are (a_{21}/a_{11}), (a_{31}/a_{11}), (a_{41}/a_{11}), and so on. The interchanges in (b) guarantees that these values are as small as possible, which helps to keep the arithmetic errors in check.

(d)   Repeat from step (a) using the second equation and column instead of the first. Continue with the other equations and columns until all the elements in the matrix A below the diagonal are zero. The matrix equations now have the form;

$$U\mathbf{x} = \mathbf{b}'$$

where U is an upper triangular matrix, i.e.:

$$\begin{pmatrix} a_{11} & a_{12} & a_{13} & \cdots & ,a_{1N} \\ \emptyset & a'_{22} & a'_{23} & \cdots & \\ \emptyset & \emptyset & a'_{33} & \cdots & \\ & & \emptyset & & \\ \emptyset & \emptyset & \emptyset & & a'_{NN} \end{pmatrix} \begin{pmatrix} x_1 \\ x_2 \\ \cdot \\ \cdot \\ \cdot \\ x_N \end{pmatrix} = \begin{pmatrix} b_1 \\ b'_2 \\ \cdot \\ \cdot \\ \cdot \\ b'_N \end{pmatrix}$$

This is easily solved by the method of back substitution.

The last equation is simply:

$$a'_{NN} \, x_N = b'_N$$

which is solved for $x_N = b'_N/a'_{NN}$. The method proceeds as follows:

(a)   Solve the last equation for x_N.

(b)   Use this value of x_N to solve the next to last equation which contains only coefficients and x_N and x_{N-1}.

(c)   Use the two values x_N and x_{N-1} to solve the next equation for x_{N-2}. Continue this process for all the other equations, working back, up to the first equation. At this point the system of equations has been solved and x_1 to x_N have been obtained.

Since each equation (row) is an independent equation it may be multiplied or divided by any arbitrary number and still remain true. Thus a direct comparison of the sizes of the coefficients in the columns of A when searching for the pivot is not necessarily the best way. Another way is to compare the size of these coefficients with the size of the other coefficients in their own equations by looking at:

$$\frac{a_{ij}}{\left(\Sigma_k a_{ik}^2\right)^{1/2}}$$

instead of a_{ij}. The subroutine on line 99Ø does this computation, and the subroutine on line 75Ø does the comparison and swapping if necessary. Try altering this subroutine to select on ordinary size only; also try removing the GOSUB from line 21Ø. This removes the partial pivoting feature and allows comparison of it in operation and not in operation. The effect is most noticeable for matrixes larger than 1Ø*1Ø.

The additional arrays C(,) and D( ) are used to hold the original values of A(,) and B( ) so that the residues of $(\mathbf{b}-A\mathbf{x})$ may be computed. They may be omitted without effecting the results, but are a very valuable guide to the accuracy of the final solution. The information on the sizes of the potential pivots and swapping is also very useful in understanding the behaviour of the system of equations being solved.

The program, named GAUSS, is given below:

```
1Ø    REM GAUSS PROGRAM WITH PARTIAL PIVOTING
2Ø    DIM A(6,6), B(6), X(6), C(6,6), D(6)
3Ø    PRINT "SOLVES THE SYSTEM OF EQUATIONS AX=B"
4Ø    INPUT "NO. OF EQUATIONS";N
5Ø    PRINT "GIVE MATRIX A (ROW BY ROW)"
6Ø    FOR I=1 TO N
7Ø      FOR J=1 TO N
8Ø        INPUT A(I,J),
9Ø        C(I,J)=A(I,J)
1ØØ     NEXT J
11Ø   NEXT I
12Ø   PRINT "GIVE VECTOR B"
13Ø   FOR I=1 TO N
14Ø     INPUT B(I),
15Ø     D(I)=B(I)
```

```
160   NEXT I
170   REM -----SOLVE EQUATIONS---------
180   M=0
190   N1=N-1
200   FOR I=1 TO N1
210     GOSUB 750
220     I1=I+1
230     FOR J=I1 TO N
240       P=A(J,I)/A(I,I)
250       PRINT "MULTIPLIER FOR ROW";J;"COL";I;"IS";P
260       FOR K=I1 TO N
270         A(J,K)=A(J,K)-P*A(I,K)
280       NEXT K
290       A(J,I)=0
300       B(J)=B(J)-P*B(I)
310     NEXT J
320   NEXT I
330   REM ------BACK SUBSTITUTE-----
340   X(N)=B(N)/A(N,N)
350   I=N
360     I=I-1
370     I1=I+1
380     S=0
390     FOR J=I1 TO N
400       S=S+A(I,J)*X(J)
410     NEXT J
420     X(I)=(B(I)-S)/A(I,I)
430   IF I>1 THEN 360
440   REM ++++ PRINT RESULTS ++++
450   PRINT
460   PRINT "ELIMINATED MATRIX"
```

```
470   PRINT
480   FOR I=1 TO N
490     FOR J=1 TO N
500       PRINT TAB(12*(J-1));A(I,J);
510     NEXT J
520     PRINT
530   NEXT I
540   PRINT
550   PRINT "NUMBER OF ROW INTERCHANGES WAS=";M
560   PRINT
570   PRINT "SOLUTION RESIDUES"
580   PRINT "X              (B-AX)"
590   FOR I=1 TO N
600     S=0
610     FOR J=1 TO N
620       S=S+C(I,J)*X(J)
630     NEXT J
640     PRINT X(I);TAB(16);D(I)-S
650   NEXT I
660   STOP
740   REM
750   REM SUBROUTINE FOR ROW INTERCHANGES
760   REM LOOKS FOR THE BEST PIVOT IN COLUMN I
770   IF I=N THEN RETURN
780   L=0
790   FOR K=I TO N
800     GOSUB 990
810     PRINT "ROW";K;"TERM";L1
820     IF L>=L1 THEN 850
830       I2=K
```

```
 840       L=L1
 850   NEXT K
 860   IF I2=I THEN RETURN
 870   M=M+1
 880   REM SWAP I2 AND I ROWS
 890   PRINT "SWAPPING ROWS";I2;I
 900   FOR K=I TO N
 910     S=A(I,K)
 920     A(I,K)=A(I2,K)
 930     A(I2,K)=S
 940   NEXT K
 950   S=B(I)
 960   B(I)=B(I2)
 970   B(I2)=S
 980   RETURN
 990   REM SUBROUTINE TO OBTAIN 'SIZE' OF TERM IN ROW K
1000   S=0
1010   FOR K1=I TO N
1020     S=S+A(K,K1)*A(K,K1)
1030   NEXT K1
1040   L1=ABS(A(K,I)/SQR(S))
1050   RETURN
1060   END
RUN
```

SOLVES THE SYSTEM OF EQUATIONS AX=B

NO. OF EQUATIONS ? 3

GIVE MATRIX A (ROW BY ROW)

?   2,   4,   3

?   1,   1,   2

?   3,   5,   2

GIVE VECTOR B

```
?    Ø,    2,    1
ROW 1 TERM .371391
ROW 2 TERM .4Ø8248
ROW 3 TERM .486664
SWAPPING ROWS 3      1
MULTIPLIER FOR ROW 2 COL 1 IS .333333
MULTIPLIER FOR ROW 3 COL 1 IS .666667
ROW 2 TERM .447214
ROW 3 TERM .371391
MULTIPLIER FOR ROW 3 COL 2 IS –1
ELIMINATED MATRIX
3            5            2
Ø           –.666667     1.33333
Ø            Ø           3
NUMBER OF ROW INTERCHANGES WAS=1
SOLUTION     RESIDUES
X            (B–AX)
 3.16667     Ø
–1.83333     Ø
  .333333    4.36557E–11
END AT LINE 66Ø
```

7.5.2 The determinant of a matrix

If this is not provided with the MAT functions on your system, one of the fastest ways of calculating the determinant of a matrix A is to reduce it to triangular form by Gauss elimination and multiply the diagonal elements of this triangular matrix together.

Adding multiples of one row of a matrix to another does not change the value of the determinant. Interchanging the rows of a matrix only changes the sign of a determinant. Thus, in terms of the elements of the eliminated matrix,

$$\text{Det}(A) = (-1)^S * a'_{11} * a'_{22} * a'_{33} * \text{------} * a'_{NN}$$

$$= (-1)^S * \prod_{i=1}^{N} a'_{ii}$$

where S is the number of row interchanges during elimination. This value is printed out at line 550 and the product may be obtained from the displayed values of the eliminated matrix or, better, calculated by adding a statement to the FOR–NEXT loop between lines 480 and 530. An example RUN is given below, assuming that the program of Section 7.5.1 was saved under the name GAUSS:

OLD GAUSS

RUN

SOLVES THE SYSTEM OF EQUATIONS AX=B

NO. OF EQUATIONS ? 4

GIVE MATRIX A (ROW BY ROW)

?	1,	4,	−2,	3
?	2,	2,	0,	4
?	3,	0,	−1,	2
?	1,	2,	2,	3

GIVE VECTOR B

| ? | 1, | 1, | 0, | 0 | (this is arbitrary for this case) |

ROW 1 TERM .182574

ROW 2 TERM .408248

ROW 3 TERM .801784

ROW 4 TERM .235702

SWAPPING ROWS 3   1

MULTIPLIER FOR ROW 2 COL 1 IS .666667

MULTIPLIER FOR ROW 3 COL 1 IS .333333

MULTIPLIER FOR ROW 4 COL 1 IS .333333

ROW 2 TERM .588348

ROW 3 TERM .812743

ROW 4 TERM .518321

SWAPPING ROWS 3   2

MULTIPLIER FOR ROW 3 COL 2 IS .5

MULTIPLIER FOR ROW 4 COL 2 IS .5

ROW 3 TERM .707107

ROW 4 TERM .938343

SWAPPING ROWS 4   3

MULTIPLIER FOR ROW 4 COL 3 IS .473684

ELIMINATED MATRIX

3	Ø	−1	2
Ø	4	−1.66667	2.33333
Ø	Ø	3.16667	1.16667
Ø	Ø	Ø	.947368

NUMBER OF ROW INTERCHANGES WAS=3

SOLUTION	RESIDUES
X	(B−AX)
−.666667	2.91Ø38E−11
−.388889	2.91Ø38E−11
−.444444	Ø
.777778	2.91Ø38E−11

END AT LINE 66Ø

The determinant is thus:

$$(-1)^3 * 3 * 4 * 3.16667 * .947368 = -36.ØØØØ22$$

The exact value is −36, so the error is the 22 in the seventh and eighth significant digits.

7.5.3 Inverting a matrix

If inversion is not provided with the MAT functions on your system, one practical way of obtaining it is to use a series of special right-hand side vectors (b) when solving a set of linear equations.

The matrix B is the inverse of the matrix A such that:

$$A*B=I$$

Now I may be considered as a set of special column vectors e_i such that:

274

$$
e_1 = \begin{pmatrix} 1 \\ \emptyset \\ . \\ . \\ . \\ \emptyset \end{pmatrix} \qquad e_2 = \begin{pmatrix} \emptyset \\ 1 \\ . \\ . \\ . \\ \emptyset \end{pmatrix} \quad \text{to} \quad e_N = \begin{pmatrix} \emptyset \\ \emptyset \\ . \\ . \\ . \\ 1 \end{pmatrix}
$$

Thus if you find a set of column vectors $\mathbf{b}_1$, $\mathbf{b}_2$ to $\mathbf{b}_N$ such that:

$$
A\mathbf{b}_1 = \mathbf{e}_1, \qquad A\mathbf{b}_2 = \mathbf{e}_2 \qquad \text{to} \qquad A\mathbf{b}_N = \mathbf{e}_N
$$

then the inverse of A is given by B, where:

$$
B = \begin{pmatrix} | & | & & | \\ b_1 & b_2 & \ldots & b_N \\ | & | & & | \end{pmatrix}
$$

There are two ways of obtaining B in practice. If you want the inverse occasionally, use program GAUSS as it is and run it N times, once for each vector e_i.

If you want inversion as an efficient feature, then modify the program to use a matrix B(,) in place of the vector B( ). Elimination is performed only once rather than N times, which means that rows of B(,) are involved instead of single values. Back substitution is performed N times, once for each column of B(,).

Taking the first approach, here is a simple example:

OLD GAUSS

RUN

SOLVES THE SYSTEM OF EQUATIONS AX=B

NO. OF EQUATIONS ? 3

GIVE MATRIX A (ROW BY ROW)

? 1,-1,2

```
? 3,0,1
? 1,0,2
GIVE VECTOR B
? 1,0,0
ROW 1 TERM .408248
ROW 2 TERM .948683
ROW 3 TERM .447214
SWAPPING ROWS 2    1
MULTIPLIER FOR ROW 2 COL 1 IS .333333
MULTIPLIER FOR ROW 3 COL 1 IS .333333
ROW 2 TERM .514496
ROW 3 TERM 0
MULTIPLIER FOR ROW 3 COL 2 IS 0
ELIMINATED MATRIX
3            0          1
0           -1          1.66667
0            0          1.66667
NUMBER OF ROW INTERCHANGES WAS=1
SOLUTION       RESIDUES
   X              (B–AX)
  0            0
 -1            0
  0            0
END AT LINE 660
```

The solution X is the first column of the inverse matrix. Now repeat for B vectors (0,1,0) and (0,0,1) to obtain (only the final part of the results are given):

```
SOLUTION       RESIDUES
   X              (B–AX)
 .4             3.63798E–12
  0            0
```

−.2	3.63798E−12

and

SOLUTION	RESIDUES
X	(B−AX)
−.2	$\emptyset$
1	$\emptyset$
.6	−1.45519E−11

respectively. Thus the inverse of the matrix:

$$\begin{pmatrix} 1 & -1 & 2 \\ 3 & \emptyset & 1 \\ 1 & \emptyset & 2 \end{pmatrix} \text{ is } \begin{pmatrix} \emptyset & 0.4 & -0.2 \\ -1 & \emptyset & 1 \\ \emptyset & -\emptyset.2 & \emptyset.6 \end{pmatrix}$$

which may be verified by multiplying them together as the result should be the identity matrix. Any deviation from this matrix will give an indication of the accuracy of the result.

Exercises

7.1 Calculate the matrix Z, such that Z=A+B+C where A,B, and C are all 4*4 matrices. Multiply the result by D, a 4*3 matrix.

7.2 This problem is designed for systems which allow re-dimensioning via the MAT statements. Dimension a matrix A to 1$\emptyset$*1$\emptyset$. Input a value of N, which is less than 1$\emptyset$, and form an N*N matrix having all the elements equal to 5. Add the N*N matrix having 5 on its diagonal and zeros elsewhere, and calculate and print the inverse.

7.3 Given a 4*4 matrix A, where:

$$A = \begin{pmatrix} 1 & 2 & -1 & 1 \\ 2 & \emptyset & 1 & 2 \\ 1 & \emptyset & 1 & 3 \\ 2 & 3 & 1 & 1 \end{pmatrix}$$

calculate and print out A^2, A^3, and A^4.

7.4   Given a 3*3 matrix A, where:

$$A = \begin{pmatrix} 2 & 1 & 3 \\ 1 & -1 & 2 \\ 1 & 2 & 1 \end{pmatrix}$$

calculate the expression $A^3-2A-9A$ and show that it is zero.

7.5   Using the program GAUSS (of Section 7.5) solve:

$$19x_1+22x_2+42x_3=25$$
$$27x_1+34x_2+56x_3=18$$
$$52x_1+41x_2+17x_3=69$$

with partial pivoting and without it. Compare the two sets of results.

7.6   Using the program GAUSS (of Section 7.5) calculate the determinant of the 3*3 matrix A, where:

$$A = \begin{pmatrix} \emptyset & 1 & -1 \\ 3 & 1 & -4 \\ 2 & 1 & 1 \end{pmatrix}$$

8
Files

Backing store of some kind is essential for any computer system. It is the medium on which the contents of the computer store, both data and programs, can be recorded magnetically and retained for long periods. There are two types of media in general use, tape and disc. Table 8.1 shows the general characteristics of the two groups. Tapes and tape units tend to be cheaper than the corresponding discs and thus provide the initial backing store for any computer configuration. This is especially true of microcomputers today and demonstrates a close historical parallel with mainframe computers over the last two decades. Initially these computers used tapes, reserving the very limited and expensive disc units for important system programs and program swapping areas. As time went on the disc units became cheaper and achieved a much higher storage capacity, so that tape was much less used. Today tapes are coming to be regarded as a back-up media for the long term retention of security copies and for the transfer of information from one computer to another. All the immediately accessible information is kept on the discs.

Table 8.1 Some characteristics of backing store media

Media	Principle computer application	Cost	Typical capacity	Comment
Tape cassette	Micro	Low	5ØK bytes	Familiar as normal Hi Fi media
Tape cartridge	Micro/mini	Medium	1ØM bytes	Data logging and professional data processing applications
Tape open reel	Mainframe	High	2ØM bytes	Large reels of half inch tape
Mini floppy disc	Micro	Moderate	3ØØK bytes	Five and a quarter inch diameter, double density, double sided
8in floppy disc	Micro/mini	Medium	1M bytes	The IBM standard, double density, double sided
Winchester fixed disc	Micro/mini	Medium	5M bytes	Eight inch diameter, more durable than floppies
Exchangeable	Mainframe	High	1ØØM bytes	Capacity up to a thousand M bytes.

Parallel developments in operating systems gave device-independent files to the programmer. This means that all types of files can be kept on the modern high density, high speed discs. For example, some files known as 'tape files' reside on disc but look like magnetic tapes to the program using them. Microcomputer operating systems are still rather minimal so that they may fit into the computer and still leave as much store space as possible for programs. Better operating systems are being developed which will soon give microcomputers most of the facilities of mainframe computers.

A *file* is the name given to a collection of data items. The collection, a file, is usually identified by a name which is given by the creator of the file. The operating system is able to associate the name with the physical location of the file so that these details are hidden from the programmer. The file may be organized in a sequential or random access manner. A *sequential* file has its items stored as a long continuous stream of data. Each of these items is obtained one at a time (i.e. in a serial way). A *random* access file has its data items stored independently so that any item can be accessed in roughly the same amount of time.

Section 8.1 discusses program files, while Section 8.2 introduces data files and describes the various file types introduced above in greater detail. Specific file organizations on particular media and their use from BASIC are included from Section 8.4 onwards.

8.1 PROGRAM FILES

BASIC programs are usually stored in the computer in some internal format which is quite close to what appears on the VDU screen, but has spaces removed and keywords replaced by symbols, and perhaps variables replaced by references to a symbol table. It is this compact format which commonly is used when programs are stored in files. The files are organized in a sequential manner with the program name and other details appearing before the program. The file may be stored on tape or disc, and the method of using it is reasonably standard.

Table 8.2 summarizes the commands which copy from store to file and back again. The SAVE and LOAD commands are fairly standard, although some of the extra parameters which they take are not. The PET takes a device number on both; if absent it assumes the files are on cassette tape. For disc it needs a special file name indicating the disc drive. Thus:

LOAD "Ø:FRED",8

will load FRED from the disc (device 8) in drive Ø.

Table 8.2 Program file commands

Action	Command examples	Comments
Saving a copy of a program in a file	SAVE "FRED"	Usual micro format, may include extra parameters.
	SAVE	For the ICL 2904 this saves a previously named program NAME FRED or NEW FRED.
Obtaining a copy of a program from a file	LOAD "FRED"	Usual micro format, the PET has a parameter to indicate the device (tape or disc) and Microsoft may include R to run the program.
	GET FRED OLD FRED	For the ICL 2904 and many mainframe computers.
Deleting a program file	KILL "FRED"	Used on disc-based micro systems only.
	KILL FRED UNSAVE FRED	Used on the ICL 2904 and many mainframe computers.
Overlaying another program from disc in place of a current one	10 CHAIN "FRED"	This is a statement, may have many extra parameters.
	10 LOAD "FRED"	Some systems, like the PET, use LOAD as a statement to give the effect of CHAIN.

There is no delete or KILL command for cassette tape; it assumes that to remove a file you re-record over it. Usually all the cassette running, recording, and rewinding has to be done manually. A typically SAVE sequence is as follows. Type in the full command, but do not press ENTER (or RETURN). Turn on the tape recorder and set it running in record mode. Wait a few seconds, then press ENTER (or RETURN) to send the command. After some minutes the system will respond OK on the VDU and the tape may be stopped.

The BBC cassette system stores program details with each block of the program recorded on tape. These are displayed while LOADing a program and provide a useful indication of its progress. In addition the command *CAT will simply build up a catalogue of the contents of a tape as the tape is played through from beginning to end. This feature is very useful for locating programs on the tape. Type *CAT and skip or rewind and then play the tape until the required program is located.

Sometimes store is limited and it is impossible to fit the complete program into it. The CHAIN statement solves this problem by calling in another program to overwrite the current one and continue executing. Consider the example of a program written in a modular way (of course) which does a calculation and produces graphics output. Only one of these modules can fit in the computer at a time so they may be CHAINED, as illustrated in Figure 8.1.

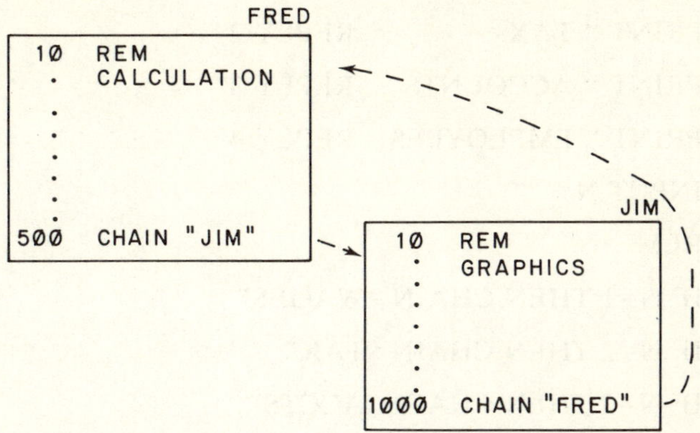

Figure 8.1 CHAINing program modules

The program starts by running FRED. Some data are requested and input, and the calculation is performed. The results must be plotted on the screen, so statement 500 calls the file JIM to overlay the current program and continue execution from the start of the graphics program. When complete, JIM overlays itself with FRED which may call for more data and continue, or just STOP. Swapping programs is a slow process but there is often no other way of running large programs.

The fine details of CHAINing vary from system to system. Most systems require each overlay to be complete with a main program, so unfortunately you cannot just swap subroutines. Quite often the original variables retain their values between overlays or, as in Microsoft, there is a COMMON statement available to designate those variables which must be preserved. Likewise some systems allow data file associations to be preserved so the overlay can continue reading or writing where the previous program left off. In any case, values to be transmitted between overlays can always be placed in temporary data files which are erased at the end of the run.

A fairly common program construction is a menu, which can be conveniently combined with CHAIN statements:

```
10   REM MAIN MENU PROGRAM

20   REM

30   PRINT " ACTION MENU"
```

```
40    PRINT " ===========”
50    PRINT " WHAT NEXT ? PLEASE SELECT ACTION.”
60    PRINT "                 TO END, REPLY 0”
70    PRINT " WAGES          REPLY 1”
80    PRINT " TAX            REPLY 2”
90    PRINT " ACCOUNTS       REPLY 3”
100   PRINT " EMPLOYEES      REPLY 4”
110   INPUT N
120   REM
130   IF N=1 THEN CHAIN “WAGES”
140   IF N=2 THEN CHAIN “TAX”
150   IF N=3 THEN CHAIN “ACCTS”
160   IF N=4 THEN CHAIN “EMPLYS”
170   END
```

There is no explicit loop back to the beginning of the display as it is assumed that each module will hand back to the start of the main program; line numbers may be included on some CHAIN statements to indicate where to start the chained program. Details may need to be added to the above example for particular computers; e.g. the PET needs the pointer to start of variables (locations 42 and 43) POKEd with the value for each CHAINed program when using the disc.

All types of file will contain some type of error detection against loss or corruption of data. This is particularly important in the case of the more fragile media, cassette tapes and floppy discs. Usually extra bits are added to each block of bytes stored, which will enable the system to detect errors when the block is read. Unfortunately an error in a single block may prevent the whole file being loaded, or the whole disc could become unreadable, at least on your equipment. Try reading the cassette or disc on another machine as it may be more tolerant; if this fails and the information is very important a dealer or computer distributor may have a system which can salvage the good parts of the data.

8.2 DATA FILES

Section 8.1 showed how programs may be stored in a file on the computer's backing store. It is the same for data, but in this case the programmer must be aware of different types of file structure and model the program to suit them. File characteristics are usually modelled on the features provided by the physical mcdia so this has to be taken into account when describing the variety of data files available in BASIC. Table 8.3 shows that Sections 8.4 to 8.6 deal with the main separate file types, and their subsections cover the variations of these types with the storage media.

Table 8.3 Combinations of file types and their storage media with references to their descriptions in this chapter. Mainframe disc sequential files are usually direct access ones used serially

File type	Storage media		
	Cassette tape	Floppy disc	Mainframe disc
Sequential terminal format (Section 8.5)	–	Section 8.5.2	Section 8.5.1
Sequential internal format (Section 8.4)	Section 8.4.2	Section 8.4.5	Section 8.6.1
Random access (Section 8.6)	–	Section 8.6.2	Section 8.6.1

Before looking more closely at file characteristics let us consider the general method of usage as illustrated in Figures 8.2 and 8.3. Data are provided to a pro-

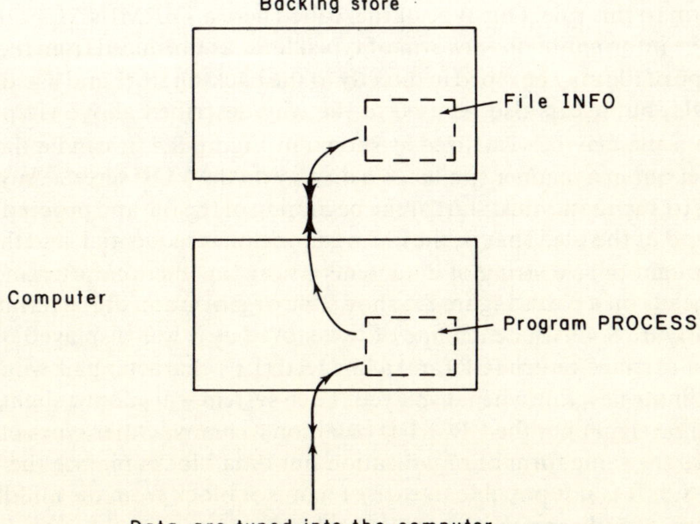

Figure 8.2 Data typed at the keyboard are accepted by a program called PROCESS which stores them in a file called INFO

284

gram called PROCESS in response to INPUT statements and after some calculation this program writes information to the file INFO in the backing store.
Another program, RESULTS, reads the information from INFO and produces
results for the VDU or printer (Figure 8.3). Most types of file give no meaningful

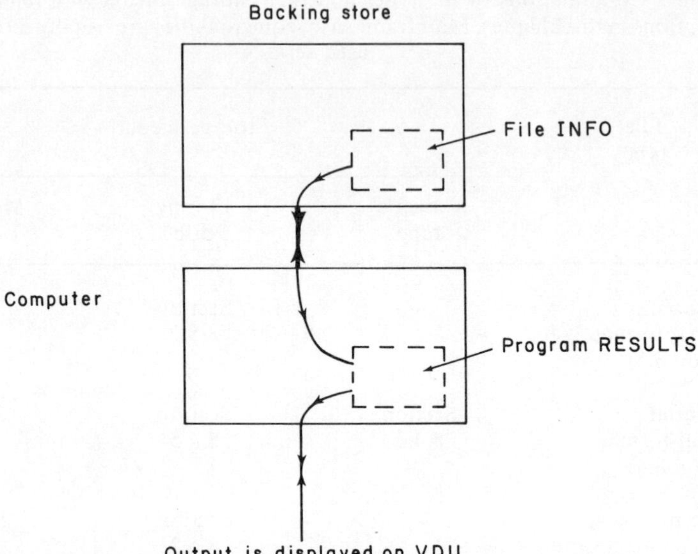

Figure 8.3 The data in file INFO are being read by the program called RESULTS and the
output sent to the VDU

information if examined directly because they are kept in internal format, so
require a program to act as an intermediary between file and user. There is an
exception to this rule. One type of file, called here a TERMINAL FORMAT file,
keeps the information in the form of typed lines as produced from the keyboard.
This type of file may be typed in directly to the backing store and listed directly on
the VDU, but it can also be used in the way described above via programs.

Such a file may be visualized as shown in Figure 8.4. It can be thought of as
being set out in a manner similar to a display on the VDU screen. Any reading or
writing to such a file must start at the beginning of the file and proceed line by line
to the end of the file. That is, the file organization is sequential, and the storage is
best thought of as a string of data items strung together one after another like a
set of beads on a cord. Figure 8.5 shows the organization of the terminal format
file of Figure 8.4. After each line of text stored as it was displayed on the VDU
comes a carriage return (CR) and a line feed (LF) character pair which gives the
approximate new line when displayed. Each system will adopt a slightly different
end of line signal but the CR, LF is common to many. Other types of sequential
file have the same form of organization but data blocks replace the lines in the
Figure 8.5. It is not possible to extract a line or block from the middle of such a
file, alter it, and replace it in the same file.

Why not? Conceptually the file is a continuous stream of values and the changed item would be longer or shorter than the original. However, in practice the file is stored in a series of blocks on tape or on disc and it is not generally possible to read to a position in the file switch to the WRITE mode for a short distance and switch back to the READ mode without corrupting data before and after the written area.

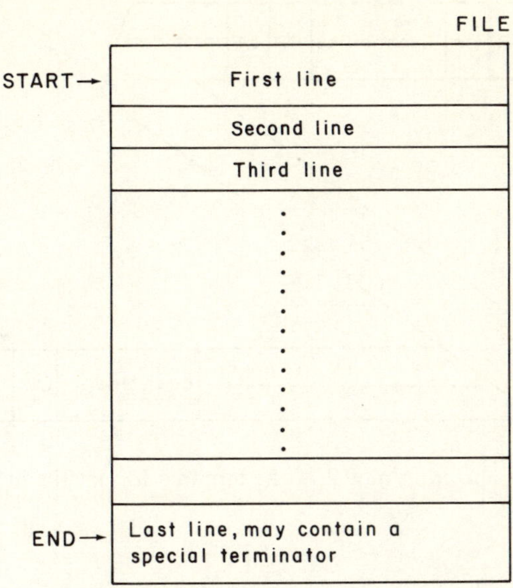

Figure 8.4 Visualization of a terminal format file

Making changes to a sequential file involves copying all the items from the original file to a new file and changing the appropriate values during this process. Sequential files, whether in terminal format or otherwise, are quite easy to use, but suffer not only from this updating defect but may prove inconvenient in certain circumstances. If such a file contained two thousand names and addresses sorted into alphabetic order by name and the program was asked to find the address of Mr Wilson who happened to be on data block 1950, then all the previous 1949 blocks would have to be skipped (i.e. read and discarded) before the desired block was obtained. This would be a time-consuming process, and demonstrates that sequential organization is no good for such an enquiry program, although it would be ideal for many tasks such as payroll printing, stores lists, and address labels.

The random access type of file organization neatly overcomes both the problems mentioned above. Figure 8.6 visualizes the organization of such a file. The data records are stored on disc according to the computer's own availability of space. Each program read or write request must specify a record number and the internal directory sorts out the actual location of the record which can then be read or written to immediately. Thus all the records may be accessed directly and all within approximately the same amount of short time, depending on the rotational speed of the disc. Maintaining the name and address file described previously in a random access organization would allow the program to find Mr

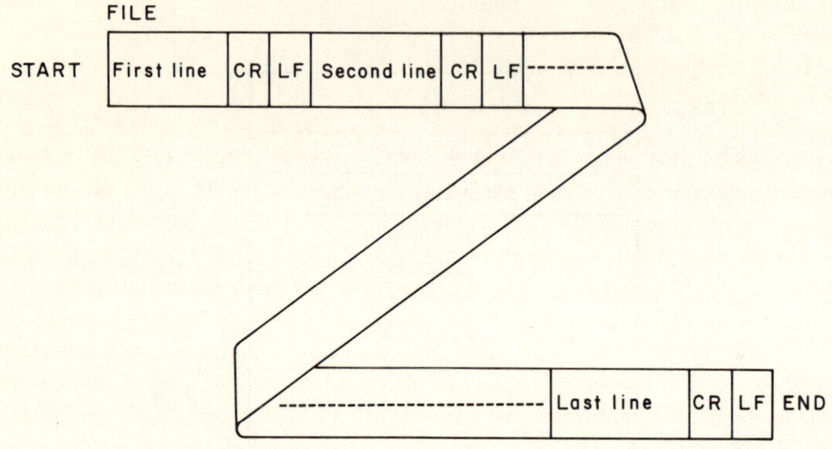

Figure 8.5 Storage organization model of the terminal format file in Figure 8.4

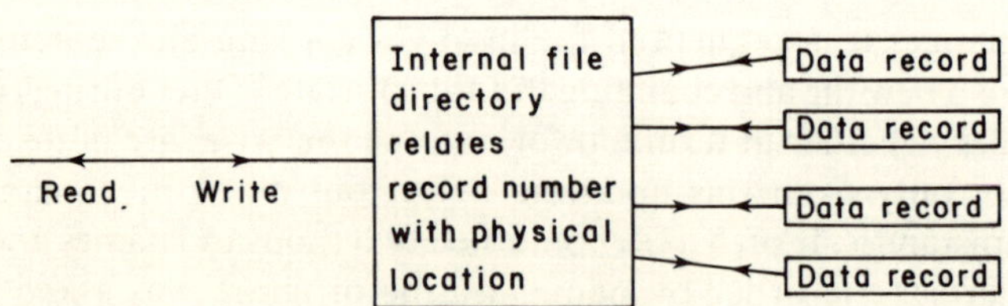

Figure 8.6 Storage organization model of a random access file

Wilson's address very quickly, and also change it if required. There are disadvantages to random access files. They usually require fixed length records, sometimes very strictly formatted; the internal file directory may limit the number of records available and thus the total file size, and it may require much more programming effort to use. Refer to the following sections for more information on the use of both sequential and random access files in BASIC.

8.3 MEDIA CHARACTERISTICS

The cheapest and simplest recording medium is cassette tape. Audio quality cassette tape recorders are used with good quality tapes. The information to be recorded on the tape is output from the computer as a series of ASCII coded characters (bytes) in a serial manner (one after the other). The zeros and ones which comprise each byte are usually transformed into two separate audio frequencies; e.g. the BBC system uses the frequency of 1200 Hz to represent 0 and 2400 Hz to represent 1. The typical data transfer speed is 300 baud which is approximately 300 bits per second, so an 8K bytes program would take at least 3.6 minutes to record or read into the computer. It would probably be a little longer as header and trailer information will be added to the program data, so between 4 and 5 minutes is an average time experienced. Thus a C60 cassette could store approximately twelve 8K programs, or around 100K bytes of data. Some computer systems have higher baud rates up to 1200 baud for a cassette interface. At this top data rate the data are packed more densely on the tape, which runs at the usual speed. Read/write times for 1200 baud will be a quarter of those at 300 baud and the same sized tape will hold four times as much data.

In certain kinds of recording media the recording surface is in contact with the read/write heads of the equipment, which causes physical wear to the magnetic coating. Both cassette tapes and floppy discs work in this way and are prone to lose information due to surface wear, so it is advisable to keep two or three copies of every important file.

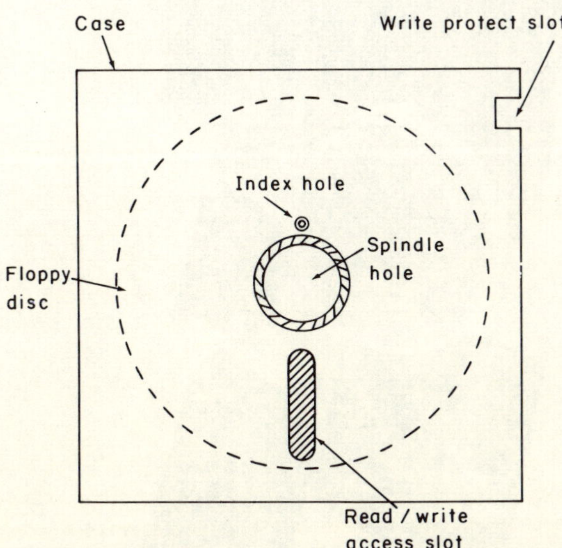

Figure 8.7 A 5¼in floppy disc. The disc is enclosed in a case with only a small part of its surface, shown shaded, visible

Figure 8.8 A range of data storage media: exchangeable disc packs and cartridges, floppy discs, cassette, and magnetic tapes. (Reproduced by permission of BASF United Kingdom Limited)

Floppy discs come in two sizes, the 8in original version developed by IBM, which is fairly standard in its data recording methods, and the popular 5¼in version which is physically similar to the larger one, but for which there are many different data recording methods. As Figure 8.7 shows, a floppy disc looks quite like a 45 r/min gramophone record sealed inside its cardboard case. It is a disc (shown dotted) of plastic coated with a magnetic material and is rotated at 36Ø r/min in its case, which has a lining of graphite coated plastic to reduce friction. Data are recorded on concentric circular tracks through the access slot cut in the outer case. To provide a reference point for the start of each track there is a small hole punched in the disc which is sensed as it passes the index hole cut in the outer case. Each track is a separate circle (unlike the spiral gramophone groove) and holds approximately the same amount of information, which means the tracks near the centre of the disc have information recorded at a higher density than tracks near the outer edge. One track of an 8in disc holds about 5ØØØ bytes of data and takes 1/36Ø minute to read or write the track, so the data transfer rate is about 24Ø,ØØØ bits per scond. Not all the space on the track can hold 'useful' data; the layout varies between systems but the IBM 8in format puts 26 sectors each holding 128 data bytes each on the complete track. This gives 3¼K bytes for data, the rest of the track being taken up with headers, data marks, data check fields, and fillers.

Figure 8.9 Cassettes for data storage. (Reproduced by permission of BASF United Kingdom Limited)

Figure 8.10 Floppy discs, sizes 8 and 5¼ inch. (Reproduced by permission of BASF United Kingdom Limited)

The actual data transfer rate from computer to disc is lower than the 19.5K bytes per second implied above, and may be reduced by the actions of computer communications hardware and software down to Ø.5K bytes per second.

An IBM 8in floppy disc has 77 tracks, so has a useful capacity of approximately 25ØK bytes per side, but this is often called 4ØØK including all the non-data information. A basic 5¼in floppy disc has 35 tracks with a useful capacity of 2.25K bytes per track, which gives a total capacity of 78K bytes per side. All types of double or quadruple density variations are available which give more than this basic value. One way of getting more useful information per track is to place holes round the inner edge of the disc to indicate where the data sectors start. This saves writing this information on the tracks and can increase useful capacity by 25 per cent; it is known as *hard sectoring* as contrasted with the *soft sectoring* described above.

The Winchester hard disc is a recent development from the large rigid discs of mainframe computers. It comprises one or more rigid disc units from 5 to 14in diameter which rotate inside a sealed container. Together with a drive unit and electronics the smaller model may replace a floppy disc unit in terms of size. The discs cannot be removed and like mainframe discs have a flying read/write head which floats over the surface disc on a cushion of air some 2Ø micro inches from it. The air cushion is produced by the disc rotating at 24ØØ r/min. Because of the floating heads there is no surface wear and by sealing the unit head crashes caused by dirt particles are eliminated. Thus Winchesters are now an extremely reliable data storage medium.

Some of the features associated with sequential files have come from the facilities provided by the mainframe tape units. These are large units designed for high speed tape reading and writing, with powerful motors to start and stop the heavy reels of tape. The tape, on reels about one foot in diameter, weigh a couple of pounds (1 kg) and record data in nine parallel tracks along the tape at densities of 16ØØ bits per inch. So one inch of tape may hold 16ØØ bytes. Data are always recorded in blocks of up to 4K bytes with a gap of $\frac{1}{2}$ in between them. The inter block gaps enable the tape unit to start and stop between blocks so features such as 'skip N blocks' or 'rewind N blocks' are available to programs. Similar instructions have come into BASIC when using some sequential files on floppy discs, but are not available for cassette tapes because the cassette tape unit has none of the hardware features required.

8.4 SEQUENTIAL FILES

Sequential files have the organization described in Section 8.2 of one item after another. There is a file header, a series of data items, and perhaps a terminator. Individual items cannot be assessed without reading all the items which come before them. Individual items cannot be replaced in the same file; a new version must be created which incorporates any changes.

BASIC provides enhanced INPUT and PRINT statements to handle sequential files which are mostly independent of the media used for file storage. Thus Section 8.4.1 describes general file usage, the particular media details being covered in subsequent sections. The additional details relate principally to file creation and linking to programs. The latter action is often called OPENing the file, and the two (link, open) will be used to mean the same in what follows.

The basic actions for file usage are:

(a)   Open the file, i.e. link it to a logical file channel. If it does not yet exist this action will create a new file on some systems; on others there must be a prior CREATE command or a special form of OPEN.

(b)   Write data to the file, or read data from the file, or append data to the end of the file (if your system allows this mode).

(c)   Close the file, which removes the link between the file and logical channel number and on most systems sends a special EOF (end of file) marker to the file.

Figure 8.11 The Commodore data cassette recorder. (This photograph was supplied by Cytek (UK) Limited of Old Trafford, Manchester, who are specialist Commodore dealers)

8.4.1 Using sequential files

There is a close similarity between the action of READ statements (see Section 4.4) which read from a serial list of data items stored in DATA statements and reading a sequential file. In this case the READ is replaced by an enhanced INPUT and the data items are no longer visible but are stored in the same way in a sequential file.

To give a flexibility to file handling BASIC uses the idea of a logical channel to the file, so that all read and write statements for that file refer to it only by the logical channel number. At the start of file usage, or before the program is run, one statement or command such as OPEN links the actual file to the logical channel number. For example:

```
10   REM FILE EXAMPLE

20   OPEN 1,1,0,"INFO"

30   INPUT #1,A,B,C
```

The above example is specific to one system (the PET) but illustrates in line 2Ø the linking of the file INFO with the channel number 1 (the first 1 after OPEN). Line 3Ø shows an enhanced INPUT taking values for the variables A, B, and C from the file linked to channel 1. Details of this file opening and linking are given in later subsections of this chapter, which may be consulted for the backing store media and system appropriate to your equipment before running the examples.

File channel designation

General form   #N:

$$or$$

#N,

where N is an expression, variable or constant which evaluates to an integer.
Some systems impose a limit on N :

$1 \leqslant N \leqslant 15$ for Microsoft
$1 \leqslant N \leqslant 255$ for PET
$1 \leqslant N \leqslant 6$ for ICL 29Ø4

In addition, the total number of files open at one time is limited by the operating system to usually less than 1Ø.

Note: BBC BASIC is different in that the value of N is *not chosen* by the programmer, but is provided by the system when the file is linked to the program.

The following statements are appropriate for sequential file usage with the addition of a file channel designation:

INPUT #N,

LINPUT #N,

LINEINPUT #N,

GET #N,

PRINT #N,

PRINT #N, USING

Here is an example of a program which works in two stages, the first to write a simple file and the second to read it back and display it on the VDU. Because you cannot 'see' what has been stored in a file on tape or disc you must have some means of examining it, as the second part of this program does.

294

```
 10   REM FILE CREATION & EXAMINATION
 20   REM ** REPLACE THIS REM BY AN OPEN STATEMENT **
 30   FOR I=1 TO 50
 40      PRINT #2, I*I
 50   NEXT I
 60   CLOSE 2
 70   PRINT "FILE WRITTEN"
 80   PRINT
 90   PRINT "REWIND TAPE & TYPE RUN 120"
100   STOP
110   REM EXAMINATION
120   REM ** REPLACE THIS REM BY AN OPEN STATEMENT **
130   FOR K=1 TO 50
140      INPUT #3, X
150      PRINT X;
160   NEXT K
170   CLOSE 3
180   END
```

Lines 20 and 120 should be replaced by appropriate OPEN statements to the same file. For illustration, file channel 2 is used for writing and 3 for reading; there is no significance in this choice.

The BBC system would use:

```
 40   PRINT #N,I*I
```

and

```
140   INPUT #N,X
```

where N was obtained from OPEN statements (see Section 8.4.4). As line numbers are not allowed on the BBC RUN statements the above program would be best executed as two programs, one from line 10 to line 100 and another from line 110 to line 180.

The action of the first part of the program is to write the squares of the numbers 1 to 50 to the file. Each PRINT statement will produce a new record (visualize as a line) in the file. The program is started by typing RUN to perform this action and will stop with the messages shown below. It is possible to add a statement number to RUN to start it from the specified line number, and this is done in this example to run the second part.

RUN

FILE WRITTEN

REWIND TAPE & TYPE RUN 12Ø

RUN 12Ø

1 4 9 16 25 36   49 64 81 1ØØ 121 144

169 (etc.)

You may notice a slight hesitation in the output after a number of values have been displayed on the VDU. This is a demonstration of the buffering action which is present in some form for all data files. Each system maintains a buffer area of store for each output device. For microcomputers this is usually 128 or 256 bytes long. When data are being written to a file it is collected in this buffer area until the buffer becomes full, when its complete contents are written as a BLOCK to the device. The buffer is then ready to collect more data, and so on. Likewise, on input, each physical block read into the computer will fill the buffer; the program reads the data it obtains from the buffer until it is empty, when a new block is read in from the tape or disc. The pause mentioned above is the evidence of the program wait while the buffer is being filled with new data from the external disc or tape. One way to avoid this erratic action is to use two buffers so that one can be filled as the other is used, and vice versa. However, this is a matter which cannot be altered from BASIC.

Let us modify the file test program to write and read two values per file record:

```
10    REM FILE EXAMPLE 2
20    REM *** REPLACE THIS REM BY AN OPEN STATEMENT ***
30    FOR I=1 TO 50
40       PRINT #2,I;",";100*I
50    NEXT I
60    CLOSE 2
70    PRINT "FILE WRITTEN"
80    PRINT
90    PRINT "REWIND TAPE & TYPE RUN 120"
100   STOP
110   REM EXAMINATION
```

```
120    REM *** REPLACE THIS REM BY AN OPEN STATEMENT ***
130    FOR K=1 TO 50
140        INPUT #3,X,Y
150        PRINT X,Y
160    NEXT K
170    CLOSE 3
180    END
RUN
FILE WRITTEN
REWIND TAPE & TYPE RUN 120
RUN 120
1          100
2          200
3          300
4          400
   (etc.)
```

This is the expected result since the two values I and 100*I are written out on line 40 and read in again on line 140. Look again at line 40, there is a "," value also sent to the file. It is there because INPUT# and PRINT# work in virtually the same way as their original INPUT and PRINT statements. That is, INPUT expects each of the values in the same line (or record) to be separated by commas. Thus:

```
10    INPUT SUM, TOT, E
```

expects:

```
? 10, -6, 42
```

as a reply from the terminal keyboard. So it is from files. If the commas are missing many BASIC systems ignore the intervening spaces and run the numbers together. Try this by removing the comma from line 40 and use:

```
40    PRINT #2, I; 100*I
```

Re-run the program:

RUN
—
FILE WRITTEN

REWIND TAPE & TYPE RUN 12Ø

RUN 120
————
11ØØ   22ØØ

33ØØ   44ØØ

    (etc.)

ERROR AT LINE 14Ø

An error occurs because the absence of the commas leads the program to take each file record as containing only one data item, so line 14Ø reads one record into X and another into Y and thus tries to read past the end of the file after half the total number of iterations of the read loop.

It is important to be able to detect the end of file as in practical use the exact number of data items in a file will not be known. Some systems provide a function EOF( ) which detects the end of file:

Microsoft: EOF(N) is –1 (true) if end of file is reached.

BBC: EOF#(N) is –1 (true) if end of file is reached.

other systems provide a special IF statement:

ICL 29Ø4:   IF END#1 GOTO 2ØØ

Others have a special status word which accepts a response each time a data transfer is made. The PET has a byte status word (ST), and different responses set different bits in the word:

PET: Status word ST   Ø is the all correct response.

                                 64 is the cassette end of file response.

100   REM EXAMPLE FRAGMENT FOR PET

110   INPUT #2, A,B,C

120   IF ST=Ø THEN 2ØØ

130   IF ST=64 THEN 5ØØ

The jump to line 2ØØ would be for normal processing and that to line 5ØØ would be for end of file actions. The advantage of a status word is its ability to monitor a range of responses and make these available to the BASIC program.

298

Here is an example using the BBC function to monitor the end of file which contains a list of names and numbers. A 'DO WHILE NOT EOF#N' loop is needed but this is not available in BBC BASIC.

```
100   REM READ DATA FROM BBC FILE ON CHANNEL N
110   IF EOF#(N) THEN 210
  .       INPUT#N, NAME$, NUMB

  .     .

  .     .

  .     .     Process input

  .     .

  .     .

  .     .

200   GO TO 110
210   REM EXIT AT EOF
220   CLOSE #N
```

Notice the slightly different form of the CLOSE statement in BBC BASIC to that normally used.

8.4.2 Files on cassette

The cassette recorder to be used for data files really needs to be under computer control as the data transfer in blocks is not continuous input or output like program files but is erratic. So the minimum needed is the ability of the computer to switch the cassette motor on or off when the appropriate manual play/record keys are switched on. It is also an advantage if the computer can sense which keys (if any) have been switched on, but the best case is when the computer has full control over all the functions of record, play, and re-wind.

The usual procedure is to start a program running and when an OPEN statement (or similar) is reached the system should request the cassette to be turned on. The cassette recorder motor under computer control should start and stop as the data are being transferred, until finally a CLOSE statement is reached. The following two systems illustrate the general features of cassette storage for data files.

8.4.3 The Commodore PET

The PET uses a rather general system for communication to all external devices which corresponds to the IEEE 488 data bus system. It has the advantage of being suitable for a very wide variety of external devices, but introduces a few extra complications on the OPEN statement which are not really necessary for simple devices. In this system all external devices have a fixed (in the computer hardware) device number from 0 to 30, some of which are shown in Table 8.4.

Table 8.4 Commodore PET device numbers and types

Device number	Device
0	Keyboard
1	Cassette 1
2	Cassette 2
3	VDU screen
4	Line printer
8	Disc drive

The device number is coupled to the logical channel number used in the program by the OPEN statement. The general form is:

OPEN logical channel no., device no., secondary address, file name

The term 'secondary address' is a little confusing in the context of tape operation because it is used as a parameter to indicate the mode to open the device. The default is 0 which is for read only, 1 is for write, and 2 is for write with an end of tape mark forced when the file is closed. File names are optional but are recommended and may have up to 128 characters. For example:

OPEN 1,2,1, "DATA FOR PAYROLL"

opens the second cassette recorder with the file DATA FOR PAYROLL in write mode and links to logical channel 1.

The following illustrates the statements which may be used for cassette tapes:

OPEN #N, D, secondary address, "file name"

PRINT #N,

INPUT #N,

    GET #N,

    CLOSE N

The buffer size is 192 characters, but a record used by one INPUT# or PRINT# must not exceed 80 characters. Remember to include commas "," or CHR$ (44) between values in the same record.

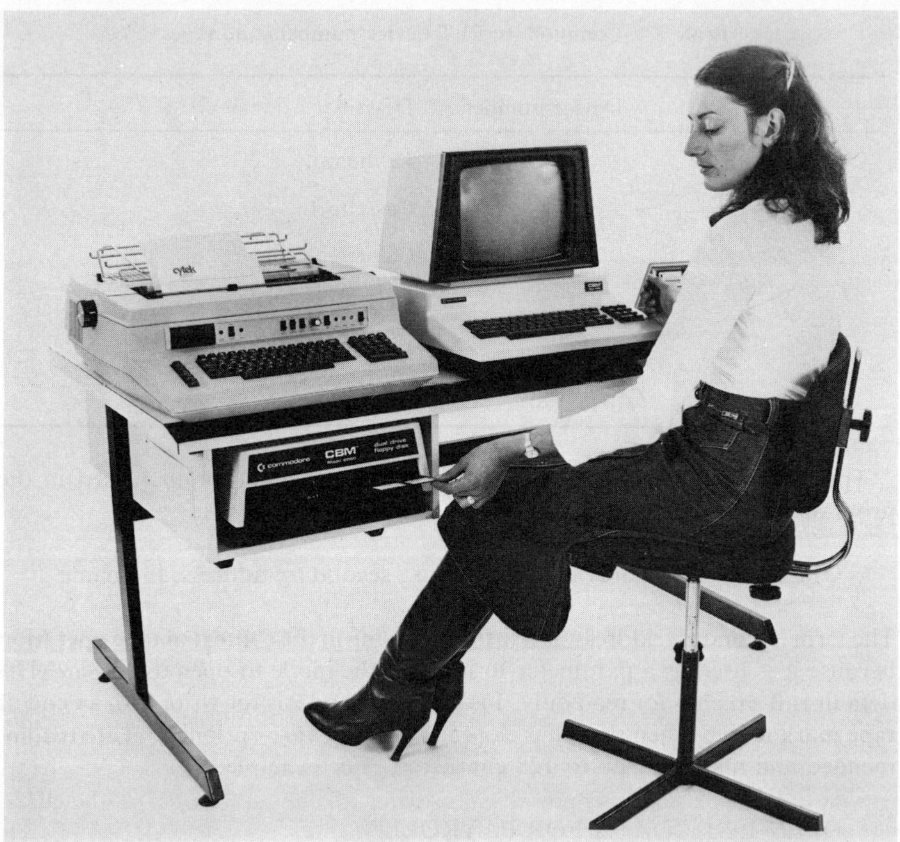

Figure 8.12 The Commodore PET computer with high quality printer, and beneath it the model 8050 twin floppy disc unit. (This photograph was supplied by Cytek (UK) Limited of Old Trafford, Manchester, who are specialist Commodore dealers)

8.4.4 The BBC system

The BBC microcomputer can run one operating system which is specially cassette based; this is the CFS (cassette filing system). The OPEN commands do not differ between this system and the disc operating system but are slightly restricted due to the tape media. There are functions which return a logical channel number chosen by the system. Thus:

    N=OPENIN("file name")

opens the file for reading only and links it to the program putting the logical channel number into the variable N:

    A=OPENIN("PROCESS")

and

    N=OPENOUT("file name")

opens a new file for writing only and again links it to the program. Thus:

    D=OPENOUT("RESULTS")

The following illustrates the statements which may be used with cassettes:

    M=OPENIN("file name")

    M=OPENOUT("filename")

    INPUT #M,

    X=BGET#(M)

    PRINT #M,

    BPUT #M,

    CLOSE #M

The function EOF#(M) is available to detect the end of file on channel M. It returns the value -1 when the end of file has been reached; otherwise it returns the value $\emptyset$. (Note that BBC 'true' is -1 and 'false' is $\emptyset$.)

File names are restricted to a maximum of ten characters in the cassette filing system, but may include special symbols (unlike variable names).

The following partial program illustrates the use of some of the above statements. It stores a list of addresses in the file called MAIL LIST. The addresses are input from the keyboard on line $14\emptyset$ and written out to the file on line $15\emptyset$ using the string variable ADD$.

```
100   REM BBC SEQUENTIAL FILE CREATE
110   N=OPENOUT("MAIL LIST")
120   INPUT "GIVE NUMBER OF ADDRESSES",M
130   FOR I=1 TO M
140     INPUT "ADDRESS", ADD$
```

```
150     PRINT #N, ADD$
160   NEXT I
170   CLOSE#N
```

The statement OPENIN opens an existing cassette file for input, and the statement OPENOUT opens a file for output from a program. Both the INPUT# and PRINT# statements can handle all types of variables for the transfer of numerics and strings between program and file. In addition the statements BGET# and BPUT# provide a means of transferring individual bytes between program and file. The following program uses BPUT to store single bytes in a cassette file:

```
10   REM BBC SEQUENTIAL FILE CREATE
20   L=OPENOUT("CHRS")
30   REPEAT
40     A$=GET$
50     BPUT#L, ASC(A$)
60   UNTIL A$="*"
70   CLOSE#L
80   END
```

The bytes are obtained as single characters from the keyboard using GET$ on line 40 and the REPEAT loop is terminated when the * key is pressed.

8.4.5 Files on floppy discs

This section covers sequential files on floppy discs; for details of random access files consult Section 8.5, although many of the disc handling statements required for random use are introduced here. The Commodore PET, BBC, and Microsoft with CP/M sequential disc file systems are introduced in the following sections.

8.4.6 The Commodore PET disc

The PET uses the IEEE 488 data bus for disc transfers as for tape use. OPEN has the same form but the file name must carry additional information, and the secondary address becomes a physical disc channel with special properties as shown in Table 8.5.

Table 8.5 PET disc secondary address options

Disc secondary address	Use
Ø	Used by LOAD command.
1	Used by SAVE command.
2 to 14	Data input/output (up to five in simultaneous use).
15	Command channel.

Commands are given on secondary address channel 15 by PRINT statements and the reply to these commands may be monitored by INPUT statements. This has its own OPEN statement which must be given before any data channels are OPENed. For example:

```
10   OPEN 15, 8, 15
20   PRINT #15, "IØ"
```

which uses logical channel 15 (the first value) to link to the disc unit (device 8) with secondary address 15 (command channel). The command is sent via the string in the print statement to initialize the disc on drive Ø. The various commands are:

N   New

I   Initialize

D   Duplicate disc

C   Copy file

R   Remove file

S   Scratch disc

$ Requests file directory (see below)

For full details consult the PET disc operating system (DOS) manual. Replies to commands are put in a special format which may be picked up by:

```
INPUT #15, EN, EM$, ET, ES
```

(logical channel 15 was chosen to correspond to the command channel as being easy to remember) where:

EN   contains Ø for correct, or an error number.

EM$ contains an error message.

ET   contains a track number.

ES   contains a sector number.

The DOS maintains a directory of files which may be obtained as follows, assuming the disc is in drive Ø:

OPEN 15, 8, 15   (opens disc and command channel)

LOAD "$Ø", 8   (requests directory to be loaded into the PET)

LIST   (displays directory)

Programs use the LOAD and SAVE commands:

LOAD   "Ø:PROCESS", 8

SAVE   "Ø:RESULTS", 8

where the Ø refers to drive unit Ø. Finally, we come to the OPEN command for sequential data files, which uses an extended entry in the previous (cassette) file name position, of:

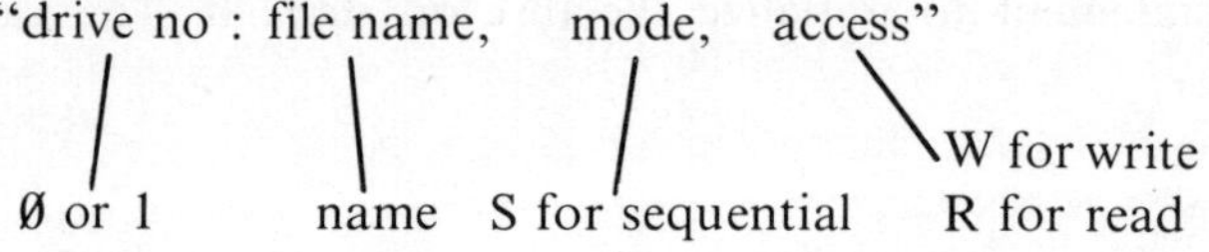

The drive numbers correspond to the two disc drives built into the unit. So an example of a data file OPEN is:

OPEN 4, 8, 1Ø, "Ø:PROCESS DATA, S, R"

which reads the file PROCESS DATA from the disc on secondary address channel 1Ø linked to logical channel 4 in the program. The program can use the statements:

INPUT #4,

PRINT #4,

GET #4,

CLOSE #4

The general procedure for PET sequential file handling may be summarized as follows:

(a) At the beginning of the program the data disc should be initialized and the command channel opened, whether the file is to be written or read:

        10   OPEN 15, 8, 15

        20   PRINT #15, "I0"

        30   GOSUB 1000

The GOSUB monitors the reply.

(b) Open a file for writing (which will replace any existing one of the same name) by:

        50   OPEN CH, 8, CH, "@0: INFO, S, W"

where CH contains the channel number, or for reading by:

        50   OPEN CH, 8, CH, "0 :INFO, S, R"

After each statement monitor the reply.

(c) Read or write using the statements INPUT#, GET#, or PRINT# and monitor the reply of each action. On reading check the status word ST which should be 0 for a correct read and 64 for the end of file.

(d) Close the file at the end of the program. The error monitor could have the form:

        500   REM SUB ERROR MONITOR

        510   INPUT #15, EN, EM$, ET, ES

        520   IF EN=0 THEN RETURN

        530   REM PRINT OUT DETAILS

        540   REM AND END, OR REQUEST ACTION

        550   REM FROM TERMINAL AND RETURN.

8.4.7 The BBC disc system

The BBC system uses floppy discs with the disc filing system (DFS). Sequential file usage is very similar in programming terms to the tape file case described earlier. The statements OPENIN and OPENOUT may be used in the same way as previously, but OPENIN now allows both input and random access and OPENOUT allows sequential writing to the file.

There are no special parameters to distinguish sequential disc files from direct access ones, but see the comment in Section 8.6.3 regarding developments of the system. The statements which may be used are:

M=OPENIN

M=OPENOUT

INPUT #M,

```
PRINT #M,
X=BGET#(M)
BPUT #M,
CLOSE #M
```

A sequential file TELEPHONE contains a set of records with names and telephone numbers. The following program would scan through the file until the required name matched the input query and would then display the telephone number.

The final design structogram is:

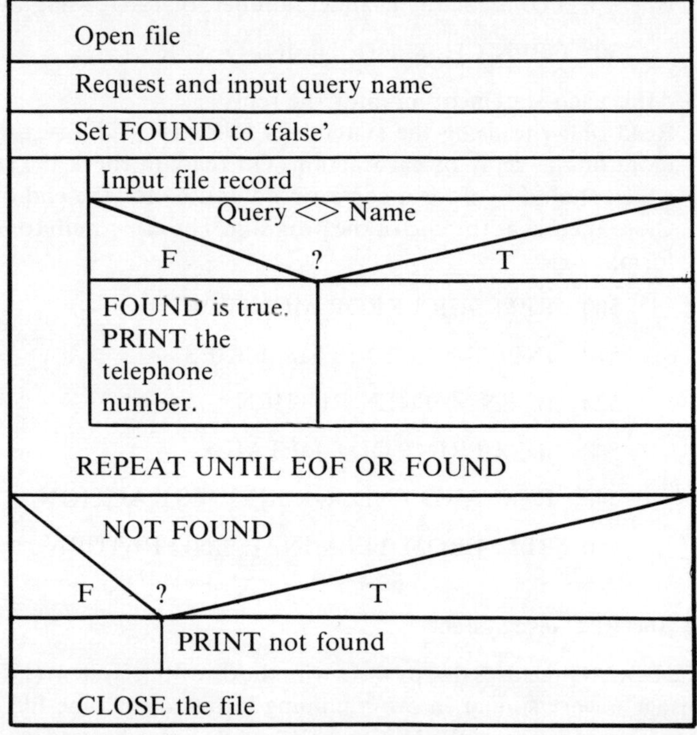

and the program may be written:

```
10   REM SIMPLE FILE DEMO
20   M=OPENIN ("TELEPHONE")
30   INPUT "PLEASE GIVE QUERY NAME";QUERY$
40   FOUND=0        :REM FALSE
50   REPEAT
```

```
 60    INPUT #M, NAM$, NUMB$
 70    IF NAM$ <>.QUERY$ THEN 100
 80       FOUND =-1     :REM TRUE
 90          PRINT "TELEPHONE NUMBER IS"; NUMB$
100    UNTIL (EOF #M OR FOUND)
110    IF NOT FOUND THEN PRINT "NAME NOT FOUND"
120    CLOSE #M
```

8.4.8 Microsoft files

This discussion applies to Microsoft sequential floppy disc files under the CP/M operating system. Section 8.5.2 gives full details of the CP/M system.

The first parameter on the OPEN statement indicates the access mode of the file, and may be I for sequential input or O for sequential output. The next two parameters are the logical channel number (from 1 to 15) and the file name. This may be up to eight characters long with an optional extension up to three characters long separated by a full stop from the first part; e.g.:

    FIRST.DAT

    DATA. PAY

    DATA. SAL

are valid CP/M file names. An OPEN statement might be:

    10   OPEN "I", #3, "DATA.PAY"

which will open the file DATA.PAY for input to the program and link it to logical channel 3. Statements which may be used for sequential disc files are:

    OPEN

    INPUT#

    LINE INPUT#

    PRINT#

    PRINT#USING

    WRITE#

    CLOSE

The WRITE# statement is extremely useful because it produces output exactly as PRINT but includes commas to separate each of the values. Thus:

```
100    PRINT #3, A;",";B;",";C
```

and

```
100    WRITE #3, A, B, C
```

have the same effect, and are required if the file is to be used as input to a program using INPUT#.

The EOF(N) function detects the end of file on channel N and the LOC function, which is used for random access, returns the number of 128 byte sectors which have been read or written in sequential mode since the file was OPENed.

There is no append mode. A file OPENed in O access mode for writing is emptied of its contents, if it already exists.

8.5 TERMINAL FORMAT FILES

Some systems allow the sequential files created as described in earlier parts of Section 8.4 to be LISTed on the VDU and edited rather like BASIC programs. In effect the storage of information in such files is exactly like the information coming from the computer terminal.

Such a file type is quite common on mainframe computers where it is stored on the large disc systems. An example of this type of file is described in the ICL 2904 system below.

Microcomputers do not generally have a sufficiently good operating system to provide such terminal format file facilities, an exception to this being the CP/M based systems. They are described in Section 8.5.2 together with a very brief summary of CP/M general file handling features.

The BBC disc system also provides these facilities. The *BUILD command allows text files to be created directly from the keyboard. These files may be displayed on the VDU by the *LIST and *TYPE commands.

8.5.1 ICL 2904 files

This system provides two types of files, the terminal format files and the internal format files which may be used in random access mode (see Section 8.6.1).

The serial terminal format files may be created by an OPEN command, which is not a statement as in many other systems, and written to, or read by, programs in the usual way. The list below summarizes the available features.

Command only:

OPEN filename, size in records (reserves space for file)

Instructions:

```
10    FILE #N: "filename"        (links file to channel)

10    INPUT #N:
```

```
1Ø   LINPUT #N:

1Ø   PRINT #N:

1Ø   FILE #N: "*"                (closes the file)
```

File names in this system are limited to a maximum of six characters. Two IF statements are provided to test for the end of file:

```
IF END #N THEN 1ØØ

IF MORE #N GOTO 1Ø
```

One very important and useful feature is the ability to return to the beginning of the file (as RESTORE in DATA statements) with the instruction RESET #N. It can do more than this; if it is given a record number as second parameter it will position the file at that record for reading or writing, thus giving random access capability:

```
1ØØ   RESET #3

1ØØ   RESET #3, 45
```

The file function LOC (#N) gives the current record number, and a useful function TYP (#N) looks ahead at the next item in the file to determine its type (1 for numeric, 2 for string, 3 for end of record, and 4 for end of file).

The other way to use files is to handle them from the keyboard directly. This system integrates file handling with program handling so that the usual commands to GET, LIST, and edit lines can be applied to data files.

In addition, a special command called TEXT is provided to create new data files. Typed responses are underlined in the example below; the system prompt is > but this changes to < during input of a file:

```
>TEXT INFO                 (new file INFO to be created)

<FIRST LINE , 2.3

<4.678 , SECOND, 7.8

<1, 2, 3,

<LAST , 67

</ / / /                   (four of / terminates input)

  INFO SAVED

>LIST                      (display current file)

  INFO

  1   FIRST LINE, 2.3
```

```
2   4.678 , SECOND , 7.8
3   1, 2, 3,
4   LAST , 67
>
```

The commands which may be used are:

LIST   lists current file, program, or data, on VDU.

KILL INFO   deletes named file (INFO) from backing store.

SCRATCH   deletes current file from computer (work area) store.

GET INFO   copies the file from backing store to (work area) store.

Files, program, or data in the work area may be altered by giving the line number followed by the new line version. Giving a line number by itself deletes a line, or use:

DELETE 1Ø,5Ø

which deletes lines 1Ø to 5Ø inclusive. To retain a changed copy of a file on backing store the original must first be KILLed, then the current file may be copied out of the work area by the SAVE command. A file in the work area may have its name changed by the NAME command.

The following simple program uses the file INFO created above. Because it is a mixture of strings and numbers all items are read as strings. The comma after A$ indicates the INPUT is to continue with the next item on the record; without it the program would read only the first item on each record.

```
1Ø   REM ICL 29Ø4 FILE DEMO
2Ø   FILE # 1: "INFO"
3Ø     INPUT # 1: A$,
4Ø     PRINT "NEXT ITEM =";A$
5Ø   IF MORE # 1 THEN 3Ø
6Ø   FILE # 1: "*"
7Ø   END
RUN
─────
     NEXT ITEM = FIRST LINE
     NEXT ITEM = 2.3
```

```
    NEXT ITEM = 4.678
    NEXT ITEM = SECOND
    NEXT ITEM = 7.8
    NEXT ITEM = 1
    NEXT ITEM = 2
    NEXT ITEM = 3
    NEXT ITEM = LAST
    NEXT ITEM = 67
LINE 70 DONE
```

8.5.2 CP/M files

Using CP/M the physical disc drives are labelled A,B, C, and so on. By convention the disc drive built into the VDU is known as A. The system disc containing CP/M should be loaded into drive A. When CP/M has been loaded as described in Section 2.1.2 the prompt will indicate the current logged drive:

```
A>
```

Typing B: or C: changes the current drive to B or C respectively.

Note that on loading BASIC by means of the MBASIC command only three data files are allowed by default, and they must use the logical channel numbers 1 to 3. More files may be requested by adding the parameter '/F: number of files' to the command; thus:

```
A>MBASIC /F:6
```

will allow up to six data files to be used within BASIC. All direct file handling, including creation, is done outside of BASIC. What follows refers to CP/M commands and editor.

When files are used it is often necessary to specify which disc drive (A,B,C) the file is on. Some commands can act on groups of files and may use an asterisk (*) to mean 'any string of characters' in the file name. Thus:

A:FIRST.PRG	refers to file FIRST.PRG on drive A.
SAMPLE.TXT	refers to file SAMPLE.TXT on the currently logged disc drive.
B:*.TXT	refers to all files on drive B which have the extension name TXT.
B:*.*	refers to all files on drive B.

Figure 8.13 The Zenith Data Systems computer running CP/M using three disc drives: one is built in next to the VDU and two in the unit on the right of the photograph. (Reproduced by permission of Martin Beer, Liverpool University)

Remember that commands must be given from the disc on which they reside, which is usually A. If this is not the currently logged disc the command must be prefixed by A:.

Sequential data files may be created in the usual way by a program as described in Section 8.4.8 or from the keyboard directly. To create a file directly use the edit ED command of CP/M with a new file name. Data may be inserted into a file by means of the I subcommand, and such insertion is terminated by a CONTROL & Z sequence. Here is an example of a complete edit (all information typed at the keyboard is underlined):

B>A:ED INFO.DAT	(ask for ED on drive A to create named file on current drive, which is B)
NEW FILE	(a file of the above name does not exist on B, so the system will create one)
:*I	(the * is the edit prompt, type I for insert)
1:10	
2:40	
3:75	(give data values, press <return> after each line)
4:-6	
5:21	
6:	(type CONTROL &Z to terminate the command)
:*E	(*prompt again, may use any edit command, use E to terminate edit)
B>	(back to CP/M and ready for a command)

The data file INFO.DAT has been created and may be displayed on the VDU by giving the command:

B>A:TYPE INFO.DAT

or if on drive A:

A>TYPE B:INFO.DAT

BASIC may be entered and the file attached to the program via OPEN as described previously. Within BASIC the data file cannot be examined or edited. There is an editor in BASIC for programs only (see Table 8.6), which is quite separate from the CP/M editor described above. Table 8.6 gives a list of the additional commands which may be given in BASIC under CP/M. Move out of BASIC to CP/M by the SYSTEM command and re-enter it again via MBASIC. To summarize file usage, either:

Load CP/M and BASIC. Create and use files from programs as described in Sections 8.4.1 and 8.4.8. Exit from BASIC if it is required to alter or display these files.

or:

Load CP/M and create or display any files. Then enter BASIC and load programs to use these files. Exit from BASIC if it is required to alter or display these files directly.

The final part of this section covers the general operations of file handling under CP/M, beginning with a summary of the editor.

Table 8.6 Additional commands in BASIC with CP/M

Example of a command in BASIC	Action
FILES "B:*.*"	Gives a list of files on disc B.
LOAD "B:MYPROG"	Loads program MYPROG.BAS from disc B.
SAVE "B:MYPROG"	Saves program MYPROG.BAS to disc B.
SYSTEM	Leave BASIC and lose any current programs not yet saved. Return to CP/M.
EDIT 35	Allows you to edit line 35 of the current program. Some editing commands are:
	L — List the current version of the line.
	SPACE — Move cursor to next character.
	D — Delete character.
	C — Overwrite existing character with next character typed.
	I — Insert characters, terminate by pressing ESC.
	RETURN — This key terminates the edit and stores the changed line.

The format of the edit ED command is:

ED filename

The edit prompt is a * and when this appears any of the following edit commands may be given. In the following $\wedge$Z means CONTROL and Z, a + or – indicates movement upwards or downwards in the file. The edit is terminated by E for normal end and save the new file or Q for quit without saving the file. When changing an existing file, after the edit this becomes the old file and is left on the disc as file "filename. BAK".

A summary of edit instructions are given below:

n A	Append n lines.
± B	Begin bottom of buffer.
± n C	Move ± n character positions.
± n D	Delete n characters.
E	End edit and close files.
n F	Find nth string: F oldstring $\wedge$Z newstring$\wedge$Z.
H	End edit, leave files open.
I	Insert characters. I string $\wedge$Z.
n J	Place strings in juxtaposition.
± n K	Remove (kill) n lines.
± n L	Move down/up n lines.
M	Macro definition
N	Find next occurrence with autoscan.
O	Return to original file.
± n P	Move and print pages.
Q	Quit with no file changes.
n S	Substitute strings: S oldstring $\wedge$Z newstring$\wedge$Z.
± n T	Type (display) lines.
± U	Upper to lower case.
n W	Write n lines.
n Z	Sleep.
± n <return>	Move and type (as LT sequence)

The CP/M file handling commands are:

Directory listing command DIR. Examples:

        DIR

        DIR B:

    DIR PROG.*

    DIR*.PRG

Display the contents of a file on the VDU, the TYPE command. Examples:

    TYPE SAMPLE.TXT

    TYPE B:FRED.APG

STAT gives statistics on files and storage. Examples:

    STAT DSK: (information on all active discs)

    STAT

    STAT B:

    STAT SAMPLE.TXT

    STAT *.TXT

Erase command ERA. Examples:

    ERA SAMPLE.TXT

    ERA *.TXT

    ERA B:*.PRG

Rename command REN (changes name of second file to first). Examples:

    REN NEWFL .TXT=OLDFL.PRG

    REN A.B=X.Y

    REN B:FRED.APG=B:JIM.BAK

PIP copies files. Example:

    PIP Z:NEW.TXT=B:OLD.PRG   (from OLD to NEW)

PIP copies files to real devices, CON: for console, LST: for printer. Examples:

    PIP CON: = SAMPLE.TXT

    PIP LST: = A.PRG

PIP copies whole discs. Example:

    PIP C: = A:*.*

Table 8.7 gives some of the keyboard control actions under CP/M. Note that within BASIC the same controls may produce quite different actions.

Table 8.7 Keyboard controls under CP/M

Keyboard control	Action
Common controls	
Rubout/delete	Delete and echo deleted character.
CTRL–U or CTRL–X	Delete a line.
CTRL–R	Used after delete to display 'clean' line.
CTRL–E	Continue on next line.
CTRL–C	Re-boot CP/M.
Others	
CTRL–H	Backspace.
CTRL–J (line feed)	Terminate input.
CTRL–M (carriage return)	Terminate command.
CTRL–P	On–off for console display to printer.
CTRL–S	Stop/re-start console output.

8.6 RANDOM ACCESS FILES

Efficient use of disc space in random access mode tends to imply certain restrictions on the length and format of the information being stored. In general, the more sophisticated the disc operating system is, the less restrictive are the constraints.

Typically, random access files have fixed format and fixed length records. For floppy discs the record length may be restricted to a sector size, perhaps 128 bytes. The information, both string and numeric, may be stored in the binary form of the internal computer representation or totally in character form.

The amount of work done by the program reflects the sophistication of the system. Basically, the programmer requires to input and output selected sets of values to named records in the file. Details of file buffers, blocks and block sizes, track and sector numbers, and conversion of numeric values should not be part of the programmer's job. However, a certain amount of such knowledge is required for most computers, even mainframe systems.

The following two sections illustrate the formatted approach to random access files. Each record in the file has the same layout as defined in the format. The result is a quite straightforward use of a random access file. The two examples chosen represent a mainframe computer, the ICL 2904, and a widely available floppy disc system, Microsoft with CP/M.

Unformatted systems differ widely; the BBC system seems to be byte (character) orientated and looks reasonable to use, but the Commodore PET system, also byte orientated, involves the user in quite a lot of detailed track and sector manipulations and is not so easy to use.

The systems usually provide access to these files by record number (byte number for BBC). The position of a record in a file may be related to its contents by means of HASH CODING a keyfield in the record. This technique is widely used in enquiry systems.

8.6.1 ICL 2904 files

The file is created and the format fixed by an OPEN command. The records are fixed length and fixed format. OPEN has the form:

OPEN filename (record format), number of records. For example:

OPEN DAFL (N, S10, 2N), 100

sets up a file DAFL to contain 100 records which have the layout of 'a number, a string of ten characters, two numbers'. The format consists of the descriptors S and N:

N for one numeric value

Sm for a string of m characters

A repeat count may be given before the descriptor, so that (N,N) is the same as (2N).

Once OPENed the following statements may be used:

10   FILE #N: "filename"

10   READ #N,L:

10   WRITE#N,L:

10   #N:"*"

The direct access statements READ and WRITE take a record number (L in the above) to indicate which record they are to operate on. Thus:

100   WRITE #2,1:A,B,C$

writes two numeric and one string value, which must match the format, to record 1 of the file on logical channel 2. Records can be written or read from the file at random so a complete updating scheme is possible. Conceptually, such a file appears like an array in the way the parts can be accessed, but since each record can hold a quite complicated structure of numbers and strings its computational uses are much richer.

The function LOC (#N) will give the current record number, so:

10 READ#2, LOC (#2)+1: A,B,C$

will read the next record in the file.

The IF END and IF MORE facilities are available together with the RESET #N,L statement described in Section 8.5.1.

8.6.2 Microsoft files

Although these random access files are stored in a binary format all information exchanged between program and file is in the form of character strings. To assist, a set of functions is provided which converts numeric values to strings, and vice versa.

Each random access file is declared in an OPEN statement with an R for its first parameter access mode (see Section 8.4.8). Thus:

10 OPEN "R", #2, "DAFL", 20

will open the file DAFL for random access with a record length of 20 bytes (default is 128), using logical channel 2.

One added complication is the buffer which is present for each file, but which must be explicitly manipulated by the program for these files. Extra actions are involved because information must be transferred between buffer and program and between buffer and file. Figure 8.14 shows the schematic effect of these actions.

The OPEN statement defines the record length in its fourth parameter and the FIELD statement defines the buffer for the file. The buffer length must not exceed the record length; all lengths are in bytes. In addition the FIELD defines string variables, which may have any names, as associated with parts of the buffer. These variables may be used in the normal way in PRINT, string functions, and so on, but may *not* be assigned any values directly. This means they cannot be used in INPUT or LET assignment statements. The only way of getting information into these variables is by using the statements LSET and RSET (see Figure 8.14). The specification for FIELD is:

FIELD logical channel no., field width AS string variable, . . .

with the latter parameter repeated as many times as required. Thus:

10 FIELD #1, 20 AS Z$, 10 AS NAME$

This sets up the buffer for the file on logical channel 1 to contain 30 bytes, the first 20 bytes for string Z$, and the next 10 bytes for string NAME$. To read such

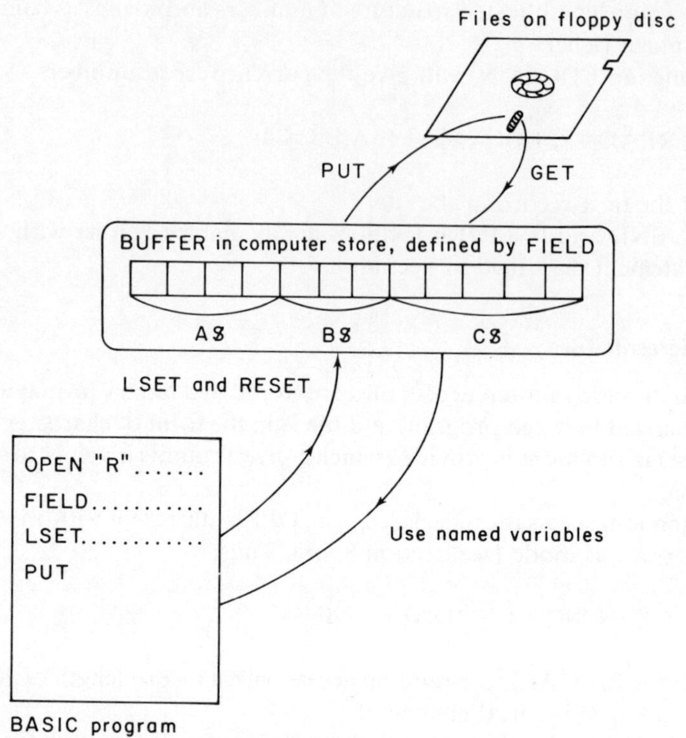

Figure 8.14 Using random access files in Microsoft BASIC

a file, first transfer a desired record to the buffer and then use the appropriate variable in the program. Thus:

    50   GET #1, 209

gets record number 209 from the file on channel 1 and puts it in the buffer, and:

    60   PRINT "NAME IS";NAME$

    70   PRINT "DETAILS ARE";Z$

The PRINT statements use the information from the buffer variables defined in the FIELD.

To write to the file discussed above information must be put into the string variables of the buffer; then the buffer can be sent to the desired record in the file. The only way to put information into the buffer variables is via LSET or RSET:

    75   LSET Z$="99–641"+"BSI 644"

    80   RSET NAME$=B$

Both have the same action, but LSET left justifies the information in the field and RSET right justifies it. Blanks pad out extra positions, or expressions are truncated if they are too long. Once in the buffer, send this to the desired record in the file:

    9Ø   PUT #1, 3Ø4

One PUT or GET acts on the complete buffer.

A summary of statements for random file use is:

OPEN "R", #1,   (opens file, specifies record length)

FILE #1,   (defines buffer)

LSET or RSET   (may be repeated many times for writing records to
PUT #1,   the file)

GET #1,   (may be repeated many times for reading records
    from the file)

CLOSE 1   (removes link between logical channel and file)

The file function LOC(N) returns the record number last used by a PUT or GET plus one, and is thus useful if you wish to use the file in a sequential mode.

Numbers may be packed or unpacked from strings using the two functions STR$(X) and VAL(A$) discussed in Chapter 4. However, special faster functions are also available, for putting numbers into strings use:

MKI$ (I%)   for integers, gives 2 byte string.

MKS$ (X)   for reals, gives 4 byte string.

MKD$ (A#)   for double precision, gives 8 byte string.

The reverse actions of these functions are provided by CVI (A$), CVS (A$), and CVD (A$).

The following program illustrates the use of random access files for a stock recording system. It has been simplified to demonstrate the essential file handling features. The shopkeeper has about 1ØØ different items in stock and wishes to record them under:

Product code number, description, number in stock, price per item

For simplicity it is assumed that the shopkeeper allocates his own product code from 1 to 1ØØ. This makes it easy to use this as the record number in the file, and the other items are stored in the record.

An enquiry and stock update system is required for this stock list. A structogram design is easily developed. Shown below are three diagrams for the final stage of the design, one for the main program and one each for the two sub-routines:

Main program

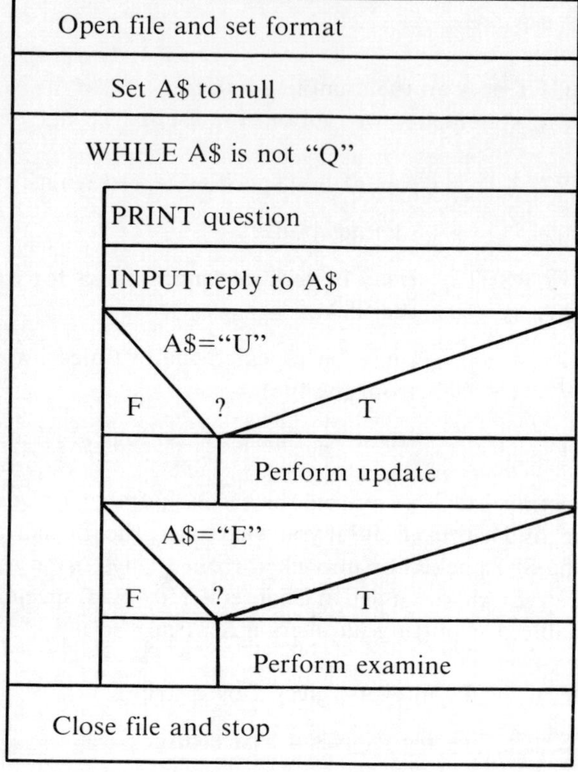

Examine subroutine

Ask for product code

INPUT reply to PC%

Use PC% to get record of this number

PRINT details of the record and RETURN

Update subroutine

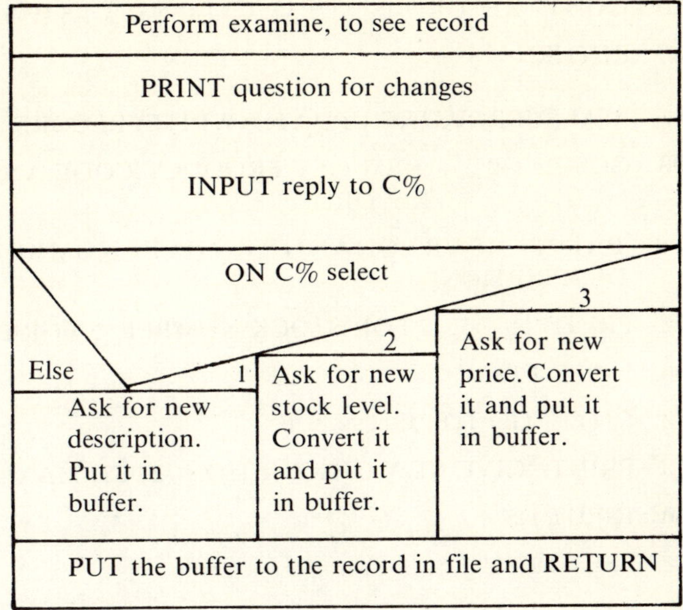


```
10    REM STOCK UPDATE EXAMPLE

20    OPEN "R", #1, "STOCK", 26

30    FIELD #1, 20 AS DES$, 2 AS SN$, 4 AS P$

40    A$=""

50    WHILE A$ <>"Q"

60        PRINT "ACTION? UPDATE OR EXAMINE OR QUIT (U OR E
          OR Q)"

70        INPUT A$

80        IF A$="U" THEN GOSUB 190

90        IF A$="E" THEN GOSUB 130

100    WEND

110    CLOSE 1

120    STOP


130    REM SUBROUTINE EXAMINE (READ) RECORD

140    PRINT "GIVE PRODUCT CODE";

150    INPUT PC%
```

```
160   GET #1, PC%

170   PRINT "RECORD IS"; DES$; CVI (SN$); CVS (P$)

180   RETURN

190   REM SUBROUTINE UPDATE (WRITE) RECORD

200   GOSUB 130      :REM GET PRODUCT CODE AND DISPLAY
                      RECORD

210   PRINT "FOR  CHANGES  GIVE  NUMBER,  1  FOR
      DESCRIPTION"

220   PRINT "         2 FOR STOCK NUMBER, 3 FOR PRICE"

230   INPUT C%

240   ON C% GO TO 250, 290, 330

250   PRINT "GIVE NEW DESCRIPTION (20 CH.MAX)";

260   INPUT D$

270   LSET DES$=D$

280   GO TO 360

290   PRINT "GIVE NEW STOCK LEVEL";

300   INPUT S%

310   LSET SN$=MKI$ (S%)

320   GO TO 360

330   PRINT "GIVE NEW PRICE";

340   INPUT P

350   LSET P$=MKS$ (P)

360   PUT #1, PC%

370   RETURN

380   END
```

8.6.3 BBC files

The BBC system supports random access files on its floppy disc unit. The full
identification for all disc files is:

: Drive . Directory . Filename

where
Drive is a number between Ø and 3 which identifies the physical disc drive.
Directory is a single character which identifies a separate section of files on the.
disc.
Filename is the name of the file containing up to 7 characters.
The following are valid names:

  : 1. A. ONEPROG

  : Ø . $. DATA 1

If the drive and directory names are not given the currently set values are used. The command *CAT which lists the details of all the files on the current disc will show these current values. The values may be changed by the commands:

  *DIR   changes the current set directory

  *DRIVE   changes the current set drive.

The filenames in OPENIN and OPENOUT statements refer to the current drive and directory.
OPENIN will open a file for random access reading and writing. Examples are:

    10   N=OPENIN ("DAFILE")

and

    10   CHAN=OPENIN (A$)

where A$ contains the file name.
The disc file system reserves 64 sectors of 256 bytes, that is 16K bytes, when a file is created by the OPENOUT statement. A buffer area of 256 bytes is reserved in the computer store for each file in use. Up to 5 files may be used simultaneously. Transfers between buffer and disc take place automatically depending upon the value assigned to PTR#.
All the file statements described in Sections 8.4.7 and 8.4.4 are available and a new file statement and function PTR# is provided which will select any *BYTE* of a file for subsequent input and output. This provides the random access feature based at the byte level of file storage. Examples are:

    100 PTR #M=1Ø

sets the file pointer to byte 1Ø;

    100 PTR #M=NUM

sets the file pointer to the value in NUM;

    100   PTR #M=PTR #M+22

sets the file pointer 22 bytes on from the previous value;

    100   PRINT PTR #M

prints out the current value of the file pointer. The buffer-disc transfers take place according to the value of PTR#. If it is set to 5000 the 20th sector containing bytes 4864 to 5119 is loaded into the buffer and reading or writing can take place from byte number 5000, but can also be directed to any position in the buffer without another disc transfer. The file random storage philosophy is completely byte orientated. Values from numeric variables are written as five bytes for a real variable and four bytes for an integer each preceded by one byte identifying its type. Strings are written as characters preceded by two bytes, the first identifying it as a string and the second giving its length. Values may also be read or written a byte at a time using BPUT# and BGET#. BPUT sends one byte to the file at the current file pointer position and BGET reads a byte from the file. For example:

    10   BPUT#N, 8

and

    10   BPUT#N, A$

will send the value 8 or the least significant byte of A$ to the file at the current pointer position, while:

    10   X$=BGET#N

reads a byte from the file into X$.

If an arbitrary mixture of variables, strings, and byte values are stored in a file then keep an index section in the file which is read into an array immediately after the file is opened. This array should record the starting position of each item in the file. Otherwise, keep to a logical fixed record format which could contain several items. For example, logical records 19 bytes long could contain two numeric values of 5 bytes each and a string of 5 bytes together with one byte header for each numeric and two for the string. If the variable REC contained the record number (0, 1, 2, 3, . . .) of each such logical record in the file then selecting a new record could be achieved with statements such as:

    50   PTR #M=REC*19

The following example will position at byte 100 in the file DAFILE and print out the next 10 bytes (characters):

```
10   REM D A FILE DEMO
20   N=OPENIN ("DAFILE")
30   PTR#N=100
40   FOR I=1 TO 10
50     PRINT GET#N;
60     PTR#N=PTR#N+1
70   NEXT I
80   CLOSE #N
90   END
```

The statements INPUT# and PRINT# work in serial mode but they can be used to read and write from the current pointer position in the file:

```
50   PTR#N=50
60   INPUT#N, A, B, C$
```

or

```
50   PTR#N=1000
60   PRINT#N, A, B, C$
```

With care, and perhaps a byte map kept in the file, it would be possible to read and write complete sets of values quite easily.

A file function EXT#N returns the length of the file in bytes:

```
L=EXT#(N)
```

8.6.4 Commodore PET files

Consult Section 8.4.6 which covers the general method of handling PET disc files, i.e. using the disc secondary addresses for command channel 15, monitoring the reply from channel 15, and using data channels 2 to 14 for data transfer.

Random access files require explicit use of a 256 byte buffer for each file. PRINT statements to command channel 15 tell the disc controller to transfer a block from the disc to the buffer, or vice versa. Data can be read or written to the buffer by INPUT# and PRINT# statements.

One complicating feature is the way the commands access data from the disc. It is done on a track and sector basis, where each sector stores 255 bytes of data and there are between 17 and 21 sectors on the 35 tracks on the standard disc drive (3040 model). Thus if you store one record per block of 255 bytes you will usually refer to that record by a number which must be translated by the program into a track and sector location. The maximum number of usable blocks is 670. If you wish you can store two or more records per block and there is a pointer provided in the buffer to enable reading and writing from the pointer position to selected parts of the buffer, and hence to individual records within a block. The layout of the disc from outer track number 1 to inner track number 35 is as follows. Tracks 1 to 17 each contain 21 sectors, track 18 is the directory track of 20 sectors and must not be used, tracks 19 to 24 each contain 20 sectors, tracks 25 to 30 each contain 18 sectors, and tracks 31 to 35 each contain 17 sectors. The total is 690 sectors, minus the 20 directory sectors, leaving 670 data sectors.

There is a large repertoire of disc handling commands provided by the PET disc system which allow very complicated manipulations. The following is an outline of one way of handling a simple one record per block structure, and the individual actions could be designed as subroutines for use in a larger program:

(a) Open the random access file on logical channel C, and for convenience use secondary address C, in the range 2 to 14:

```
10   OPEN C,8,C"#"        (open and reserve buffer)
20   OPEN 15, 8, 15       (open command channel)
```
(check error reply)

(b) Read a record. First translate the record number to track T and sector S values; the drive number D is 0 or 1:

(convert to obtain T and S)
```
100   PRINT#15,"U1:" C;D;T;S        (reads a block from disc to
                                     buffer)
110   PRINT#15,"B-P:"C;1            (set buffer pointer to start
                                     of buffer)
```
(check error reply)
```
120   INPUT#C, list                 (read values from buffer)
```

(c)   Write a record:

    (convert to T and S)

    200   PRINT#15, "U1:"C;D;T;S   (read a block to buffer)

    210   PRINT#15, "B–P:"C;1   (position buffer pointer)

    (check error reply)

    220   PRINT#C, list   (write values to buffer)

    230   PRINT#15, "U2:"C;D;T;S   (write out buffer to disc)

    (check error reply)

(d)   Close the file:

    300   CLOSE C

    310   CLOSE 15

8.7 FILE MAINTENANCE

Techniques for handling the data in large files go much beyond the basic techniques described earlier in this chapter. Therefore this section provides a few suggestions for those who wish to put BASIC programs to use in the data processing environment.

The essentials of file maintenance are searching for a particular record and updating the records. Updating is the adding, deleting, or changing of existing documents.

Data processing deals with large amounts of data, although 'large' is not quantifiable in general. It is easy to see that once the data have grown too large to fit into the computer store they can be considered 'large', and quite different techniques are required for sorting and searching than those already discussed in earlier chapters.

Data held in random access files are conceptually the same as being held in an array, and the techniques described earlier apply reasonably well. If you want a very efficient search mechanism to reduce disc transfers to a minimum then use a *hash addressed* file. The record key (identification part of the record) is processed to produce a number called the hash address, which is then used as a record number to store the record. This works well until a different record key produces the same number; then some method must be used to place this new record. One way is to put it into the nearest free record past the occupied one. Of course the retrieval mechanism must take this into account when searching for a record.

A simple hash method for a name field would add the ASCII values of the letters together and divide by a prime number a bit larger than the maximum number of records expected. Take the remainder which must lie between 0 and the prime number; this is the hash address for that record. Consult the extensive literature on the subject for full details.

Sequential files are most commonly used for large data storage, often on grounds of cost or because random access files may be severely limited in size by the system or technology used.

There is no quick way of locating a desired record from a sequential file apart from scanning it serially. However, one way of speeding up the process, on average, is to build up a list of search queries. Then scan the file and pick out the matching records as they are encountered. If, say, ten queries were satisfied in only one complete scan of the file then the searching process is much faster on average than if the ten were processed individually. It all depends on the nature of the enquiries. Can they wait until such a list has been built up and processed?

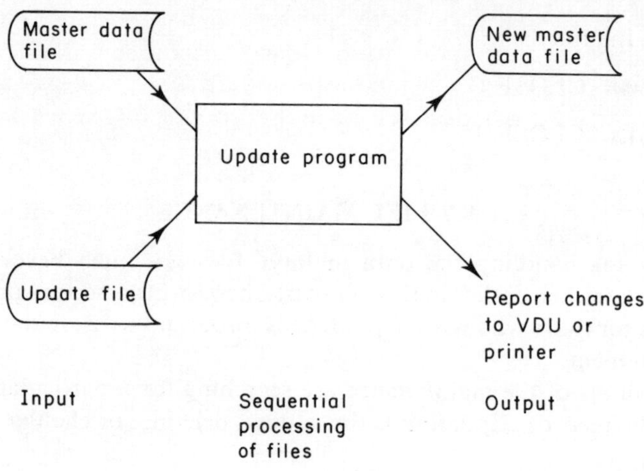

Figure 8.15 Updating a master file. After a satisfactory update the new master file will replace the original file

File maintenance follows the above method. How often the main data file is changed will depend on several factors. Usually it is not altered each time one item requires modification. A list of changes is built up and then applied to the main data file to produce a new data file (see Figure 8.15). The list of changes is usually small enough to be in store, but may also be kept in a file, the 'update file'.

There is usually a requirement that the main file is kept sorted on some key of the records it contains, so the most efficient update method is to sort the update items also. Applying the update to the main file is in many respects the merging of two files. If both are sorted then the resultant new main file will also be sorted. This is one way of building up a large sorted file from scratch. Repeatedly apply the sorted update information as it is obtained, starting with an empty main file.

One major sequential file sorting method uses a merge with a number (more than two) of files, each of which contains many groups of records. Each group might have initially fitted into the computer store, so is sorted within itself. It is called the *polyphase* method; consult *Concise Survey of Computer Methods* by Peter Naur (Studentlitteratur, 1974) or other works on data processing for further details.

Certain *ad hoc* methods will often work quite well. For example, if only two sequential files are available with two real cassette tape recorders then the following technique will sort data in a large file. Some data are read into store from file 1 and sorted, and then output to file 2. This is repeated, so when the end of file 1 is reached, file 2 contains small sequences of data sorted within each sequence. Repeat the exercise going from file 2 back to file 1 but use a different store area work size. Repeat again from file 1 to 2, and so on. Going one way, say from file 1 to file 2, the sorting area can be kept fixed at perhaps 100 records, but going the other way it must vary each time (say, between 51 and 79 records). Otherwise a periodicity will occur causing the entire data never to be sorted; this will end in sequences repeating at the product of the sorting area sizes. Continue the process until no more sorting is required. It is a lengthy process but does work in the end.

PART IV
General Summary

A summary which may be profitably used by those who have completed Part I. A useful background to computer operations and BASIC is given.

9
Program development

Together with new material, this chapter brings together a number of items mentioned earlier with the purpose of illustrating the direct and very useful program development features provided by BASIC. As with other chapters, there is a warning that not all BASICs will have all the features described here.

Development of programs leads inevitably to a debugging stage somewhere in the process, and the action of debugging is one of the most difficult to define clearly. It is a skill acquired mainly through practice, and some programmers seem to develop an intuition about program faults which is impossible to communicate to others. The first two sections of this chapter concentrate on some simple techniques of fault finding to help you get started in program development, and the third section describes one way of building up a complex program.

9.1 DEBUGGING

Debugging is the act of finding and removing errors from programs.

9.1.1 Simple errors

The kinds of errors which occur most frequently are connected with simple typing errors or a slight misunderstanding about the effects of some BASIC statements like FOR–NEXT loops. Some of the typing errors are noticed by the system when it checks the syntax of each statement. That is, it examines each statement in detail to determine if it is a valid BASIC statement. Some BASICs (the best for beginners) check each line the moment that it is sent to the computer, thus:

```
10   Y=6*X+5Z+2                    <press return or send>

>SYNTAX ERROR
```

and the line must be corrected to:

```
10   Y=6*X+5*Z+2
```

However, if the line had been typed as:

```
10   Y=X*6+Z5+2
```

to mean the same as the one above, there would be no error reported as it is syntactically correct, even though you may actually mean it to be:

```
10   Y=X*6+Z*5+2
```

Many BASICs only check for syntax errors when RUN has been typed. This is a little unfortunate, as those starting programming who are most likely to make trivial mistakes are then presented with a whole list of error messages. This is enough to make many would-be programmers abandon hope of ever succeeding. If you find yourself in this situation the golden rule is to ignore most of the error messages and concentrate only on the first one or two in the list. It is very common that an incorrect statement at the beginning of a program can cause other, later statements, to be regarded as incorrect although they are quite all right. Correcting the first one or two errors may remove many others, so that typing RUN again gives only errors which are genuine.

The sort of errors which generate this 'knock-on' effect may arise from faulty declarations of variables at the program beginning. So:

```
10   DIM AA(10), B1(20,5), C1(2,3)
```

with statements like:

```
100   BB(16,1)=2*C(1)+20
```

cause problems because B1( ) not BB was declared an array and C1( ) not C( ) was declared. Either you have mis-spelt the array name in the declaration on line 10 or have started to use new array variables on line 100. A pitfall exists here for the unwary, because BASIC is in my view overgenerous in that if it finds a new array being used it will assume it has a default dimension 10, or 10,10 for a two-dimensional array, and not report a fault. If you did not intend to use a new array but by mistake typed BB instead of B1 you may not get a fault reported.

To summarize: syntax checking will pick up any obvious errors and mis-spellings in any of the words such as INPUT, PRINT, and so on, but it may not do this until you type RUN. Thus it is often advisable to try out any constructions you are unsure of, in a few lines, perhaps separately from the program being developed. The two areas which often cause difficulty are FOR–NEXT loops and arrays.

In FOR–NEXT loops you do not alter the variable—the system takes care of all that. If in doubt always include PRINT statements to demonstrate what is happening:

```
10   REM LOOP TEST
20   INPUT "STARTING VALUE";S
30   INPUT "TERMINATING VALUE";T
40   INPUT "STEP LENGTH";S1
50   PRINT "LOOP IS: FOR I=";S;"TO";T;"STEP";S1
```

```
60    FOR I=S TO T STEP S1
70      PRINT "IN LOOP FOR I=";I
80    NEXT I
90    PRINT "OUT OF LOOP"
100   END
```

This program is a rather elaborate one, but demonstrates exactly what happens in a FOR–NEXT loop. Even a simple test, as:

```
10    FOR I=1 TO 5
20      PRINT I
30    NEXT I
```

may be sufficient to get over any uncertainty you may have concerning loops. In a similar way devise simple programs to demonstrate what happens when you use array elements. Input values, alter array elements, and print out the changes at each stage.

The other point with error detection which you may have noticed is that most BASIC systems give very terse messages to indicate an error. The reason is that the correct diagnosis of an error may be quite complicated and require a larger BASIC compiler/interpreter. It is quite possible, and very desirable, to provide good error diagnostics but very few compilers/interpreters in any computer language prove to be satisfactory in this respect. Thus the new user of any BASIC system has to discover, often by trial and error, what the error messages are likely to mean. Again this is a good reason for trying out a few statements at a time rather than writing a long program before starting to debug it.

Finally, check for the simple typing errors such as the substitution of 1 for I or l (the letter), or the substitution of O (the letter) for Ø (zero, the number). These frequently occur in combination with other characters which make the differences difficult to notice. Thus AO may be written instead of AØ, or I=1+1 instead of I=I+1.

9.1.2 Diagnostics

When a program has been accepted as correct by the BASIC system and runs producing results, it must be validated using data with known results. This is fundamental to the acceptance of the program. The test data should exercise all, or as many as possible, of the various execution paths in a program. A modular approach allows the testing of individual parts quite easily, but beware of the use of global variables between modules. Inadvertant changes in such variables by one module could cause other apparently correct modules to fail.

The state of program variables and execution paths may always be displayed by PRINT statements, which can be so easily added and deleted in BASIC.

338

Remember also the use of immediate PRINT statements (i.e. without a line number, see Section 2.4) for displaying values after an execution error or after a normal END. For example, a program which calculates the roots of a quadratic equation is producing incorrect results. There are two roots to the quadratic equation:

$$ax^2+bx+c=\emptyset$$

which are given by:

$$\text{Root}_1 = \frac{-b+\sqrt{(b^2-4ac)}}{2a}$$

$$\text{Root}_2 = \frac{-b-\sqrt{(b^2-4ac)}}{2a}$$

The incorrect program is:

```
10   REM QUADRATIC, ROOTS OF
20   INPUT "COEFFICIENTS";A,B,C
30   D=B*B-4*A*C
40   IF D<∅ THEN 100
50     D=SQR (D)
60     R1=-B+D/2*A
70     R2=-B-D/2*A
80     PRINT "TWO ROOTS ARE";R1;R2
90   STOP
100  PRINT "IMAGINARY ROOTS ONLY"
110  END
RUN
COEFFICIENTS? 1, -5, 6
TWO ROOTS ARE 5.5∅   4.5∅
```

This is incorrect, as the roots of this particular quadratic $x^2-5x+6=\emptyset$ are known to be 2 and 3. (You can check that $(x-2)(x-3)=x^2-5x+6=\emptyset$.)
  Try an immediate PRINT of the internal values:

PRINT D; A; B; C

1   1   −5   6

which is correct, so examine the calculation of R1 and R2 in lines 6Ø and 7Ø. There is no further information which can be usefully displayed here, but in more complicated programs there may be many variables to be examined.

Try calculating what R1 actually produces:

R1 is $-(-5)+\frac{1}{2}*1$ which is $5+\frac{1}{2}$

whereas it should be:

$$\frac{-(-5)+1}{2*1} \text{ which is } \frac{5+1}{2} \text{ gives } 3$$

Thus lines 6Ø and 7Ø should be:

6Ø   R1=(−B+D)/(2*A)

7Ø   R2=(−B−D)/(2*A)

9.2 INVESTIGATING ERRORS

Assuming that syntax errors can be located sooner or later with the information provided by the compiler/interpreter, this section concentrates on the means of locating execution errors. In many systems, when an execution error occurs the program stops and displays an error message or error number. There are no other facilities available and the programmer has to rely on PRINT statements and careful examination of the program to detect the cause of the error. When only an error number is given the full error message may be obtained by typing in a command or special symbol. On the BBC system, for example, the command is REPORT.

The following sections describe two other major facilities which are very useful for error handling. The first enables the tracing of line numbers as the program executes. The second gives facilities for the program to monitor and handle its own errors. This is a rather exotic feature, and is not intended to be used for the 'ordinary' errors which occur during program development but those which may occur when the program is in service. These may be generated by bad keyboard input or by electrical noise on lines causing strange characters to be presented to the program. Rather than halting and re-starting the program, it is possible to take some action and continue with program execution.

9.2.1 Tracing execution

Programs with more than a few IF statements, FOR–NEXT loops, and subroutines soon build up a large number of execution paths. It is not always possible to determine which path was being taken just prior to an error unless a number of internal variables are PRINTed at many stages in the program. Some systems provide an easier way of obtaining this information using a TRACE command, which causes the interpreter to print out the line number of each statement as it is executed. Thus a complete 'history' of the program execution path is available when an error is encountered.

```
10   REM TRACE DEMO
20   TRACE
30   I=10
40   FOR J=1 TO 2
50     I=I+1
60     PRINT J;I
70   NEXT J
80   END
RUN
[30]   [40]   [50]   [60]        1        11
[70]   [50]   [60]   2     12
[70]   [80]
OK
```

The above program demonstrates Microsoft's TRACE statement which may also be used as a command, in immediate mode. The statement numbers appear in square brackets to distinguish them from other output, which may be internal values for diagnostic purposes such as J and I above in line 60. The statement NO TRACE switches the tracing facility off.

BBC BASIC uses TRACE ON and TRACE OFF to control its tracing, but also provides TRACE N where N is a statement number. Only those lines with numbers less than N will be traced.

Tracing slows down program execution speed considerably and can generate a lot of output. Either wait for the program to get near the error area and halt it (by some 'break' key), switch on TRACE and CONTINUE the program, or place TRACE, NOTRACE statements in the program in the suspected error area.

Remember that the interpreter may optimize the BASIC which is provided as input, so that not all the expected lines will appear. This is true of the FOR statement at the beginning of a FOR–NEXT loop in the above example.

9.2.2 Error routines

(Advanced feature, omit until Part III has been covered.)

As discussed in the introduction to this section this is quite an exotic facility designed to allow 'correct' programs to handle faults which may appear in the computer environment from a variety of sources.

Microcomputers, being small and portable, rely on local power supplies for their operation. Unlike mainframe computers which may have regulated power supplies, micros must accept the normal power supply which is quite likely to have 'spikes' on it from other appliances and fluctuating voltage levels. Electrical noise may also be generated by radio frequency pickup on unscreened cables or connectors.

Portability is a new feature for computers which leads to micros being used more by non-experts. This is a good thing, but it means that the chances of incorrect input are much higher. Although the input values in such circumstances should be carefully screened it is possible that invalid values can be missed and cause a serious program error later.

Only experience will indicate the type of error likely to occur in both the above circumstances and whether there is anything which can be done to recover from it. The following describes the mechanics of the error handling facilities, the design of the appropriate routine being different for each case.

The normal program state causes the program to halt when an error is detected. Internal values are usually retained so that immediate PRINT statements can be used. However, it is possible to set a global condition so that whenever an error is detected a jump is made to a special error routine. This has the form:

```
10   ON ERROR GOTO 500
```

and line 500 will be the start of the error handling section. When this statement is in effect, execution continues through the error routine which may finally transfer control back to where the error occurred, or elsewhere in the program. The ON ERROR statement has a 'whenever' type of action which means it will be obeyed from any point in the program when an error occurs. The error trapping action may be switched off, to return to normal by a statement ON ERROR OFF or similar. (Microsoft use ON ERROR GO TO 0 for this purpose.)

The following illustrates an error trapping routine:

```
10   REM

20   . . .

30   . . .

40   ON ERROR GO TO 200

50
```

```
200   REM ERROR ROUTINE
210   IF ERR=11 THEN 240
220   PRINT "ERROR"; ERR; "AT LINE NUMBER";ERL
230   STOP
240   PRINT "DIVISION BY ZERO FIXED UP-CHECK INPUT"
250   Z=1.0E-20
260   RESUME
```

Microsoft and BBC BASICs contain two variables (or functions), ERR and ERL, which contain the error number and line number of the error respectively. In the example above the error checking is switched on at line 40, and when an error occurs control passes to line 200. This is set up to monitor a divide by zero error, so if anything else occurs the information is printed out on line 220. When the divide by zero error is found, the text on line 240 is output and the value of a variable (Z) is set to avoid the error. The statement on line 260 causes control to go back to the error line and repeat it.

Variables such as ERL, ERR, or special IF statements should be available to determine the error details within the error routine. Once appropriate action has been taken, which can include switching future error trapping off, the execution control is routed back to the program perhaps using a statement like RESUME, or if this is absent using a GO TO. Do not use a RETURN statement as the routine was not called in the correct subroutine manner.

9.3 DEVELOPMENT STRATEGY

One purpose of this book, like many others covering programming language, is to describe how the language works and what the statements in the language do. In parallel with this aim, it tries to teach the techniques of program design and construction.

A major difficulty with design is the uncertainty about the details of the solution, so the refinement method advocated here is one which tries to put off for as long as possible decisions concerning these details. However, even quite general decisions made at the outset do tend to imply certain later low level features. Therefore there is not as much freedom as might be imagined once the design has commenced. Indeed, different top level decisions for solving the same problem will probably not converge to a similar solution. Only experience will indicate which approach is likely to reach the 'best' solution, if such a one exists.

To build up some idea of the details of a solution the author has found the following experimental method helpful on occasion.

The problem may involve some unfamiliar computational features such as file handling or complex nested loops or special printing. In this case it is best to run an experiment and develop a prototype before designing the final product. Set out in the usual way to sketch out a design, which may involve only a part of the solution which is the obscure area, and then go to the computer, type it in, and run it. Debug the program, and spend as much time as is necessary to satisfy

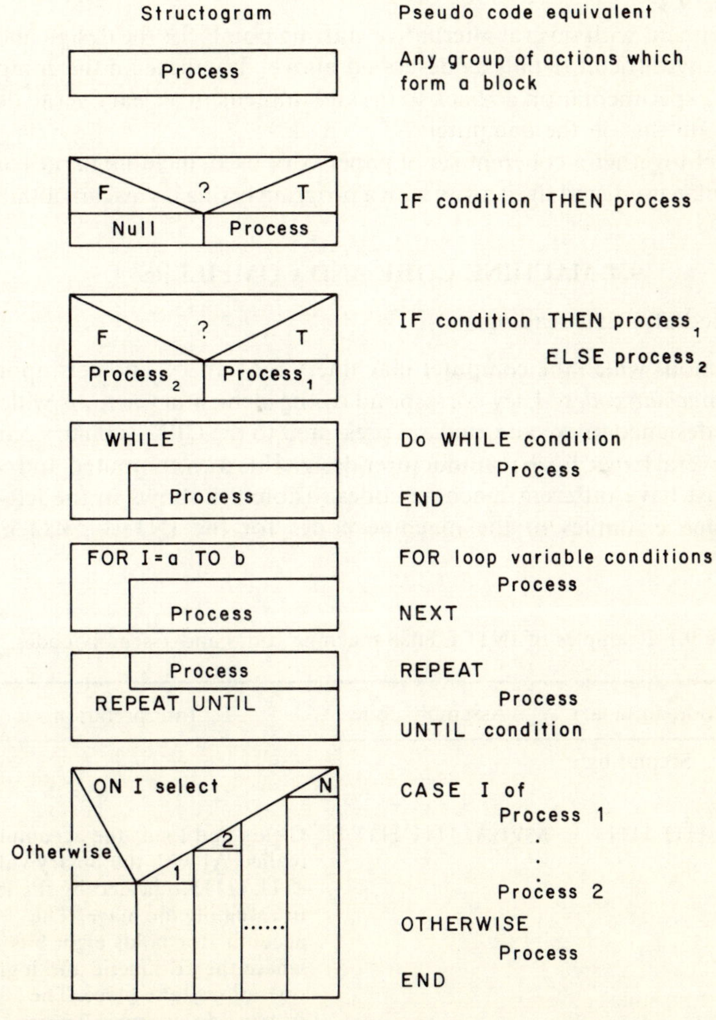

Figure 9.1 Structograms and Pseudo code (see also Figure 3.1)

yourself as to the best way of achieving a solution. At this stage do not be tempted to add the rest of the solution round the part just developed. If you do so you will find the structure of the program forming a 'heap' rather than something more elegant and understandable. Leave the solution for a little while, perhaps overnight, so that you are not too closely involved with the details just programmed and set out afresh to design the complete solution. This time accommodate all the proper details of error checking, user interface, and so on. The result should be something to be proud of, which can be happily passed to friends and colleagues.

In summary:

(a) Design top-down using structograms or pseudo code. These are given in Figure 9.1.

(b) Experiment with several alternative starting points for the design and also with any difficult details as described above. Try these on the computer.

(c) After experimentation go back to (a) and implement a clear overall design. Program this on the computer.

(d) Collect together a coherent set of paperwork used, including notes on any formulae used, and file it away with a program listing if you can obtain one.

9.4 MACHINE CODE AND COMPILERS

(Best omitted at a first reading.)

The instructions which the computer machinery recognizes, and acts upon, are known as *machine codes*. They correspond to the elementary actions which the machine is designed to execute, and are presented to the CPU as binary patterns in one or several bytes. Each manufacturer designs his own computer, and consequently most have different machine codes. Table 9.1 shows in the left-hand column some examples of the machine codes for the INTEL 8080 microcomputer.

Table 9.1 Examples of INTEL 8080 machine codes and assembly codes

Machine code, in binary		Assembly code	Interpretation
First byte	Second byte		
0011 1110	1111 1111	MVI A, 1111 1111 B	Clears and loads the accumulator (called A) with the binary value 1111 1111, indicated by the letter B in assembly language. The accumulator holds eight bits and is where the arithmetic and logical operations take place. The instruction occupies 2 bytes.

1000 0110	ADD M	Adds the contents of a store location (which is eight bits) to the value already in the accumulator. The location (address) of the store is held in a register called M. The instruction occupies 1 byte.
1101 0011 0000 0001	OUT 0000 0001 B	Copies the result in the accumulator onto some output wires, called the data bus. The number 0000 0001 identifies which output device is required, and is put on to a set of wires called the address bus. Other parts of the computer then take action to handle this output. The instruction occupies 2 bytes.

As you might imagine, a machine code is very difficult to write correctly, because it is so easy to make a mistake when using binary numbers. Actually, the binary numbers can be written in a more compact form as hexadecimal numbers for keyboard input, but many programming problems still remain. To eliminate some of these, an easier representation has been devised, in which the binary codes are replaced by mnemonic codes that a programmer finds easy to read and remember. This, together with a few other helpful programming features, forms what is known as an *assembly language*. The centre column in Table 9.1 illustrates some assembly language instructions.

Because of the close relationship between assembly language and machine code it is easy to construct a program which will accept assembly language as input and produce machine code as output. Such a program is called an *assembler*. It operates as follows: firstly, a program is written in assembly language instructions which are input to the computer; secondly, the assembler checks the input and performs the translation which produces machine code as output. Finally, this machine code is loaded into a suitable part of the computer core and executed.

Although many programs are written in assembly language they tend to be quite long, require considerable skill to produce, and are intimately connected with the details of the particular computer machinery. For example, the following fragment of BASIC would require at least 100 assembly language instructions for the INTEL 8080 to produce the equivalent effect, namely, the multiplication of two numbers:

```
10   INPUT A,B

20   LET C=A*B

30   PRINT C
```

Although a compiler acts in a similar fashion when translating from a high level language, such as BASIC, into a machine code, the gap is so much greater

346

that a compiler is a very much more complicated program than an assembler.

There are a number of ways in which compilers may be written. The essence of an interactive language like BASIC is the ability to edit the program easily, to display the program when required, and to execute the program on command. All these activities may be done in any order, and are usually repeated many times during the construction and correction of programs.

One approach, called pure compilation, takes each BASIC line as it is received and translates it to a machine code. At the end of the program the resultant machine code is certainly complete and ready for execution. However, large tables and lists are needed during the line by line translation to keep track of the original variable names and statement numbers so that the compiler can guarantee a complete program. For example, records must be kept to indicate that 1Ø GO TO 51Ø has been encountered before line 51Ø has been typed in. Equally, earlier lines could be changed or deleted before the program is finished. This approach produces final machine code ready to execute, but the interactive requirement on the compilation process requires very large tables which take up a lot of computer store.

Another approach, called pure interpretation, would be to retain the BASIC program as typed in to the computer, and only translate it line by line when it is being executed. Thus, when a loop is encountered the statements are repeatedly translated over and over again, because the system just translates the next statement it reaches so that it may be executed, and does not retain the machine code (which is probably not even produced). The advantage of having the input program available for editing and display is set against the very slow execution speed. While compilers can check each statement as it is received and immediately report errors, interpreters can only do so at run time, which is a serious disadvantage.

A practical translation system lies somewhere between the two approaches outlined above. Figure 9.2 indicates the main actions of such a system, which may be called a compiler or interpreter in the literature. Some types of internal representation are used which retain the line by line layout of BASIC, but contain much of the preparation necessary for the execution. Below are a few lines of a BASIC program together with the internal format used by the ICL 29Ø4 computer. The program is:

```
1Ø    REM SIMGLE EXAMPLE
2Ø    P=3.14159
3Ø    INPUT R
4Ø    A=P*R*R
5Ø    C=2.Ø*P*R
6Ø    PRINT R,A,C
7Ø    END
```

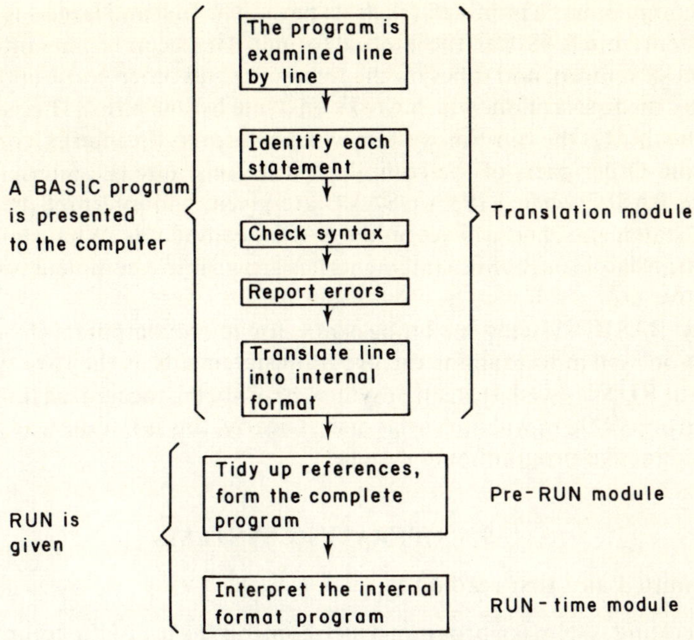

Figure 9.2 The stages in program translation and execution

and the internal form is:

K!SIMPLE EXAMPLE

P′3.14159K=

L!R′!

A′P′R′*R′*K=

C′2.ØP′*R′*K=

P!R′,A′,C′!

E!

Later, when RUN is given, the internal format may be interpreted by a run-time system. The internal format closely follows the structure of the original BASIC, and so may be edited and listed back as BASIC without too much difficulty. On conversion to the internal format quite a lot of error checking can be performed on each BASIC statement. While the speed of execution is not as good as the pure compiler, described above, it is very much better than the pure interpreter.

The compiler has a number of distinct parts. The first and largest is the translation system from BASIC to the internal format. The second comes into operation when RUN is given, and tidies up the references and other 'loose ends' not completed by the first section, which works on a line by line basis. This is the pre-run part. The third is the run-time system which interprets the internal format during execution. Other parts of the compiler will reconstitute the internal format to produce BASIC when LIST or SAVE are given, will interpret the immediate BASIC statements, and will act on the BASIC commands. What started out as a simple translator for BASIC statements has grown into a complete system for full interactive use.

Many BASIC systems including some for microcomputers do not use the translation system to examine the program statements as they are typed in, but wait until RUN is given. Instead of syntax errors being recognized immediately, a whole group of them will appear at once. Clearly, this is not the way to provide a good interactive programming system.

9.5 OPERATING SYSTEMS

(Best omitted at a first reading.)

The operating system is a program which controls the use of the computer. All, or part, of it is resident in the computer store whenever it is executing programs. It provides an environment in which the rest of the software, including user programs, can run. In effect, it separates the nasty details of the hardware from the user of the computer.

If the computer is a powerful one which has many terminals attached to it, the operating system is a time-sharing one. That is, it gives a share of the computer time to each user terminal. It also maintains the appearance that each user has the sole use of the resources of the computer. Possibly the only effect of other users on such a system is when most of the terminals (VDUs) are in use and a quite noticeable slowing down in response is apparent.

Another task of a modern operating system is to provide a file system. This concerns the types of file which may exist, as well as the data formats for tape and disc, the naming conventions for these files, and how they may be accessed by programs. Within the operating system various utilities will be provided to manipulate the files, such as copy, erase, rename, print, and edit. Sometimes only certain types of files, called graphic or terminal format files, may be edited at the VDU. In effect, these files appear as they were typed into the system; the other types are purely for internal, i.e. program, use and would make no sense if displayed on the VDU.

Many microcomputers which supply BASIC do not have a clearly separate operating system. The computers have been designed for one purpose, to run BASIC, and the many features required of an operating system have been built into the BASIC system. This is the case in the Commodore PET microcomputer. When the power is switched on, BASIC is loaded automatically and provides all the facilities required for the development and execution of programs.

It is possible to 'step out' of the BASIC system on the PET (By means of SYS 64785 command) and to find a simple operating system, which is called a monitor. This provides a very limited number of facilities for machine code programs. Such BASIC systems, as illustrated in Figure 9.3(a), are typical of software designed for the computer to do specific functions, which in this case is the provision of BASIC only. Many microcomputer systems are like this, and are loaded into the 'naked' computer which either has no monitor or a very simple one. These systems must then cope with the most elementary hardware details themselves.

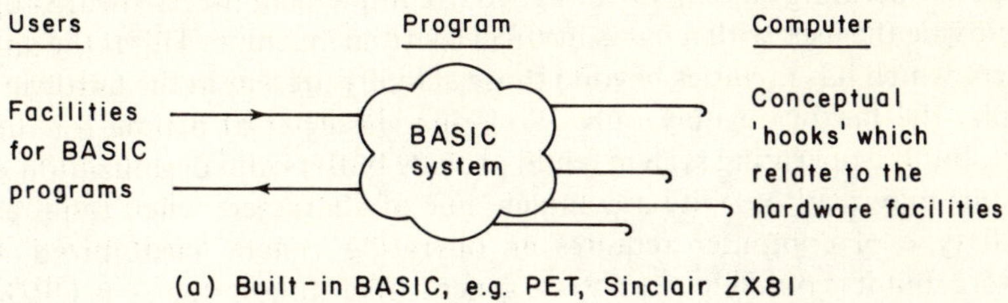

(a) Built-in BASIC, e.g. PET, Sinclair ZX81

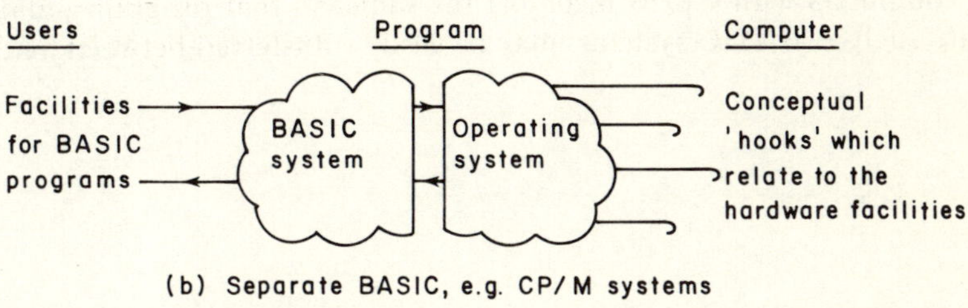

(b) Separate BASIC, e.g. CP/M systems

Figure 9.3 BASIC operating systems

One widespread operating system, which is clearly separate from BASIC, is the CP/M operating system for microcomputers. Section 8.5.2 describes the loading procedure, which first requires CP/M to be loaded before BASIC.

Let us look in some detail at the problem of getting a program to execute. Before execution, the program must be loaded into the store by the operating system, or the equivalent part of a BASIC system where this is on its own. How is this initial system itself to be loaded so that it can load programs? The answer lies in a very simple program called a bootstrap, written in machine code. Early computers of the 1950s had a series of switches by means of which the operator could key in manually the bootstrap, but, luckily, modern microcomputers have it built into a special read-only memory (ROM), and switching on will activate it and thus initiate the loading of the full system.

The main function of the first operating systems was to avoid 'booting' each separate program into the computer. They quickly developed to allow a batch, or series, of programs to be submitted to the computer. When one program had finished, control would pass to the operating system which was then able to load and execute the next one.

Gradually new facilities were added. Standard routines handled the input and output devices and simple error recovery actions developed. Job control language (JCL) emerged as a series of commands for selecting the options available for running any particular program. As terminals on-line to the computer began to be used, the JCL developed into a more comprehensive series of commands which took advantage of the interactive nature of the communication between user and computer.

Modern operating systems are designed to complement the hardware; together they provide the user with what is in effect a virtual machine. This is the name for a system which has facilities beyond those actually present in the hardware. For example, the hardware may only allow one character at a time for input or output, but the operating system could provide buffers and organization so that programs may read or write a complete line of characters when required.

Each type of computer requires an operating system 'customized' for its hardware, but it is possible to take one general operating system, e.g. CP/M, and adapt it to fit a number of different computers. The user appearance of the different computers with CP/M is almost the same, so that programs, and other software such as BASIC systems, may be easily transferred between machines.

Appendix I
Solutions to the exercises

Solutions to the exercises for Chapter 1

1.1   (a)   Z=6, B=2, A=2

        (b)   A=–5, B=5, Q=–5⅓

        (c)   B=Ø, A=½, Z=8

        (d)   A=11Ø

1.2   (a)   LET A=B+C*C

        (b)   LET A=(A+B)/C

        (c)   LET Y=(X+A)/(Y–B)

        (d)   LET Z=1/(1–1/(A+B))

1.3   The program seems to put assorted values in the variables A,B,C, and D. Then finds the total and average value in Z. The program prints the average value from line 7Ø.

1.4
```
10  INPUT A
20  INPUT B
30  INPUT C
40  INPUT D
50  Z=A+B+C+D
60  Z=Z/4
70  PRINT Z
80  END
```
or
```
10  INPUT A,B,C,D
50  Z=A+B+C+D
60  Z=Z/4
70  PRINT Z
```

352

                80   END

1.5   10   INPUT M,T,R
            20   I=M*T*(R/100)
            30   PRINT I
            40   END
    or
            10   PRINT "PLEASE INPUT MONEY, TIME, RATE"
            20   INPUT M,T,R
            30   I=M*T*(R/100)
            40   PRINT "FOR £";M;"OVER";T;"YEARS"
            50   PRINT "AT A RATE OF ";R;"%"
            60   PRINT "THE SIMPLE INTEREST IS";I
            70   END

Solutions to the exercises of Chapter 2

2.1   10   INPUT M,T,I
            20   R=1+I/100
            30   P=M*R**T*(R-1)/(R**T-1)
            40   PRINT "FOR A LOAN";M;"OVER";T;"YEARS"
            50   PRINT "AT A RATE OF";I;"%"
            60   PRINT "THE ANNUAL REPAYMENTS ARE";P
            70   END

2.2   10   INPUT L,H,W
            20   PRINT "BOX L=";L;"H=";H;"W=";W
            30   REM FIND VOLUME
            40   V=L*H*W
            50   REM FIND SURFACE AREA
            60   S=2*(W*H+H*L+W*L)
            70   REM FIND COST IN PENCE

```
 80  C=5+S*0.02
 90  REM
100  PRINT "THE VOLUME IS";V
110  PRINT "WITH SURFACE AREA";S
120  PRINT "AND COST (IN PENCE) IS";C
130  END
```

2.3 Add to the solution to exercise 2.2:

```
 85  C=C+(S-W*L)*0.005
```

2.4
```
 10  PRINT "TAXHAVEN CREDIT CARD LIMITED"
 20  PRINT "-----------------------------"
 30  PRINT
 40  REM BALANCE IS B
 50  I=B*8/100
 60  PRINT "PREVIOUS BALANCE ";B
 70  PRINT "            INTEREST ";I
 80  PRINT
 90  PRINT "ITEM                              COST "
100  PRINT "----                              ---- "
110  T=B+I
120  FOR J=1 TO 3
130     INPUT A$,C
140     PRINT A$,C
150     T=T+C
160  NEXT J
170  PRINT "                        ---- "
180  PRINT "                TOTAL    ";T
190  PRINT "                        ---- "
200  PRINT
210  PRINT "MINIMUM PAYABLE ";T/10
```

220   END

Lines 120 to 160 may be replaced by the lines:

120   INPUT A$,C

124   PRINT A$,C

126   T=T+C

130   INPUT A$,C

134   PRINT A$,C

136   T=T+C

140   INPUT A$,C

144   PRINT A$,C

146   T=T+C

These have the same effect as the loop, which is described in detail in Chapter 3.

Solutions to the exercises of Chapter 3

3.1
```
10   INPUT M
20   C=25
30   IF M<=2 THEN 50
40     C=C+2*(M-2)*8
50   PRINT C
60   END
```

To accommodate the additional feature modify line 40 to become:
```
40   C=C+INT (2*(M-2+.49))*8
```

3.2

PRINT headings
FOR N=1 to 10
PRINT N,N*N,N*N*N
END

```
10   PRINT "NUMBER", "SQUARE", "CUBE"
20   FOR N=1 TO 10
```

```
3Ø      PRINT N,N*N,N*N*N
4Ø   NEXT N
5Ø   END
```

3.3

| PRINT headings |
| FOR N=1 TO 1Ø |
| Set base value to 1 |
| FOR I=1 TO 5 |
| Multiply base value by N |
| PRINT base value, not on new line |
| PRINT for a new line |
| END |

```
 1Ø   PRINT "POWERS OF N"
 2Ø   PRINT "-----------"
 3Ø   PRINT
 4Ø   FOR N=1 TO 1Ø
 5Ø      S=1
 6Ø      FOR I=1 TO 5
 7Ø         S=S*N
 8Ø         PRINT S;
 9Ø      NEXT I
1ØØ   PRINT
11Ø   NEXT N
12Ø   END
```

3.4

INPUT N
Set up factorial=1
WHILE N>1
Factorial=factorial *N
N=N–1
PRINT results
END

```
10    INPUT N
20    F=1
30    IF N<=1 THEN 70
40      F=F*N
50      N=N–1
60    GO TO 30
70    PRINT "THE FACTORIAL IS";F
80    END
```

Notice how the WHILE loop has to be transformed into an IF statement and a GO TO statement. The above program does not retain the value N which should be copied to another variable (say M) if its value is required. It also will return (incorrectly) F=1 for negative values of N which should be guarded against if these values are expected.

3.5

Set count=Ø and sum=Ø
INPUT first mark
WHILE mark greater than or equal to zero
Sum=sum plus mark
C=C+1
INPUT next mark
Average=sum/C
PRINT results
END

```
10   REM  INPUT  MARKS  AND  END  WITH  A  NEGATIVE
        NUMBER
20   REM C=COUNT OF NUMBER OF MARKS READ
30   REM S=SUM OF MARKS READ
40      C=0
50      S=0
60      INPUT M
70      IF M<0 THEN 120
80         S=S+M
90         C=C+1
100        INPUT M
110  GO TO 70
120  A=S/C
130  PRINT "THE AVERAGE IS";A
140  END
```

Note the WHILE loop transform to IF and GOTO statements. A translation from WHILE to GO TO–IF statements requires that the IF statement start the loop. There is no construction for arbitrary jumps, so a modification to:

```
50   . . . . . . . . . . . . . . . .
60   INPUT M
70   IF M<0 THEN 110
80      S=S+M
90      C=C+1
100  GO TO 60
110  . . . . . . . . . . . . . . .
```

is not permitted by structured programming. It does not seem wrong, but in a more complex situation can lead to errors very easily so is to be avoided.

3.6

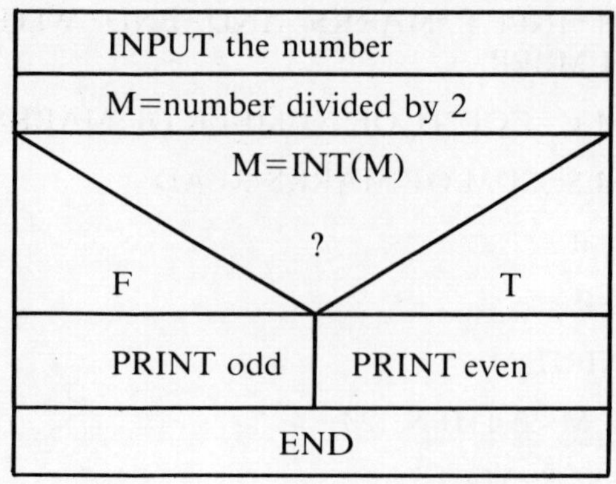


```
10   REM TEST FOR EVEN OR ODD
20   INPUT N
30   M=N/2
40   REM
50   IF M=INT(M) THEN 80
60      PRINT N;"IS AN ODD NUMBER"
70   GO TO 90
80      PRINT N;"IS AN EVEN NUMBER"
90   END
```

3.7


```
10   REM SUM EVEN NUMBERS
20   REM C IS COUNTER, S IS THE SUM, N IS THE NUMBER.
30   C=1
40   S=0
50   N=2
```

```
60    IF (S+N)>100 THEN 110
70      S=S+N
80      C=C+1
90      N=N+2
100   GO TO 60
110   PRINT "THE SUM IS";S;"AFTER";C-1;"VALUES"
120   END
```

3.8

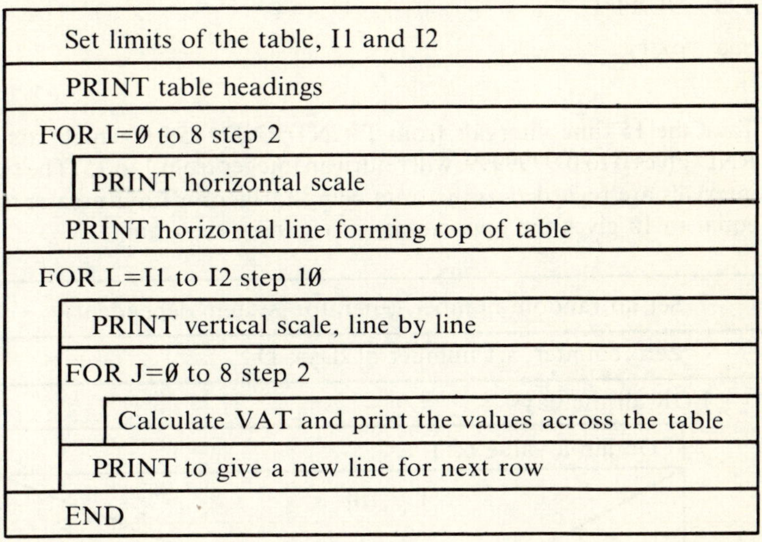

| Set limits of the table, I1 and I2 |
| PRINT table headings |
| FOR I=0 to 8 step 2 |
| PRINT horizontal scale |
| PRINT horizontal line forming top of table |
| FOR L=I1 to I2 step 10 |
| PRINT vertical scale, line by line |
| FOR J=0 to 8 step 2 |
| Calculate VAT and print the values across the table |
| PRINT to give a new line for next row |
| END |

```
10    REM VAT TABLE GENERATION
20    REM RATE IS 15%
30    I1=0
40    I2=200
50    PRINT "VAT FOR";I1;"P TO ";I2+8;"P"
60    PRINT "----------------------------"
70    PRINT
80    FOR I=0 TO 8 STEP 2
90      PRINT TAB(10+I*3);I;
100   NEXT I
110   PRINT "        +----------------------------"
```

```
120   FOR L=I1 to I2 STEP 10
130     PRINT L;TAB(6);"I";
140     FOR J=0 TO 8 STEP 2
150       V=INT (0.15*(L+J))
160         PRINT TAB(10+J*3);V;
170     NEXT J
180     PRINT
190   NEXT L
200   END
```

3.9   Take the 15 time intervals from T=INT(RND*15+1) which, assuming RND gives 0 to 0.9999999, will return an integer from 1 to 15. The first ten intervals are regarded as the train being early, only for T greater than or equal to 10 gives the opportunity of catching the train.

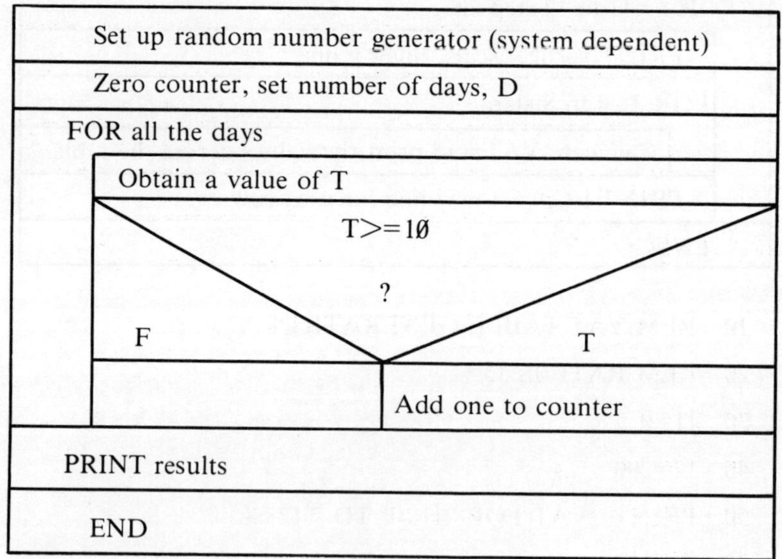


```
10   REM TRAIN SIMULATION
20   REM SET UP RANDOM GENERATOR
30   INPUT "PLEASE INPUT A NUMBER" ;N
40   RANDOMIZE N
50   REM
```

```
60    C=Ø
70    D=2Ø
80    FOR I=1 TO D
90      T=INT (RND*15+1)
100       IF T>=1Ø THEN C=C+1
110   NEXT I
120   PRINT "YOU CAUGHT THE TRAIN ON" ;C;" OCCASIONS"
130   END
```

<table>
<tr><td rowspan="9">3.10</td><td colspan="2"> 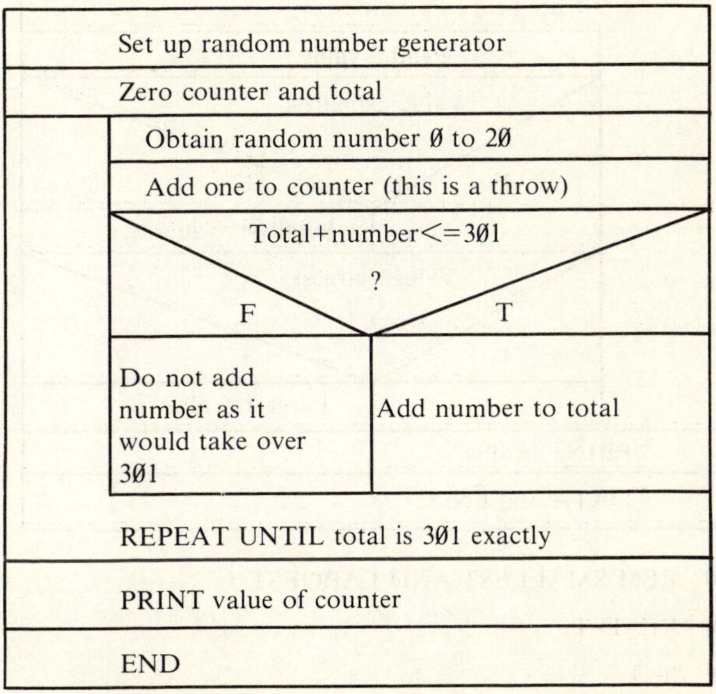Set up random number generator</td></tr>
<tr><td colspan="2">Zero counter and total</td></tr>
<tr><td colspan="2">Obtain random number Ø to 2Ø</td></tr>
<tr><td colspan="2">Add one to counter (this is a throw)</td></tr>
<tr><td colspan="2">Total+number<=3Ø1 ?
F   T</td></tr>
<tr><td>Do not add number as it would take over 3Ø1</td><td>Add number to total</td></tr>
<tr><td colspan="2">REPEAT UNTIL total is 3Ø1 exactly</td></tr>
<tr><td colspan="2">PRINT value of counter</td></tr>
<tr><td colspan="2">END</td></tr>
</table>

```
10    REM DARTS SIMULATION
20    INPUT "PLEASE INPUT A NUMBER" ;N
30    RANDOMIZE N
40    S=Ø
50    C=Ø
60      L=INT (21*RND)
70      C=C+1
```

362

```
 80    IF (S+L)<=301 THEN S=S+L
 90   IF S<>301 THEN 60
100   PRINT "OK - SCORE IS 301 AFTER" ;C;"THROWS"
110   END
```

Solutions to the exercises of Chapter 4

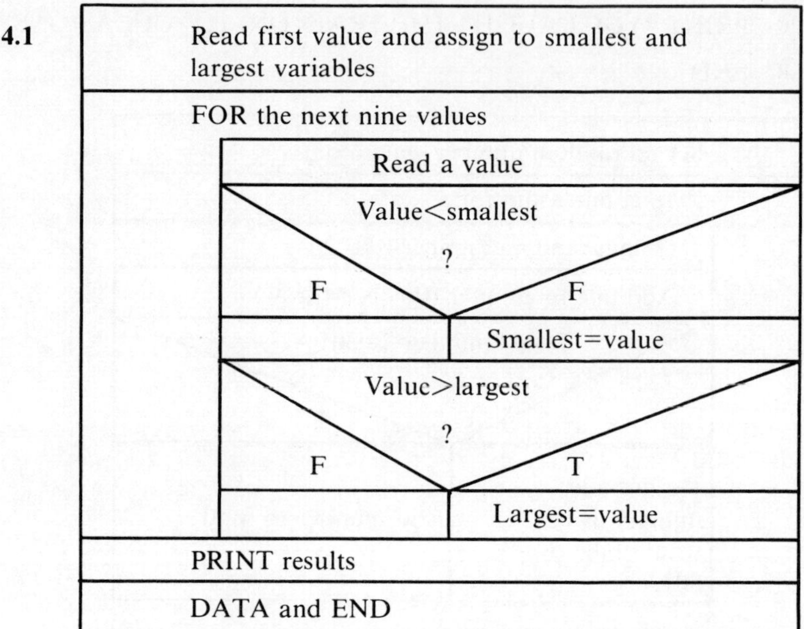


```
 10   REM SMALLEST AND LARGEST
 20   READ T
 30   S=T
 40   L=T
 50   FOR I=1 TO 9
 60     READ T
 70     IF T<S THEN S=T
 80     IF T>L THEN L=T
 90   NEXT I
100   PRINT "SMALLEST VALUE IS" ;S
```

```
110   PRINT "LARGEST VALUE IS" ;L
120   DATA 10,0,19,20,7,39,267,4,1,500
130   END
```

4.2

Set DIM statement for marks, and number of pupils
Zero total S, and PRINT heading
FOR the number of pupils
READ name and PRINT name
INPUT mark and add to total
PRINT average
RESTORE data list, and PRINT heading
FOR the number of pupils
READ name, and PRINT name and mark
DATA and END

```
10    REM CLASS MARKING LIST (ASSUME 5 PUPILS)
20    DIM M(5)
30    N=5
40    S=0
50    PRINT "GIVE MARK FOR EACH OF THE FOLLOWING"
60    FOR I=1 TO 5
70      READ A$
80      PRINT A$;
90      INPUT M(I)
100     S=S+M(I)
110   NEXT I
120   PRINT "CLASS AVERAGE IS" ;S/N
130   RESTORE
140   PRINT "THE FULL LIST IS"
150   FOR I=1 TO 5
160     READ A$
```

364

```
170     PRINT A$,M(I)
180   NEXT I
190   DATA "JOANNA","LARA","SARAH","DAWN",
      "ESTHER"
200   END
```

4.3

<table>
<tr><td colspan="4">Set DIM statement for attendance, and number of pupils</td></tr>
<tr><td></td><td colspan="3">FOR the number of pupils</td></tr>
<tr><td></td><td></td><td colspan="2">Set array element to zero for pupil total</td></tr>
<tr><td></td><td colspan="3">FOR each of the days of the week</td></tr>
<tr><td></td><td></td><td colspan="2">Set daily total (S) to zero</td></tr>
<tr><td></td><td></td><td colspan="2">FOR the number of pupils</td></tr>
<tr><td></td><td></td><td></td><td>READ attendance</td></tr>
<tr><td></td><td></td><td></td><td>Add to daily total (S)</td></tr>
<tr><td></td><td></td><td></td><td>Add to pupil total</td></tr>
<tr><td></td><td></td><td colspan="2">PRINT the daily total</td></tr>
<tr><td></td><td colspan="3">PRINT heading</td></tr>
<tr><td></td><td colspan="3">FOR the number of pupils</td></tr>
<tr><td></td><td></td><td colspan="2">READ name, PRINT name and pupil total from array</td></tr>
<tr><td></td><td colspan="3">DATA and END</td></tr>
</table>

```
10    REM REGISTER (3 PUPILS FOR EXAMPLE)
20    DIM N(3)
30    M=3
40    FOR I=1 TO M
50      N(I)=0
60    NEXT I
70    FOR D=1 TO 5
80      S=0
90      FOR I=1 TO M
100       READ P
```

```
110      S=S+P
120       N(I)=N(I)+P
130    NEXT I
140    PRINT "FOR DAY";D;"TOTAL IS";S;"PUPILS"
150  NEXT D
160  PRINT "INDIVIDUAL ATTENDANCE IS"
170  FOR I=1 TO M
180     READ A$
190     PRINT A$;N(I);"DAYS"
200  NEXT I
210  DATA 0,1,1
220  DATA 1,1,1
230  DATA 1,1,1
240  DATA 1,0,0
250  DATA 1,0,1
260  DATA "PETER","JOHN","DAVID"
270  END
```

```
4.4   10   REM STRING HANDLING (MICROSOFT FUNCTIONS)
      20   A$="ANN"
      30   B$="KENNY"
      40   C$=A$+" "+B$
      50   PRINT C$
      60   REM
      70   PRINT LEFT$(A$,1);" ";LEFT$(B$,1)
      80   REM
      90   D$="MS"
      100  E$="201 TOWNEND ROAD, CREWE"
      110  PRINT D$;" ";C$        :REM PRINTS NAME
      120  J=INSTR(1,E$,",")      :REM FIND POSITION OF COMMA
      130  PRINT LEFT$(E$,J)      :REM PRINTS ROAD PART
```

140   J=LEN(E$)–J

150   PRINT RIGHT$(E$,J) :REM PRINTS TOWN

160   END

Lines 100 to 150 illustrate the splitting up of the address string to print the road and town on different lines as is usual. The comma is located and parts to the left and right of it are printed on different lines.

4.5   The design and program is based on the solution technique that one name is selected and all the other names in the list are permutated with it. The next name is selected, and so on. Thus a pair of nested FOR–NEXT loops fits this solution very well.

<table>
<tr><td colspan="4">Define DIM string array</td></tr>
<tr><td></td><td colspan="3">FOR all the names</td></tr>
<tr><td></td><td></td><td colspan="2">READ the names into the array</td></tr>
<tr><td colspan="4">Set week counter to zero</td></tr>
<tr><td></td><td colspan="3">FOR all the names</td></tr>
<tr><td></td><td></td><td colspan="2">FOR the rest of the names</td></tr>
<tr><td></td><td></td><td></td><td>Increment week counter by one</td></tr>
<tr><td></td><td></td><td></td><td>PRINT week and two names</td></tr>
<tr><td colspan="4">DATA and END</td></tr>
</table>

```
 10    REM ORDINARY ROTA (FOR EXAMPLE 5 NAMES)
 20    DIM N$(10)
 30    N=5
 40    FOR I=1 TO N
 50      READ N$(I)
 60    NEXT I
 70    W=0
 90    FOR I=1 TO N
100      FOR J=I+1 TO N
110        W=W+1
120        PRINT "WEEK";W;" ";N$(I);"AND";N$(J)
```

130   NEXT J

140   NEXT I

150   DATA NAME1,NAME2,NAME3,NAME4,NAME5

160   END

Real names may be substituted in line 150, but the existing names will illustrate the systematic generation of the rota when the program is RUN.

Quite a lot of thought is required to produce a simple program which includes the restriction that no name may appear on the list for more than two consecutive weeks. The solution has the same form as above, but selects the names rather differently. Use the modified lines:

10   REM MODIFIED ROTA (LIMIT MAX 2 WEEKS PER NAME)

90   FOR I=1 TO N−1

100   FOR J=1 TO N−I

120   PRINT "WEEK";W;" ";N$(J);"AND";N$(J+I)

4.6   The solution assumes the words are separated by one comma, semicolon, full stop, or blank space. Note that quotes round the input are required if it contains a comma, unless a LINPUT or similar statement is used in the program.

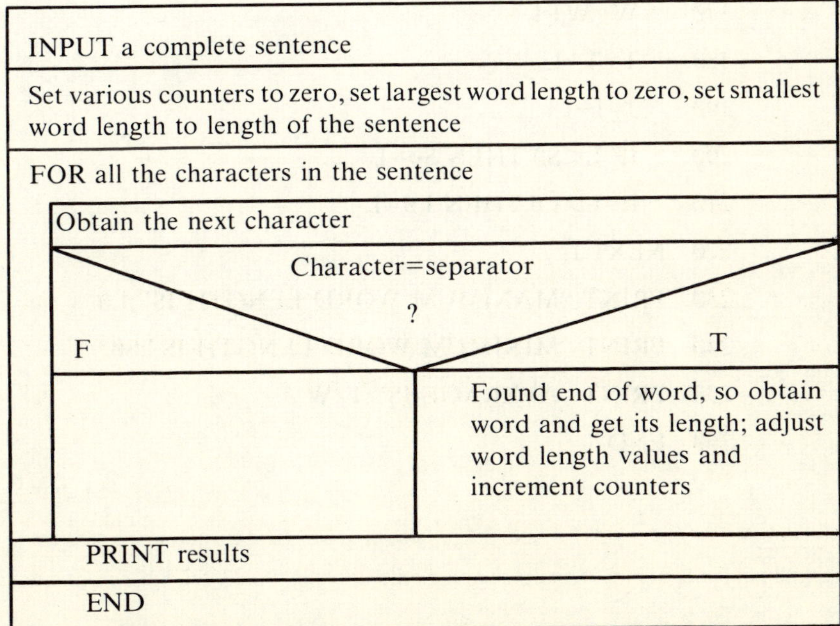

```
10   REM SENTENCE ANALYSIS (MICROSOFT TYPE
     FUNCTIONS)
20   INPUT S$
30   S=LEN (S$)
40   SØ=S
50   LØ=Ø
60   J=1        :REM WHERE WORD STARTS
70   T=Ø
80   W=Ø        :REM COUNTS WORDS
90   FOR I=1 TO S
100     A$=MID$(S$,I,1)
110     IF A$=" " THEN 160
120     IF A$="." THEN 160
130     IF A$=";" THEN 160
140     IF A$="," THEN 160
150     GO TO 220
160     L=LEN(MID$(S$,J,I-J))
170     W=W+1
180     T=T+L
190     J=I+1
200     IF L<SØ THEN SØ=L
210     IF L>LØ THEN LØ=L
220   NEXT I
230   PRINT "MAXIMUM WORD LENGTH IS";LØ
240   PRINT "MINIMUM WORD LENGTH IS";SØ
250   PRINT "AVERAGE IS";T/W
260   END
```

4.7	Initialize array (word table)

Structure very similar to the FOR loop box of exercise 4.6, except that when a word is found put in a different process box (shown below) to update word table
INPUT next sentence

REPEAT UNTIL NULL sentence
PRINT results of accumulated values
END

Word found process:

Set flags F (found)=Ø
Does word found match those already in table?
REPEAT UNTIL found or end of table

F=1

F	?	T
Add new entry to word table and check not over the size	Increase word count for appropriate entry for appropriate entry	

```
1Ø    REM MANY SENTENCES WORD FREQUENCY PROGRAM

2Ø    REM (FOR EXAMPLE HERE THE ARRAYS HAVE SIZE 2Ø)

3Ø    DIM W$(2Ø),W(2Ø)

4Ø    FOR I=1 TO 2Ø

5Ø    W$(I)="" "       :REM WILL HOLD WORDS

6Ø    W(I)=Ø           :REM  WILL  HOLD  CORRESPONDING
                        FREQUENCY

7Ø    NEXT I

8Ø    WØ=1             :REM TOP OF WORD TABLE POINTER

9Ø    INPUT S$         :REM GET FIRST SENTENCE OR PHRASE

1ØØ     S=LEN(S$)
```

```
110    J=1
120    FOR I=1 TO S
130      A$=MID$(S$,I,1)
140      IF A$=" " THEN 190
150      IF A$="." THEN 190
160      IF A$="," THEN 190
170      IF A$=";" THEN 190
180      GO TO 340
190        B$=MID$(S$,J,I-J)
200      J=I+1
210      F=0
220      K=1
230        IF B$=W$(K) THEN F=1
240        K=K+1
250      IF F=0 AND K<W0 THEN 230
260      IF F=1 THEN 330
270        W$(W0)=B$
280        W(W0)=1
290        W0=W0+1
300        IF W0 <=20 THEN 340
310          PRINT "WORD TABLE EXCEEDED"
320          STOP
330        W(K-1)=W(K-1)+1
340    NEXT I
350    INPUT S$
360  IF S$<>"" THEN 100
370  REM
380  REM HAVE WORDS IN W$( ) AND THEIR COUNTS IN W( ),
390  REM USE A SORT AS DESCRIBED TO SORT INTO
     ALPHABETIC
```

```
400  REM ORDER. DON'T FORGET TO APPLY THE SAME
     ACTIONS TO
410  REM W( ) AS YOU DO TO W$( ).
420  REM
430  PRINT "WORD", "FREQUENCY"
440  FOR I=1 TO WØ-1
450     PRINT W$(I),W(I)
460  NEXT I
470  END
```

4.8 For simplicity the data are not assumed to be ordered in any way, so a simple search is used. The program is capable of many elaborations; one adopted here as an example of the sort of feature which may be included is to re-try the search with a shortened query string. This will pick up an entry even if there is some mistake in the spelling of the query.

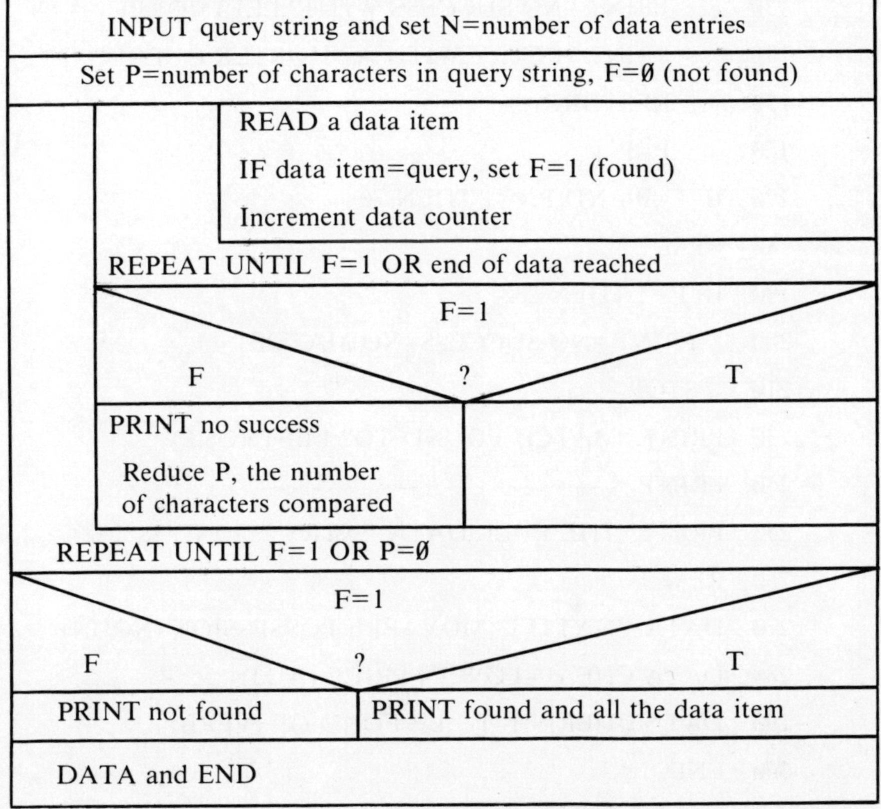

```
10    REM DATA RETRIEVAL
20    INPUT "QUERY TOPIC";Q$
30      P=LEN(Q$)
40      N=3      :REM NUMBER OF DATA INFORMATION
                  ITEMS,A
50    REM         PRACTICAL PROGRAM MAY HAVE
                  HUNDREDS
60    F=0
70      I=1
80        READ A$
90        IF LEFT$(A$,P)=LEFT$(Q$,P) THEN F=1
100       I=I+1
110      IF F=0 AND I<=N THEN 80
120      IF F=1 THEN 170
130        PRINT "NO SUCCESS WITH";LEFT$(Q$,P)
140        PRINT "RETRY WITH A SHORTER QUERY"
150        RESTORE
160        P=P-1
170   IF F=0 AND P>=1 THEN 70
180   REM
190   IF F=1 THEN 230
200     PRINT "NO SUCCESS-NO MATCH"
210     STOP
230   PRINT "MATCH FOUND TO";LEFT$(Q$,P)
240   PRINT "----------------------"
250   PRINT "THE FULL DATA ENTRY FOUND IS";A$
260   REM
270   DATA CHATTEL-MOVABLE POSSESSION (NOUN)
280   DATA CHEAP-LOW IN PRICE (ADJ)
290   DATA CHERISH-TO BE FOND OF (VERB)
300   END
```

Solutions to the exercises of Chapter 5

5.1

<table>
<tr><td colspan="3">Define the conversion formula as a line function</td></tr>
<tr><td></td><td colspan="2">INPUT with prompt the first value</td></tr>
<tr><td></td><td></td><td>PRINT the results using the function</td></tr>
<tr><td></td><td></td><td>INPUT the next value</td></tr>
<tr><td></td><td colspan="2">REPEAT UNTIL value is zero (small)</td></tr>
<tr><td></td><td></td><td>END</td></tr>
</table>

```
10   REM DEFINE FN CALL IT C FOR CONVERSION
20   DEF FNC(X)=32+180*X/100
30   REM
40   INPUT "CENTIGRADE";C
50     PRINT "FAHRENHEIT=";FNC(C)
60     INPUT "CENTIGRADE";C
70   IF ABS(C).GT.1.0E-7 THEN 50
80   END
```

5.2   The layout of each letter produced in this solution is as follows: top right is your name and address followed by the date; below this is the name and address of the recipient on the left of the sheet; immediately below this the letter begins DEAR . . . and ends YOURS SINCERELY with enough blank lines to sign it and leave some space before the next letter begins. The program assumes the letter text is stored in DATA statements, and the names and addresses are input from the terminal. In practice, one or both of these data streams would originate from a file.

Level 1

Input any standard information such as the date and name of the products
   which is described in the letter.
Input a set of names and addresses.
While names to be processed.
   Compose and print the letter.
Endwhile

374

Refinement 1.1.   Input any standard . . . letter.

Print prompts and input date, product name if required, and any other information required.

Refinement 1.2.   Input a set of names and addresses.

Print for number of names, and input N.

For the N items

Input the name.

Input the three lines of address
(road, district, town).

end for.

Refinement 1.3.   Compose and print the letter.

Print your name and address on the right, with the date below it.

Print recipient name and address on the left, below it print DEAR name.

For the number of text lines.

READ a text line.

PRINT the text line.

end for.

Print YOURS SINCERELY on the right.

Print a number of blank lines.

The above form a reasonable description for level 2, but a practical point is that the computer store will limit the number of names and addresses input in refinement 1.2, so perhaps iterate the major part of the program using (say) 2Ø names and addresses at a time. In outline, level 2 becomes:

Level 2

(1.1) for fixed data.

Repeat for sets of names and addresses.

(1.2) for a set of names and addresses.

While names to be processed.

(1.3) for the letter.

endwhile.

Request, any more sets of data?

Until no more sets of data.

The major elaboration now required is to expand letter printing. The action of READing and PRINTing a string occurs at least twice (for your address and the text), so this may be expanded.

Refinement 2.1

Obtain the start print position L and the number of repetitions K.

For the K repetitions.

READ a string.

PRINT the string from position L.

end for.

It is also useful to have a block producing blank lines.

Refinement 2.2

Obtain number of blank lines required K.

For the K repetitions.

PRINT

end for.

Note that the level 2 actions above could equally well have been drawn as structograms. A final level could be described, or drawn as structograms, in which decisions as to variable names, loop counters, etc., are made. The resultant solution is given by the program:

```
10    REM LETTER PRODUCTION PROGRAM
20    DIM N$(2Ø),A$(2Ø,3)
30    REM
40       GOSUB 12Ø
50       GOSUB 16Ø
60       FOR I=1 TO N
70          GOSUB 25Ø
80       NEXT I
90       INPUT "MORE SETS OF NAMES (YES OR NO)";B$
100   IF B$="YES" THEN 5Ø
```

```
11Ø    STOP
12Ø    REM SUBROUTINE FOR INPUT FIXED DATA
13Ø      INPUT "GIVE DATE";D$
14Ø    REM ANY OTHER INFO ALSO HERE
15Ø    RETURN
16Ø    REM SUBROUTINE FOR SET OF NAMES
17Ø      INPUT "NUMBER OF NAMES";N
18Ø      FOR I=1 TO N
19Ø        INPUT N$(I)
2ØØ        FOR J=1 TO 3
21Ø          INPUT A$(I,J)
22Ø        NEXT J
23Ø      NEXT I
24Ø    RETURN
25Ø    REM SUBROUTINE TO PRINT LETTER
26Ø      RESTORE
27Ø      K=4
28Ø      L=3Ø
29Ø      GOSUB 44Ø
3ØØ      PRINT TAB(35);D$
31Ø      PRINT N$(I)
32Ø      FOR M=1 TO 3
33Ø        PRINT A$(I,M)
34Ø      NEXT M
35Ø      PRINT "DEAR";N$(I);","
36Ø      K=1Ø
37Ø      L=1
38Ø      GOSUB 44Ø
39Ø      PRINT
4ØØ      PRINT TAB(35);"YOURS SINCERELY"
```

```
41Ø     K=1Ø
42Ø     GOSUB 5ØØ
43Ø   RETURN
44Ø     REM SUBROUTINE FOR READ/PRINT
45Ø   FOR P=1 TO K
46Ø     READ B$
47Ø     PRINT TAB(L);B$
48Ø   NEXT P
49Ø   RETURN
5ØØ     REM SUBROUTINE FOR SKIPS
51Ø   FOR P=1 TO K
52Ø     PRINT
53Ø   NEXT P
54Ø   RETURN
55Ø   DATA
56Ø   DATA
         .   .
         .   .
         .   .
         .   .
         .   .
         .   .
         .   .
         .   .
         .   .
71Ø   END
```

your name and address (4 lines)

text of letter (1Ø lines in this example)

5.3   Where there are multiple values for each data item (in this case, a person) and ordering is carried out it is often easier to sort a list of pointers and not move all the multiple data items around.

Level 1

Read data into two arrays;A$( ) for the name and B( ) for the number.

Set an index array I( ) to point to initial values of the items stored.

Sort on the values of B( ) which are pointed at by I( ); move values in I( ), not A$( ) and B( ).

Print the list in the order indicated by I( ).

Apart from reading the values, the other three actions (set index, sort, print) are covered completely in Section 4.5.3. They will be taken as subroutines with slight modification of the variable names to adapt to this problem. This is a case of top-down development with a very clear view of what is available at the bottom level of functions/subroutines.

The final program is:

```
10   REM INDEX SORT
20   DIM A$(10),B(10),I(10)
30   FOR K=1 TO 10
40      READ A$(K),B(K)
50   NEXT K
60   REM SORT
70      GOSUB 900
80   REM PRINT
90      GOSUB 120
100  STOP
110  REM
120  REM PRINT SUBROUTINE
130  FOR K=1 TO 10
140     PRINT A$(I(K));B(I(K))
150  NEXT K
900  REM SORT SUBROUTINE (INDEXED SORTING)
910
```

} program in Section 4.5.3 with the modification given below

```
1120   RETURN
1130   DATA

         .

         .

         .

1140   END
```

Modifications required to Section 4.5.3 are:

```
 910   FOR L=1 TO 10
1040   FOR I=10 TO 2 STEP-1
1060      IF B(I1)<=B(I2) THEN 1100
```

Solutions to the exercises of Chapter 7

7.1
```
 10   DIM A(4,4),B(4,4),C(4,4),D(4,3),Z(4,4)
 20   REM
 30   PRINT "GIVE THREE MATRICES A,B,C"
 40   MAT INPUT A,B,C
 50   MAT A=A+B
 60   MAT Z=A+C
 70   MAT PRINT Z;
 80   REM
 90   PRINT "GIVE MATRIX D"
100   MAT INPUT D
110   MAT A=Z*D
120   MAT PRINT A;
130   END
```

7.2
```
 10   DIM A(10,10),B(10,10)
 20   INPUT N
 30   MAT A=CON(N,N)
```

380

```
40    MAT A=(5.)*A
50    REM
60    MAT B=IDN(N,N)
70    MAT B=(5,)*B
80    REM
90    MAT A=A+B
100   PRINT "MATRIX IS"
110   MAT PRINT A;
120   REM
130   MAT B=INV(A)
140   PRINT "INVERSE IS"
150   MAT PRINT B;
160   END
```

7.3
```
10    DIM A(4,4),B(4,4)
20    REM
30    MAT READ A
40    MAT B=A*A
50    PRINT "SQUARE IS"
60    MAT PRINT B;
70    REM
80    MAT B=B*A
90    PRINT "CUBE IS"
100   MAT PRINT B;
110   REM
120   MAT B=B*A
130   PRINT "FOURTH POWER IS"
140   MAT PRINT B;
150   REM
160   REM ASSUMES THE INPUT IS BY ROWS
170   DATA 1, 2,-1, 1, 2, 0, 1, 2, 1, 0, 1
```

```
180   DATA 3, 2, 3, 1, 1
190   END
```

7.4
```
10    DIM A(3,3), B(3,3), C(3,3)
20    REM
30    MAT READ A
40    MAT B=A*A
50    MAT C=B*A
60    MAT B=(2.)*B
70    MAT C=C-B
80    MAT A=(9.)*A
90    MAT C=C-A
100   PRINT "MATRIX A**3-2A**2-9A IS"
110   MAT PRINT C;
120   REM
130   DATA 2,1;3, 1, -1,2,1,2,1
140   END
```

7.5   The solutions, and the differences between using pivoting and not using it, depend very strongly on the accuracy of the computer being used. The following solution gives residuals on the order of 10^{-8}:

$$x_1 = 5.003106553$$

$$x_2 = -5.072538054$$

$$x_3 = 0.98897173$$

7.6   The GAUSS program performed two swaps (3 to 1, 3 to 2) during the elimination to give:

$$
\begin{array}{ccc}
2 & 1 & 1 \\
0 & 1 & -1 \\
0 & 0 & -6
\end{array}
$$

Thus the determinant is $(-1)^2 * 2 * 1 * (-6) = -12$.

Appendix II
ASCII character codes

The ASCII code is defined as a 7 bit code and thus has a range from Ø to 127, with the character assignments as shown in the following table:

ASCII character codes

Decimal	Character	Decimal	Character	Decimal	Character
ØØØ	NUL	Ø43	+	Ø86	V
ØØ1	SOH	Ø44	,	Ø87	W
ØØ2	STX	Ø45	–	Ø88	X
ØØ3	ETX	Ø46	.	Ø89	Y
ØØ4	EOT	Ø47	/	Ø9Ø	Z
ØØ5	ENQ	Ø48	Ø	Ø91	[
ØØ6	ACK	Ø49	1	Ø92	\
ØØ7	BEL	Ø5Ø	2	Ø93	]
ØØ8	BS	Ø51	3	Ø94	↑ or ∧
ØØ9	HT	Ø52	4	Ø95	← or -
Ø1Ø	LF	Ø53	5	Ø96	`
Ø11	VT	Ø54	6	Ø97	a
Ø12	FF	Ø55	7	Ø98	b
Ø13	CR	Ø56	8	Ø99	c
Ø14	SO	Ø57	9	1ØØ	d
Ø15	SI	Ø58	:	1Ø1	e
Ø16	DLE	Ø59	;	1Ø2	f
Ø17	DC1	Ø6Ø	<	1Ø3	g
Ø18	DC2	Ø61	=	1Ø4	h
Ø19	DC3	Ø62	>	1Ø5	i
Ø2Ø	DC4	Ø63	?	1Ø6	j
Ø21	NAK	Ø64	@	1Ø7	k
Ø22	SYN	Ø65	A	1Ø8	l
Ø23	ETB	Ø66	B	1Ø9	m
Ø24	CANCEL	Ø67	C	11Ø	n
Ø25	EM	Ø68	D	111	o
Ø26	SUB	Ø69	E	112	p
Ø27	ESCAPE	Ø7Ø	F	113	q
Ø28	FS	Ø71	G	114	r
Ø29	GS	Ø72	H	115	s
Ø3Ø	RS	Ø73	I	116	t
Ø31	US	Ø74	J	117	u
Ø32	SPACE	Ø75	K	118	v
Ø33	!	Ø76	L	119	w
Ø34	"	Ø77	M	12Ø	x
Ø35	#	Ø78	N	121	y
Ø36	$	Ø79	O	122	z
Ø37	%	Ø8Ø	P	123	{
Ø38	&	Ø81	Q	124		
Ø39	'	Ø82	R	125	}
Ø4Ø	(	Ø83	S	126	~
Ø41	)	Ø84	T	127	DELETE
Ø42	*	Ø85	U		

Notice the abbreviations:

LF Line feed   FF Form feed   CR Carriage return

The above codes and the three below are frequently used:

ESCAPE   CANCEL   DELETE

Some of the others are:

SOH	Start of heading	STX	Start of text
ETX	End of text	EOT	End of transmission
ENQ	Enquiry	ACK	Acknowledge
BEL	Bell	BS	Backspace
HT	Horizontal tabulation	VT	Vertical tabulate
SO	Shift out	SI	Shift in
DLE	Data link escape	DC1 to DC4	Device ON/OFF controls
NAK	Negative acknowledge	SYN	Synchronous idle

Many systems use a byte value (8 bits) for the code and use the additional values 128 to 255 for special graphics and cursor control characters. Others interpret the above control characters (decimal Ø to 31) in different ways to the standard. Consult your computer manual for full details. On many microcomputer keyboards, pressing the two keys CTRL and A generates the ASCII code ØØ1, CTRL & B generates the code ØØ2, and so on through to CTRL & Z, which generates the code Ø26. Thus most of the ASCII data control codes may be easily generated from the keyboard if required.

Appendix III
BASIC commands

The following are a list of the most commonly used BASIC commands. Note that many BASIC statements may be used in the immediate mode (see Section 2.4) and thus act like commands.

Details of the commands vary between systems and not all commands are provided on any one system.

AUTO	Provides an automatic statement number prompt, usually in tens for typing in BASIC programs.
BYE	On multi-user computer systems (not usually micros) this terminates a session.
CLEAR or CLR	Clears all program variables.
CLS	Clears the screen (or only the text display).
CLG	Clears the graphic display part of the screen.
CONT	Continues program execution after it has been stopped. Values of the variables are retained and used when execution resumes.
CONTINUE 500	Enhanced version of CONT which resumes execution from the specified line number (mainframe computers only).
DEL or DELETE	Deletes the whole of the current program.
DELETE 10,20 DELETE 10-20	Deletes lines 10 to 20 inclusive from the current program.
EDIT 20	Edits line 20 of the current program (Microsoft only).
GET PROG	Used on mainframe computers to load the program into store from backing store.
HELLO	Used on multi-user systems to identify a user to the system and start a session.
HELP	Calls for information on BASIC statements or commands.
KILL DATA	Deletes the named file from backing store on mainframe computers.
KILL "DATA"	As above, Microsoft version.

LIST	Lists the current program to the VDU.
LIST 20	List only line 20, or some systems list from line 20.
LIST 20–40 LIST 20,40	List between the specified lines.
LIST ,100 LIST –100	List from the beginning until line 100 is reached.
LLIST	Options as above, but output directed to the printer, not VDU.
LOAD	Loads the next program from the cassette tape (Microsoft uses CLOAD).
LOAD "PROG"	Loads the named program from cassette or disc. Additional parameter can be given to identify device, etc.
NAME PROG2	Names the current program with the new name given (mainframe computers).
NAME PROG1 AS PROG2	Names the program on disc with the new name (Microsoft only).
NEW	Clears away any current program and on micros re-starts the BASIC interpreter afresh.
NEW PROG	Clears away any current program and names the new one PROG (mainframe computers only).
OLD	Reverses the effect of NEW, provided no new lines have been typed in (BBC only).
OLD PROG	Same as GET for mainframe computers.
RENUMBER RENUM RESEQUENCE	Renumbers the statement numbers of the current program, usually in steps of 10 but options may be available to select other values.
RUN	Starts execution of the current program from the beginning. Usually clears all variables before starting, unlike CONT.
RUN 500	As RUN, but starts execution from line 500.
SAVE	Saves current program onto cassette tape (Microsoft uses CSAVE).
SAVE	Some mainframe computers save the current program, previously NAMEd, to backing store.
SAVE "PROG"	Saves the current program to disc or cassette tape.
SCRATCH or SCR	As DELETE.

SYSTEM   Exits from BASIC and returns control to CP/M (Microsoft only).

UNSAVE PROG   As KILL PROG.

Appendix IV

Glossary of terms

Some of the specialist terms mentioned in this book are explained below: in many cases a full technical explanation appears also in the text.

Address	The identification code for memory locations which is used to select a location for reading and writing.
Adjoint matrix (square matrix only)	Is a square matrix whose elements are the cofactors of the original matrix. A cofactor is the signed determinant with one column and one row of the original matrix removed.
ANSI	American National Standards Institute.
Arithmetic logic unit	The part of the computer hardware which performs a variety of arithmetic and logical operations under the control of function inputs from the controller executing the machine code.
Artificial intelligence	Is the (desired but not yet attained) capability of a device to perform functions normally attributed to human intelligence.
ASCII	American Standard Code for Information Interchange.
Assembler	A program which translates from assembly language to machine code and is much smaller than a compiler for a high level language.
Assembly	A language using (slightly more) readable mnemonics for the machine code instructions used directly by the computer. There is approximately one assembly statement to each machine code instruction.
Backing store	The long term storage area for programs and data. Usually on the magnetic media: rigid discs, floppy discs, cassettes, and tapes.
Bit	A binary digit, which can have only the values $\emptyset$ or 1.

388

Bootstrap (also bootstrap loader)	A technique for loading the first instructions into the empty computer memory after it is powered on. This very simple group of instructions can then be executed to load the rest of the initialization program, which can then be used to load any other programs including the operating system. The bootstrap is likely to reside in special ROM memory.
Byte	The fundamental grouping of bits which the computer handles as a single unit; is eight bits in length.
Compiler	A program which translates a program written in a high level language (such as BASIC) into a low level language (assembly or machine code).
Compiler tables and lists	During the compilation process a lot of temporary information is generated and a work area comprising tables and lists is required.
Cursor	The marker on the VDU screen which shows where the next character typed from the keyboard will appear.
Determinant (square matrix only)	Is a single numerical value derived from a sum of products of all the elements.
Diagonally dominant	For each row of the matrix the diagonal element is greater in magnitude than the sum of the other elements in the row.
Disc controller	A device which controls the head positioning and read/write actions of a disc.
Editor	A program which manipulates all types of text in programs (and perhaps data files) and allows the user to make changes, additions, and deletions.
Execution control	The path of control during execution of a BASIC program, i.e. which statements have been, or will be, executed after RUN is typed.
Hexadecimal	Number system with base 16; the allowed digits are from 0 to 9 and the letters A to F.
IEEE 488 Data bus	A group of 24 parallel wires (or connections) with defined properties for the transmission of data between instruments and computers.
Ill conditioned	Applied to numerical problems to indicate that small changes in the numerical values of the problem can cause large changes in the solution of the problem.

Immediate (in BASIC)	This means that the statement or command will be executed once the SEND or RETURN key is pressed.
Interactive	Direct and immediate communication between the computer and the user at a terminal.
Interpreter	A program which processes a high level language program statement by statement to cause the execution of each statement as it is processed; it may not produce low level language output as the compiler does.
Inverse of a matrix (square matrix only)	Is the matrix derived from the original matrix so that when multiplied with the original matrix the identity matrix is the result.
Left justifies	The items in different zones or on different lines are aligned to the left of the zone or line.
Local variables	Variables which only have a meaning (exist) in a limited region of a program, and do not interfere with variables of the same name outside this region, e.g. in BASIC some block functions can have local variables.
Logical channel	The logical address of a link to a computer input/output unit. The actual machine address is matched to the logical address by the BASIC system.
Logical operations	The comparison of statements which have values equivalent to TRUE and FALSE, using the operations AND, OR, and exclusive OR.
Low resolution graphics	The generation of lines, curves, and blocks of colour by means of symbols and characters rather than tiny dots.
Mainframe	A powerful computer, physically large, capable of supporting many terminals simultaneously.
Matrix	A two-dimensional array; a table of values in which the position of the value in the table is important.
Memory (another name for store)	The immediate area where programs and data are kept during processing.
Microelectronic circuits	The arrangements of transistors and other components connected together which are reduced in size and manufactured onto silicon chips.

390

Minimal BASIC standard | A document of the European Computer Manufacturers Association defining a basic core set of the BASIC language; standard ECMA–55 was published in 1977 and is available free from: ECMA, 114 Rue du Rhone, 1204 Geneva, Switzerland.

Modules | Indicates the semi-separate parts of a program such as subroutines and functions.

Nested | One item inside another; usually applied to BASIC FOR–NEXT loops to indicate that one is completely inside another.

Numerical stability | Slight pertubations of the values in a stable numerical problem do not give radically different solutions.

On-line | Used to describe a terminal which is connected to a computer and is being serviced by it. This is always the case for single-user microcomputers.

Program | A sequence of instructions or statements properly organized to perform a particular job. In BASIC the statements are obeyed one after another in the order indicated by the statement numbers.

RAM (random access memory) | A memory that can be both read and written to in normal operation.

Random access | Items accessed in approximately the same amount of time without having to read or write neighbouring items.

Record key | That part of a record which is used to identify it, e.g. a name could be the record key for a name and address record.

Recursion | Applied to a subroutine or block function or procedure; it means that it calls itself as part of its execution.

Responses | The time between giving a command and the results appearing on the VDU or printer.

ROM (read only memory) | Contains data fixed permanently into it as part of the manufacturing process and does not require power to retain the information.

Security printing | Usually a reference to the printing of potentially valuable documents such as cheques.

Sequential	Access to items in a serial manner.
Serial	One thing after another.
Stack	A section of computer store used in a 'last in, first out' manner; the top of the stack is the last data value stored and is the first to be removed.
Status byte	One byte is set to contain values by the hardware to indicate the state of an input/output operation, i.e. whether it is ready to receive new data.
Stepwise refinement	The action to generate the more detailed (lower) design levels when using structured programming.
Store	See memory.
Structured design	The name given to a specific approach to program design, which proceeds from general actions through to detailed actions.
Syntax	The rules governing the statement in a language; i.e. what may appear where in the statement layout.
Vector	A simple (one-dimensional) array; a list of values whose positions are important.

Index

XOR, 205

ZER, matrix function, 254
Zones, see PRINT columns, 76
ZX81 numeric functions, 69